# THE
# DOOMED DEMOCRACY

*Czechoslovakia in a Disrupted Europe*
*1914-38*

Thomas Masaryk led the struggle for recognition of the Czechoslovak independence movement by the Allies. His plans for a multi-national republic were based on the French and American models. *Karel Hájek, Prague*

# THE
# DOOMED DEMOCRACY

## Czechoslovakia in a Disrupted
## Europe 1914-38

*by*

# VĚRA OLIVOVÁ Pavova

*Translated by*
GEORGE THEINER

## SIDGWICK & JACKSON
### LONDON

ISBN 0 283 98083 4

Printed in Great Britain by
Morrison & Gibb Ltd
London and Edinburgh

# Contents

6 *Contents*

# Illustrations

7

# Introduction

The First Republic of Czechoslovakia has been described by a British historian as 'in many ways the most satisfactory and most successful of the Succession States'. It was indeed in its time more democratic and socially progressive than Britain herself. Its bi-cameral legislature was elected by direct and secret ballot in a system of suffrage which drew no distinctions of sex, race, religion or property. If the principle of proportional representation adopted produced a plethora of political parties, it meant at least that most minority interests could find their spokesmen in parliament. This served as a useful safety-valve for the national minorities in particular who could hardly consider themselves unrepresented when in the elections of 1920, 1925 and 1929 they had between thirteen and twenty 'minority' parties to choose between, quite apart from the 'national' parties which they could vote for instead if they thought their interests were better served by doing so. Governments were always composed of coalitions and this made for stability and eliminated extremism. Compared with the difficulties in forming coalition governments experienced by some Western countries, notably Holland, the Czechoslovak experiment was comparatively free from friction or delay. When coalitions could not immediately be formed a caretaker government of officials stepped in under the aegis of the President. It would, of course, have stood no chance of taking office if it had not enjoyed the broad support of the major parties.

The Communist Party was at no time suppressed. In 1925 it had the second largest representation of any party in the Chamber of Deputies – a remarkable phenomenon in a bourgeois state. If it took no part in the government, that was originally its own choice. But it played a full part in parliamentary business and local government. The Party's training in parliamentary democracy in the First Republic stood it in good stead when the thaw set in in the mid-sixties and after.

Schools were better and more democratic than in Britain. 'There is no democracy without education,' said Masaryk. He himself preferred British education because it formed character. But the high academic standards in Czech schools could be traced back to Comenius and all had the same opportunities. In the years before the National Health Scheme Czechoslovakia was in advance of Britain in social services too. The new state got down very quickly to passing a series of progressive social laws which included the 8-hour day, unemployment insurance, protection of women and children, family allowances, holidays with pay, housing and agrarian reform. After the redistribution of land the people 'owned' their country.

In foreign affairs Czechoslovakia was a loyal member of the League, in which her Foreign Minister, Edvard Beneš, played a distinguished part. She was at no time aggressive in her foreign policy and was not involved in any major international complications between the settlement of her dispute with Poland over Teschen and the Sudeten German crisis. She developed good relations with Austria and Germany at the time of the Weimar Republic and if she did not do so with Hungary it was because she knew that her existence depended on the preservation of the *status quo* which Hungary was pledged to overthrow. In her loyalty to the Europe of Versailles Czechoslovakia was more consistent than those who had created it.

Given the circumstances that the peacemakers saw no difficulties in placing $3\frac{1}{2}$ million Germans under Czechoslovak rule (mainly because there was no alternative; they could not be included in Austria and had never belonged to Germany) the Czechoslovak government treated its largest minority very reasonably. The Germans in Czechoslovakia were better provided with schools than the Czechs and Slovaks themselves. If the Germans boycotted the new state at the outset they had only themselves to blame. But in 1928 1,137,000 Germans voted at the provincial elections for the 'activist' parties who were for participation in the government. The 'negativists' only polled 349,000 votes. The Germans in Czechoslovakia would never have posed an international problem if it had not been for the rise of Hitler and the failure of France and Britain to stand up to him.

As for the Slovak question this would also have found its own solution if there had been no outside interference. The problem was of the same order as ours with the Irish, Welsh or Scots which still face us today (and which we are always determined to solve on our own). The President was half-Slovak and the Prime Minister from 1935–8 fully Slovak. In Britain we have had several Scottish Prime Ministers and one outstanding Welshman. It will always be for debate whether a disgruntled national or regional minority serves its cause best by having its own little provincial empire or whether it does better by infiltrating the central apparatus, thus influencing national policy. Probably the Slovaks would have had a harder time to make their influence felt in the central apparatus (partly because they had not had the necessary training and experience to do so) but 20 years is not a very long time to do it in.

Finally, Czechoslovakia had as its President and guarantor a truly enlightened and humane man of great perceptiveness who in this respect towered head and shoulders above the Piłsudskys and Horthys, not to speak of the Mussolinis, Hitlers and Stalins of his time.

And yet in spite of all this and of the fact that Britain once liked to think of herself as the midwife or godmother of Czechoslovakia, no British historian has yet presented us with a full account of the fortunes of the young republic from 1918, the year of its birth, to 1938, the year of its betrayal and dismemberment. Moreover it took some 25 years before any British historian ventured to embark on a study of the diplomatic history of this period. And even in those British histories which deal with the international events of the time the Czechoslovak Republic is usually mentioned only at its birth and in its death-throes. The positive and constructive period in between is ignored and now almost forgotten.

For this reason the present volume, which deals with the history of the First Czechoslovak Republic in its European setting, is much to be welcomed, even if the large space necessarily given to international problems inevitably means that we have to content ourselves with a rather summary version of domestic developments. But we should be grateful for this book for another reason as well. Dr Olivová is a Czech historian of the post-war school and she can therefore write with less emotion about the period than could the few authors on whom we British have been brought up. Not that Dr Olivová is not a fervent patriot; in spite of her restrained treatment of the events it is clear that like all her countrymen she feels deeply about them. What is most revealing in this book, which is most lucid and readable in Mr Theiner's excellent translation, is that the author shows how profoundly the whole history of Central Europe, and indeed of Europe itself, has been affected by the betrayal by the Entente of the principles for which they claimed to be fighting. When at the Locarno discussions the French failed to obtain British support for a guarantee of her Central European allies the fate of Czechoslovakia, as of Poland, was sealed. Again and again one asks the question – why did the Allies create these states if they were not prepared to defend them? And what was the use of Britain continually reaffirming the principle of 'no commitment' when the Treaty of Versailles, to which she had been a signatory, was bound to involve her in commitments and, in fact, did at a time when she was not prepared for them, when friendly powers in that part of Europe on whom she might have relied had been eliminated. The First World War had started in this part of Europe – in the Austro-Hungarian Empire – and Britain had been at once involved in it. The excuse may have been that Belgian neutrality had been violated, but how could Britain, Belgium or no Belgium, have stood aside and allowed the Central Powers to dominate Europe? It would only have meant the commitment to fight a defensive war at a later stage when Britain would have been isolated and immeasurably inferior to her enemies. One could not use the reluctance of the electorate as an excuse for non-involvement. The British electorate is notoriously apathetic about foreign affairs and was even more so between the wars. The Anglo-French Treaty, committing Britain to defend France against unprovoked aggression by Germany, which could have and did involve untold commitments, was passed in 1919 without any fuss on the part of the public.

In conclusion I venture to query one or two of Dr Olivová's interpretations of the events in a book with so much of which I am in agreement. I believe that, like other modern Czech writers, she tends to exaggerate the effect of the World Economic Crisis on Czechoslovakia. Evidence suggests that the Republic weathered it a great deal better than its neighbours. If the social discontent had been as great as she suggests the Communist vote would surely have risen by leaps and bounds. But figures disprove it. In 1925 the Party polled 13·2 per cent of the votes; in 1929, 10·2 per cent; in 1935, 10·3 per cent. The crisis was, of course, felt worse in the territories inhabited by the Germans, where the light industries were centred, and this partly accounted for the enormous number of votes cast for Henlein's Sudeten German Party which amounted in 1935 to 15·2 per cent of the whole.

She also perhaps attributes to ruling circles in Britain more selfish motives than they actually held. Although Neville Chamberlain would certainly have welcomed a settlement with Germany which would have brought Britain economic advantages, and although he was most unenthusiastic about any idea of co-operation with the U.S.S.R., his main preoccupation was to try to preserve peace. If he sought to do this at the expense of Czechoslovakia and the other smaller countries of Central Europe this was not only because he knew and cared little about them. The plain fact is that he was terrified of Hitler and sincerely believed that unless some accommodation was reached with him the whole of Europe including the people of Czechoslovakia would be enveloped in an appalling catastrophe. His folly lay in the fact that he did not realize that by standing firm and encouraging the French and the Czechs to do so he could have saved the situation without bloodshed.

# *Prologue*

On 28 June 1914, several shots rang out in a picturesque little town of mosques, Orthodox churches, and noisy market-places, on the charming embankment of the Milyachka river. The town was Sarajevo and the shots were the alarm signals of a new era. Within a few days the world was aflame with the fires of a great war that would sweep Europe, Asia, Africa, and even America, tangibly and bloodily confirming the unity of the world.

The outbreak of the war saw the start of a struggle for world power that had been in the making since the end of the nineteenth century, a struggle in which an old world power – Britain – was faced by a new power – Germany. The beginnings of this conflict can be traced to the year 1871, when, under Prussian leadership, 'the second German Empire' was born. The unification of Germany brought great economic growth and unprecedented prosperity to the German people, and a tremendous population explosion scattered the citizens of this new empire throughout the world. Colonies of emigrants, maintaining contacts with their native land, came into being in Africa, Asia, and America.

This new European power, strong both in a political and an economic sense, demanded its 'birthright on the Planet', aiming to create a world colonial empire – *Grossdeutschland*. It was this that brought Germany into direct conflict with Britain.

Britain had enjoyed world domination throughout the nineteenth century. Strong and independent, she had not needed any allies. Her rivals were France, who had conflicting interests in Africa and Asia, and Russia, who threatened British hegemony particularly in India and Central Asia. Wars against both these powers had ended in absolute British victory, and Britain had no quarrel with Bismarck's Germany, which was following an exclusively European policy. On the contrary – a Germany in the process of unification was a valuable economic partner and a useful counterweight to France and Russia. The common Anglo-Saxon origin of the two nations also played its part in good Anglo-German relations.

It was Kaiser Wilhelm's Germany, turning itself into a naval as well as a land power, and striving to dominate the world, which infringed these relations. Feeling threatened in her 'splendid isolation', Britain concluded alliances with her former rivals, now very much weakened, who were also beginning to suffer from the effects of German expansion. Germany, on the other hand, strengthened her position by concluding alliances with Austria-Hungary and Italy.

Thus, in 1914, two new power groupings, the Entente and the Central Powers, which had been formed at the turn of the century, stood facing each other. The camp of the former was larger, but it lacked unity and tradition, being linked chiefly by considerations of defence. To these were added individual aspirations, such as the French desire to avenge their defeat by the Prussians at Sedan in 1870 and regain Alsace-Lorraine, and Russian ambitions in the Balkans. The Entente had neither a common goal nor an ideological programme.

The Central Powers on the other hand were more of an entity, though even they were not without their discords. Italy, for instance, at a crucial moment proclaimed her neutrality, and later went over to the enemy camp; Turkey took her place at the side of the Central Powers. Germany had all the advantages of a state whose actions are governed by the dream of world domination. Moreover, it had the exceptionally effective, if un-official, ideological programme provided by the pan-German movement. As for Austria-Hungary and Turkey, they saw in war an opportunity to halt the disintegration of their empires.

The devastating world war unleashed by the Sarajevo as-sassination resulted in a highly unstable political situation, which gave rise to countless minor problems. One of these was the Czech question, forming part of the complicated problem of Central, Eastern, and South-Eastern Europe as a whole. The very fact that it was in this region that the immediate cause of the war was to be found testified to the inner conflicts prevailing there.

The war created the kind of situation Czech politicians had thought about throughout the nineteenth century, a situation offering the possibility of a new deal for this part of Europe. Exactly what its future was to be no one knew, either before the war or when it broke out. It was only as the war progressed that this question received a concrete – and unexpected – answer.

To those whose entire lives have been spent in the Czechoslovak Republic its existence seems necessary and is taken for granted. Yet as recently as the years leading up to the First World War, the idea of an independent Czechoslovak state was just so much pie in the sky: that generation was used to the idea of the Austro-Hungarian monarchy. That is not to say that people were blind to its failings, that they were not dissatisfied, and did not seek ways and means to remedy them. However, none of these remedies took into account the breaking up of a great and time-honoured empire. Under the relatively stable European conditions of the nineteenth and early twentieth century, the very idea was unimaginable.

Czech politics were aimed at achieving equality and a certain autonomy within the Habsburg monarchy, against German, and later also Hungarian, domination. Negotiations towards this end were constantly in progress with the Government in Vienna.

The rise to prominence of Imperial Germany was to influence the Habsburg monarchy and Czech policy as much as it influenced world development as a whole. As she grew increasingly more powerful, Germany developed ever closer ties with the Danubian Empire, forging strong economic, political, as well as ideological links between the two countries. Though Austria-Hungary on the one hand tried to resist this, on the other she found the prospect of sharing Germany's immense boom attractive and tempting.

Wealth, prosperity, success – this 'economic miracle' of the Second Empire gave the German nation a welcome feeling of strength, fortifying its pride and self-esteem. Contacts with less prosperous, less civilized peoples evoked feelings of superiority, especially in the younger German generation. The Germans, it was thought, were the world's élite, destined to rule and govern. 'We are entitled to demand that our nation be a *Herrenvolk* which takes its rightful share in the world without relying on the charity of others. *Deutschland wach auf!*' demanded the young Germans organized in the Grossdeutscher Bund. The call for the unity of all Germans and their alliance as an essential condition of world domination was a pan-German theory that inspired the young generation in Austria as well as in Germany itself. Its influence was greatest where the Second German Empire bordered on the Habsburg monarchy and where the growing strength of the Czech nation tended to weaken German positions.

In these circumstances, Czech policy increasingly became a struggle against the growing German influence in Austria-Hungary and against her pan-German theories which were seen as directly endangering the aspirations of a people that had so recently undergone a renascence. The old problem – the problem of the existence of a small nation – reared its head again with renewed urgency.

At the turn of the century, Czech politicians, whatever their allegiance, had attempted to solve this problem within the framework of the Austro-Hungarian Empire, working on the assumption that the Czechs alone could not defend themselves against the growing German expansion. This could only be resisted by Austria-Hungary as a whole. Their differences of opinion concerned the ways and means by which to achieve this Austrian resistance to the influence of the German Reich.

Conservative Catholic circles, together with the Czech nobility, recommended full and faithful support of the Habsburg dynasty, which was also afraid of German influence, believing that the Hohenzollern monarchy would pose a threat to its own position. The Habsburgs relied on international Catholic solidarity and on the Vatican in their struggle against the German ruling dynasty, and the Czech nobles and Catholics hoped that in return for their loyal support the Austrian authorities would grant Bohemia a certain measure of autonomy.

At the other extreme to the Catholic movement stood the Social Democrats, led by Bohumír Šmeral. Having adopted a common policy with the German Social Democratic Party at their Congress in Brno in 1899, they were working towards a democratization of Austria, based on 'universal, equal and free suffrage, with all the feudal privileges abolished, for it is only in such conditions that the working classes, which in actual fact form the real basis of the state and of society, can come into their own'. The Social Democrats therefore demanded that:

'1. Austria be transformed into a democratic, federal state.

'2. Instead of the historical crown lands, autonomous regions should be created, according to the nationality of their inhabitants.

'3. All the autonomous regions of any single nation form one national union which is to have full autonomy in administering its affairs.'

The internal reform of Austria was also the aim of Masaryk's 'realistic group', whose demands were, however, far milder than those put forward by the Social Democratic Party. In the mid-nineties Masaryk had repeatedly stressed the need for keeping the Austro-Hungarian Empire intact:

'Should Austria suffer defeat in a European conflagration, and should she disintegrate as a result, we would be swallowed up by Germany, with whom we have been in contact for thousands of years. What that would mean, anyone can guess.

'. . . our policy cannot hope to succeed unless it be based on a strong and genuine interest in the fate of Austria as a whole, though of course I do not see this interest as a blind, passive loyalty *à la Es gibt nur eine Kaiserstadt*, and so on, but rather as a cultural and political endeavour in keeping with the needs of our people and aimed at the uplifting of Austria and the improvement of its political administration.'

In his programme Masaryk reiterated the need for the pains-taking daily work which would remove the political short-comings of the Austro-Hungarian Empire. He did not at that time demand any far-reaching internal changes, nor did he regard the monarchy as presenting any obstacle.

'The European monarchies today sleep quite calmly next to the French Republic . . . Monarchy still has many stages of development before it, from the absolutist, constitutional form (with aristocratic and *bourgeois* oligarchy in various degrees and combinations) to the parliamentary and more popular, and perhaps even social, form . . .'

Masaryk's views underwent a gradual change following the Russian revolution of 1905, and at the time of the Balkan crisis. These events were the first to mar European stability and indicate the possibility of future changes. The increasing danger represented by Germany, whose influence on Austria was constantly growing, became ever clearer to Masaryk, who studied the pan-German movement and was well aware of the threat it posed. He concentrated on trying to find a defence against it.

He looked first towards Russia, studying the conditions there and publishing his findings in his *Russia and Europe*, a voluminous book that came out in 1913. While rejecting Russian tsarism as as well as Prussian militarism, Masaryk nevertheless differentiated between them. He wrote that, 'Russian tsarism is less horrible than the Prussia of the Hohenzollern in that it is just a rough fist, whereas the German form of tsarism is a fist combined with learning, force combined with conviction and using propaganda for its purposes.'

In the revolution of 1905 he saw an opportunity for the inner rebirth of Russia, which would become a *bourgeois*-democratic society like the countries of Western Europe. A democratic Russia seemed to him a possible pillar in the struggle against Prussian pan-German militarism, as well as a basis for far-reaching social reform in Central Europe.

At the same time Masaryk kept investigating the possible ways in which the countries of Central Europe might develop on their own and find their own defence against pan-Germanism. He was grappling with the age-old dilemma of small nations.

'The problem of a small nation is the problem of the Czech people', he began a lecture on this subject in 1905, asking his listeners, 'What is to be done? We must pool all our resources, do what the poor do. The operative word is associate, band together. Look at the workers! What a wretched group they were, but they improved their lot by banding together. Today everyone will tell you that association is of the utmost importance for those who find themselves in danger . . .'

Masaryk, in 1905, still did not have any clear idea of what concrete political line to take, but in 1908 he made some changes in the proofs of his *The Czech Question* which showed in what direction his search was proceeding. In contrast to his old theory of gradual, non-violent evolution and progress, we find the following sentiment: '. . . there is justification for reform by revolution: no progress would ever have been achieved without revolutions.'

He reiterates this idea in his work *Russia and Europe*, where he says: 'Revolution may be one of the necessary means, in which case it is morally justified; it can become a moral obligation.' Masaryk, of course, did not think of revolution in terms of class warfare but rather as the use of force as a means of achieving certain political aims. Shortly before the war the Social Democrats made a *rapprochement* with the young generation of 'realists' on this platform, which strengthened Masaryk's group politically.

A fourth important current in Czech politics was the group led by Karel Kramář, its policy anchored in a broadly based international political concept rather than a concern with internal reforms within the Austro-Hungarian Empire. Kramář made use of the pan-Slav and Russophile tendencies that had exerted a strong influence on Czech politics in the nineteenth century, adapting them to the needs of the time.

He, too, saw the problems facing a small nation:

'We are too small to be able to carve our own destiny. We're not living on an island but are encircled by enemies. And we can only hope to influence the big powers who have the final say on matters that vitally affect small nations like ours via some large grouping such as the Slavs.'

Kramář's neo-Slavism was conceived as a defence against pan-Germanism. It was based on the new Russian policy, which, since the defeat of Russia by Japan, was increasingly turning away from Asia and towards South-Eastern and Eastern Europe. Another important contributing factor was the 1905 revolution, which brought about a change from absolutism to a constitutional monarchy in Russia. It was the aim of the neo-Slavonic movement to prise Austria-Hungary away from Germany and from her influence. The Slav nations were then to act within the monarchy as a mediator and guarantor of the new Austro-Russian alliance.

In 1908, the year of the sixtieth anniversary of the first Slav Congress in 1848, a new Slav Congress was held in Prague on the initiative of the National Council. Meeting in July, the Congress came out against pan-Germanism and in favour of equality and national as well as cultural freedom for all nations.

> 'All we want [said Kramář, outlining the programme of the movement] is that all Slavs should feel that we have common interests, that the Slav peoples are a single large entity whose vitality is imperilled if one or the other of its branches withers, that Russia will suffer if the Poles succumb in their struggle against Germanism, that both the Poles and the Russians will suffer if we Czechs fail to fulfil our task as the Slav vanguard, and that all of us suffer when the great, mighty Russia is weakened.'

The Congress elected a Slav Council, with Kramář at its head, to implement its programme.

The earnestness of these neo-Slavonic moves is shown, among other things, by Kramář's visit to St Petersburg, carried out in preparation for the Congress with the knowledge and approval of the Austrian Government. Together with Russian politicians, Kramář drank the health of the Austrian Emperor, and direct Russo-Austrian talks were held at the same time.

However, all these promising attempts to bring about an alliance between Austria and Russia were wrecked that very same year by Austria's annexation of Bosnia and Herzegovina. Austria took this step with Germany's backing, and the success of the operation was first and foremost the success of Germany's expansionist policy in the Balkans and Asia Minor.

Following this crisis, Kramář's neo-Slavonic programme began to aim at the creation of a federation of Slav nations under Russian leadership. Shortly before the outbreak of the First

World War, Kramář actually submitted such a plan to the Russian Government, but the moment Austria declared war on Russia in 1914, this policy, based as it was on Austro-Russian collaboration, was doomed to failure.

The adherents of the various concepts of Czech policy were at loggerheads with one another. The Catholic stream was viewed by all the rest as being Germanophile, while both the Kramář group and other Czech nationalists considered the Social Democrats to be un-Czech. The Social Democrats, on the other hand, justifiably criticized their opponents for their jingoistic attitudes, which combined recollections of the past glories of Czech history with hopes for a future that relied on the reactionary Tsarist regime in Russia.

Masaryk found his chief antagonist in Kramář, who considered the former's realism to be nothing more than fruitless academic philosophizing. Moreover, Kramář strongly disagreed with Masaryk on the Slav question, accusing him of lacking patriotism and of betraying his own nation. Masaryk did, in fact, frequently condemn the extreme nationalism which lay at the centre of Kramář's political creed. Kramář, in turn, was quite justified when he referred to Masaryk as a man who was more closely linked with Western culture than with the Slav tradition of the Czech nation, whereas Masaryk saw Kramář's Slavonic ideas as mere fantasies, based on an idealization of Tsarist Russia. The catastrophic defeat Russia had suffered at the hands of the Japanese in 1905 had convinced Masaryk of Russia's fatal inner weakness. And, unlike Kramář, he did not consider the end of absolutism in Russia to be sufficient in itself to overcome this weakness. He kept pointing out that Russia had no real Slav policy and that for her the small Slav nations of Central, Eastern, and South-Eastern Europe were merely pawns in the struggle for power in that area.

But for all these fundamental differences and conflicting views, the four main political currents in Bohemia had one thing in common: a well-founded fear of German expansion, a fear  of the aggressiveness of Kaiser Wilhelm's military and pan-German advisers who were clearly preparing to make a bid for world domination. It was this aspect of the situation that was in the forefront, demanding urgent solution, at the time when the

Austro-Hungarian monarchy entered the war at the side and under the leadership of its German ally.

The shots that rang out in Sarajevo brought discussion and argument to an end; now it was time to act.

# CHAPTER I

# THE BIRTH OF A NEW EUROPE

## The Big Powers at War

When the war broke out it was not possible to forecast the outcome because the two camps were fairly evenly matched. Not even the likely duration of the war could be foretold, though experts on both sides thought more in terms of a quick, modern war than a long struggle. In a short war it would be above all the military preparedness of the combatants, their strategy, and technical equipment that would count.

Czech and Slovak politicians now found themselves very much at sea. Although the war had been long in the making, no one in the Czech political camp had really expected it. It is, after all, a human trait to believe in the unpleasant only when it is actually upon us, and when the war came, it was clear that no Czech politician had managed to draft a concrete programme for the eventuality of a world conflagration. The Catholic circles, naturally enough, continued to support the Habsburg monarchy.

The collapse of the Second International placed the Social Democrats in a critical situation. While before the war the various parties belonging to the International had coined radical slogans calling for the prevention of war by fomenting civil strife, once the world conflict broke out they found themselves too weak to act accordingly. Instead of 'make war on war', the overwhelming majority of the parties of the Second International voted in favour of war loans, i.e. in support of the war. This was the case with the Austrian, and also the Czech, Social Democratic Party. Nor did Masaryk's group have any ready-made programme to deal with the new situation, and as for Kramář's programme, that was obviously negated by the fact that Austria and Russia were now at war.

So with their nation reduced to impotence by the harsh realities of world war, unhappy Czech soldiers left for the front to join the jubilant Germans. The nostalgia typical of the Slavs and the helpless feelings of the Czech soldier were dramatically expressed in the melancholy tone of the popular song:

'Your red kerchief is waving goodbye,
We're fighting the Russians and we don't know why.'

With no effective political leadership to guide them, the people created their own myth about their national destiny. The old, nineteenth-century Russophile tradition, fortified immediately before the war by Kramář's neo-Slavonic movement, bore fruit once the first shock caused by the outbreak of hostilities had worn off. It produced a spontaneous, naïve, but at the same time immensely powerful sympathy for Russia, which was sparked off by the first Austrian defeats, with Russian forces advancing towards the frontiers of the Empire. In the imagination of the frustrated Czechs and Slovaks, Russia was a great Slav brother who would not permit their nations to be annihilated.

The pan-Slav sentiments of the Slav peoples within the Habsburg monarchy were used by the Tsar's military leaders for propaganda purposes, paving the way for their armies as they pushed forward into the Austro-Hungarian Empire. A proclamation issued by the Russian C.-in-C., Grand Duke Nikolay Nikolayevich, which was printed in nine languages including Czech and Slovak, asserted that Russia was about to give back the nations of the Austro-Hungarian Empire their rights and ensure justice for all 'so that each and every nation may develop and maintain the precious heritage of their forefathers – their language and their faith – and, in unison with their brothers, live in peace and accord with their neighbours'.

In the popular interpretation, this general statement, aimed above all at the Orthodox nations of the Balkans, was seen as a promise to re-establish Czech independence. In the Czech lands as well as in Slovakia other manifestos of a similar nature – forgeries turned out by over-enthusiastic Russophiles – went the rounds, being copied over and over again and passed on by word of mouth.

Thus it was with hopes running high that the Czech and Slovak nations awaited the arrival of the approaching Russian forces. The best geese were set aside for the liberators. And at the front, Czech and Slovak troops began to desert to the Russians.

The Austrian Government countered this growing Russophile movement with severe measures, both in the field and at home. Military courts were set up to deal with those who distributed pro-Russian propaganda, sentencing the offenders to long terms of imprisonment and even to death. Karel Kramář, the leader of the Czech pan-Slav movement, was one of those tried and condemned for treason.

Meanwhile, with the help of German forces, the Austrians succeeded in halting the Russian advance, breaking through the Russian front at Gorlitz in May 1915. Czech hopes were dashed, and the authorities strengthened the police régime in the country by instituting a harsh military dictatorship. Yet the Russophile movement proved to be of great value to the Czech and Slovak people in their wartime resistance to the Habsburg monarchy, boosting their morale and providing them with their first, hard-won political experience, misguided though it was in so far as it was based on a completely unrealistic appraisal of the true state of affairs in Tsarist Russia.

The Allies had shared out their military tasks in such a way that Britain and France carried on the war against Germany, while Russia made it clear that she considered Balkan affairs and the problem of Austria-Hungary to be predominantly her own concern. Russia's chief interest centred on the Balkans, with the question of Istanbul figuring uppermost. She wished to enlarge her empire by the annexation of territories with Ukrainian and Polish inhabitants. Especially interested in the Orthodox Slav nations, Russia tried to solve the problems of the other Slav peoples at the time of her military successes – that is, in the latter half of 1914 and the first half of 1915 – by way of autonomy within an Austro-Hungarian Empire suitably reduced in size.

When, after the battle of Gorlitz, the Russian front started receding from the Czech lands, the Russian Government understandably lost interest in the Czech question. In consequence the Western front became increasingly important in Czech eyes. As the Russophile movement failed, carrying Kramář down with it, Masaryk's group, which had emigrated in 1914, gained in importance.

As has already been said, when the war broke out Masaryk had no concrete political programme. He was then only beginning to find his bearings, and towards the end of 1914, at the age of sixty-four, he left Prague for the West. He first of all turned to the leading power in the Allied block, Britain, and he sent their leaders his first plans for the creation of an independent Czechoslovak state. This first draft, completed by Masaryk in October 1914, is known to us only indirectly, from the notes of Professor Seton Watson.

The plan, which proposed linking the historical Czech lands, Bohemia and Moravia, with Slovakia, was based on the assumption that Germany would be unconditionally defeated and crushed, and that Russia would occupy the territory of the future Czechoslovakia, to become her immediate neighbour, as would also an autonomous Poland. In his plan Masaryk also dealt with the economic and financial problems involved. The programme was conceived as an ideal, and it was the younger Czechs and Slovaks especially who believed it would be successfully put into practice.

A second, more precise, and broader plan was drafted in May 1915. Called by Masaryk 'Independent Bohemia', it was handed to the British Government in the form of a confidential memorandum. It starts off by stating that the conflict concerned in particular the following three European powers: Britain, Russia, and Germany. In the Allied camp it was Britain who played the decisive role, France having been weakened in the course of the past century and forced to seek an alliance with Russia in order to withstand Germany. It was against these two Allied powers that Germany's war effort was chiefly aimed – against Britain on the seas and against Russia on land.

German expansion – so the argument ran – above all into Asia, was inspired by the idea of pan-Germanism. This *Drang nach Osten*, its true aims hinted at by the slogan 'Berlin-Baghdad', gave exceptional importance to the problem of Austria-Hungary, and to the small nations within the Empire who were resisting the attemps to drag the monarchy into to assist Germany's plans. Germany was most alarmed that these small nations were at the same time demanding their independence; not only the Czechs but the people of Poland and Serbia as well. And there remained the problem of the Balkans and Turkey.

Since the creation of independent Czech and Serbo-Croat states 'would prevent Germany from colonizing the Balkans and Asia Minor', such a step was in the best interests of the Allies. So ran Masaryk's argument in his first outline of an independent Czechoslovakia.

The memorandum also contained another important statement: 'The attempt to solve these questions . . . which concern the world in this war . . . is the real aim of a resurrected Europe.' Indeed, Masaryk gave a part of his memorandum the heading, 'The Aim of the Great War: a Resurrected Europe.'

Masaryk simultaneously took the first informative and organizational steps in Rome and Geneva. Especially important were the links he forged with the representatives of Czech and Slovak *émigré* colonies in Britain, France, America, and Russia. Hitherto they had lacked contact with one another, while their contacts with their land of origin were purely personal ones. Masaryk became a clearing-house for Czech views.

Another of Masaryk's major concerns was the building up of an intelligence network connecting him with Bohemia. It was at his instigation that an underground organization called the Mafia was established, providing him with detailed information on developments not only in the Czech lands but throughout the Austro-Hungarian Empire. This information, which concerned the internal policy of the Viennese Government as much as the attitude and morale of the Czech as well as the Slovak people, was important to him for two different reasons. On the one hand, passing such information on to the Allies improved his standing with them, and on the other hand the information itself helped to determine his own political strategy which, if it were to succeed, would have to be in keeping with developments at home.

Masaryk, however, did not act officially as a Czech political spokesman, the chief reason for this being that in 1914 and for the greater part of the following year, Czech and Slovak policy at home was quite clearly Russian-oriented. In his drafts submitted to the British Government, Masaryk invariably emphasized the strong pro-Russian sentiments of the Czechs and Slovaks, but he could do nothing to gain effective support in the West for a Russian solution of the Czech question because Russia categorically refused to allow her allies to interfere in what she saw as exclusively her affairs in the Balkans, or in Central Europe. Apart from this, Masaryk doubtless did not feel like coming out on the side of Russia in this respect, owing to his dislike and distrust of the Tsarist regime.

This attitude earned him the disfavour of the Russian Government, and Kramář, in a message sent from Prague at the beginning of 1915, urged him not to do anything which might impair his, Kramář's, plans for a Slav empire dominated by Russia. In the circumstances Masaryk feared, rightly, that if he spoke out against Russia in the West, the political leaders at home might disown him.

There was yet another very important reason for Masaryk's reticence. This was the standpoint adopted by Britain. Masaryk concentrated his efforts on London, where he moved his headquarters in May 1915, but the British Government had never taken much interest in continental politics. It was only Italy's entry into the war on the Allied side, and perhaps also that of Rumania, that caused the British to ask Masaryk for his memorandum on the Czech question. Since their two new allies had been promised parts of the Habsburg Empire, the Entente was forced to take an interest in the future of the rest of Austria-Hungary. Italy declared war on the Habsburg monarchy at the end of May 1915, and on Germany, formerly her chief ally, in August of the same year. In this connection Masaryk's programme was undoubtedly of some value to Britain, even though she, being a naval power, did not have any direct interest in the setting up of an independent Czechoslovak state and was reluctant to give Masaryk the support he needed. However, Masaryk's ideas fell on more receptive ground in a completely unexpected quarter – in France.

Ever since the outbreak of hostilities, France had carried the main burden of the fighting on the European Western front. Her attempt at a breakthrough in Champagne ended in failure, as did Joffre's great offensive. As a continental power, France also took greater interest in the internal situation of the Central Powers. That was why the detailed reports and documents on developments inside Austria, brought to Paris from Prague in September 1915 by Dr Edvard Beneš, one of the chief organizers of the Mafia, were gratefully received by the French Ministry of War, where Beneš's former university professor at Dijon, Professor Eisenmann, now worked in the Information Section. France accordingly gave Masaryk the necessary political support, and it was in Paris that he made his first public appearance.

The immediate impulse for this was provided by the events on the Eastern front, where Russian troops continued to retreat after their defeat at Gorlitz, and by the arrest of Kramář in Prague and the silencing of the Russophile faction that resulted from it. 'To wait for the Russians', Masaryk stressed, 'would be a mistake. They have no political programme, there is disorder and evident treachery in their army, their administration is in a state of chaos, and they have no interest in our affairs.' This being the case, Czech political leaders at home gave Masaryk, through the Mafia, the go-ahead for his action.

On 14 November 1915, Masaryk's group in Paris, which enjoyed the support of Ernest Denis, a professor at the Sorbonne, issued an official statement on behalf of the newly-formed Czech Committee in Exile. The statement was signed by Masaryk and by Josef Dürich, a member of Parliament for the Agrarian Party who had come from Prague as a representative of the Russophiles. The statement also bore the signatures of the representatives of Czech *émigrés* in Russia, America, France, and Great Britain, and of Slovaks living in the United States.

'All the Czech parties have hitherto demanded independence within the Austro-Hungarian Empire; the fratricidal war [the war against Russia] and the ruthless repressive measures taken by Vienna force us to seek independence regardless of Austria-Hungary. . . . Our aim is the establishment of an independent Czechoslovak state. . . .'

This statement marked the beginning of Masaryk's independent political campaign abroad.

Immediately afterwards, Masaryk's cause was joined by Dr M. R. Štefánik, a Slovak with whose active co-operation the Czech Committee became the Czechoslovak National Council, the supreme organ of all Czechs and Slovaks living and working outside Austria-Hungary. Štefánik's participation demonstrated the unity of the future Czechoslovak state, and this was of great political significance both at home and abroad.

Thanks to Štefánik's extensive social and political contacts, Beneš as well as Masaryk himself now had access to the most influential French politicians, their own contacts having hitherto been confined chiefly to the universities. And it was through Štefánik that Masaryk was able to arrange his first audience with the French Prime Minister, Aristide Briand. The official communiqué issued after this meeting announced that France supported the Czechoslovak independence movement.

The movement now concentrated all its efforts on France. That country, which was in the middle of a difficult and bloody war, had a material as well as a political reason for backing the Czechoslovak initiative. France needed soldiers, and Czech units had already been formed there, although their numbers were negligible. It was hoped to augment these Czech forces by volunteers from the ranks of Czech prisoners-of-war in Russia, where they were far more numerous. In the summer and autumn of 1916, negotiations took place between the Czechoslovak National Council and the French Government on the transfer of Czech and Slovak prisoners-of-war from Russia to the Western front. Then in December, an agreement was signed on the formation of an independent Czechoslovak Army.

The Czechoslovak political campaign, however, had one more aspect which France could not fail to appreciate. Masaryk's extensive lecture programme, both in France and in Britain throughout 1916, had an impact that exceeded the limits of a mere political struggle. In his lectures Masaryk gave increasing emphasis to the ethical aspect of the Allied cause which he had already underlined in his memorandum to the British Government. The slogan of a resurrected Europe that was to result from an Allied victory provided the Allies with an ideological weapon they had hitherto lacked, creating a powerful counterweight to the pan-Germanism of the enemy. Its importance grew as events on all fronts gave the Allies fewer and fewer grounds for believing in a speedy and victorious conclusion to the war.

The Eastern front had been in retreat ever since May 1915, while on the Western front the issue remained undecided. Nor was the year 1916, in which both sides had hoped to gain victory, decisive. In the West, the fighting still continued on French territory, with terrible casualties on both sides. The 'hell of Verdun' was followed by an Allied attempt to breach the German front on the Somme, but to no avail. The Central Powers, in their turn, launched a futile offensive in Italy.

In the East a Russian offensive led by Brusilov was intended to relieve the Western and Southern fronts. After a series of successes which achieved a breakthrough in the enemy front, Russian troops advanced as far as the Carpathians. There, however, they were halted, three offensives by Brusilov in succession proving abortive.

In the Balkans the Central Powers had occupied Serbia in 1915. By the end of the following year they had taken Rumania, at the same time intensifying their air and naval campaigns.

The Allied camp showed signs of fatigue as the war dragged on, seemingly without any hope of a successful conclusion. While in the earlier stages of the war there had been something of a balance of power, now the Central Powers seemed to be in the ascendancy.

It was at this moment – at the end of 1916 and the beginning of 1917 – that attempts were made to negotiate an end to the war. The Central Powers went over to the 'peace offensive', turning to President Wilson with a request for mediation. The initiative for this move had come from Vienna. Wilson accepted, opening negotiations with the slogan 'peace without victory', while a number of countries, and in particular the continental big four, Germany, Austria-Hungary, France, and Russia, investigated the possibilities of concluding a separate peace.

All this led to a profound crisis within the Allied camp. And it automatically jeopardized Masaryk's entire campaign, for a peace without victory would at best mean the maintenance of

Peace without
victory bad

SPLiT

the *status quo*, in other words, the continued existence of the Austro-Hungarian Empire. Such an outcome would wreck everything Masaryk and his friends had been working for.

Masaryk's movement was at the same time being weakened from within. After co-operating with Masaryk for a time, the representative of the Russophile branch of the movement, Dürich, left Paris for Russia. With the political and financial support of the Tsarist government he founded a separate National Council, which became the sole recognized organization of Czechs and Slovaks in Russia. The Czechoslovak movement was thus split into two, one in the West led by Masaryk and the other in the East headed by Dürich. Masaryk consequently lost the support of the large colony of *émigrés* in Russia, as well as tens of thousands of soldiers who had deserted from the Austrian Army into Russian captivity.

Russia had a vested interest in the break-up of the Czechoslovak resistance movement into two separate factions. Since she considered Austria-Hungary to be her own affair, she was naturally keen on making Russia the centre of the Czechoslovak movement, merely as part of her own foreign policy. And by isolating Masaryk, Russia was at the same time limiting Western, and in particular French, influence on the solution of the Austro-Hungarian problem. Moreover, Masaryk's plans were now imperilled even in the West, and by the nation that had hitherto been his strongest supporter – France.

The disintegration of the Czechoslovak movement had put a stop to the transfer of Czech and Slovak fighting men from Russia to the Western front, and as a result France had quickly lost interest in the whole business. And, perhaps even more important, since the end of 1916 France had been seeking ways to make peace. One of the most promising was direct negotiation with Austro-Hungarian representatives, and consequently, reaching some sort of agreement with the Habsburg monarchy, rather than disrupting it from within and defeating it at battle, now became the chief aim of the French. This explains why France began to give markedly less support to Masaryk in his efforts to win independence for his nation after the war.

The Austrians, too, tried to smooth the way to a settlement.

The new Emperor Charles, who ascended the throne in November 1916 on the death of Franz Josef, introduced new policies. In a government reshuffle Count Clam-Martinic became the Premier and Count Czernin, Minister of Foreign Affairs. Both of them were members of the Czech aristocracy. These changes were intended to signify that the Czechs had assumed a leading role in the monarchy. And in a further attempt to achieve domestic peace by way of national justice and a settlement with the Czechs, the new Emperor amnestied Karel Kramář, Rašín, Klofáč, and others who had been sentenced to death for their Russophile political activity.

The Emperor's policy was sympathetically regarded by the Allies, in particular by France. Masaryk's worst fears now came to be realized, and Czech politicians at home dissociated themselves from his campaign.

Woodrow Wilson had in the meantime approached both warring sides with a request that they put their claims and proposals on paper in preparation for a peace conference. The Czechoslovak National Council in Paris launched a campaign aimed at getting the issue of an independent Czechoslovakia included on the agenda. It succeeded only partially, the Allies agreeing on a more general and rather ambiguous formulation. They demanded 'the liberation of the Italians, Slavs, Rumanians and Czechoslovaks from foreign domination'. Yet even though this permitted a variety of interpretations, the National Council had good reason to consider it a success, for it was the first official proclamation by the Allies that they were interested not only in the Czech but also the Slovak question.

However, this statement was angrily countered by the official organ of the Czech politicians at home, the Czech Union.

'In view of the reply given by the Allies to the President of the United States, Wilson, in which the countries in a state of war with our Empire have, among other things, listed "the liberation of the Czechs from foreign domination" as one of the goals they seek to achieve by force of arms, the Praesidium of the Czech Union refutes this insinuation, which is based on completely erroneous premises. We declare categorically that, as always in the past, the Czech nation today and in times to come sees its future and conditions for its development only under the Habsburg rule.'

The pro-Austrian stand taken by Czech politicians at this time was also clearly to be seen from a number of propaganda articles and studies published in *Austria Nova* and in the monthly *Das Neue Österreich*.

So it was that as 1916 ended and 1917 began, Masaryk's movement was increasingly swimming against the tide of international developments, losing the Allied support that was essential for its success. And as the chances of Austria-Hungary's survival improved, it found itself disavowed in Czech political circles.

This possibility of imminent defeat brought with it the unenviable prospect of 'the migrant life of an exile after the war'. Masaryk wrote at this time:

'Often when I think about it, it occurs to me whether I ought not to return home. If we were to lose, and our people at home did not do anything, perhaps that would be the best course of action. They would undoubtedly hang me, but at least I would see my wife again, who I fear will not live to see the end of the war. . . .'

## The Year 1917

The war was now in its fourth year. As 1917 began, it seemed that peace would not be long in coming. Then two things happened in quick succession to thwart these hopes.

Firstly, the 'peace offensive' of the Central Powers failed as a result of Germany's refusal to comply with Wilson's suggestion for a specification of the individual countries' war aims. Unlike the Allies, Germany did not agree openly to state her demands, thus confirming the suspicion that her peace initiative was in fact no more than another form of offensive. Germany had counted on an end to hostilities and the calling of a peace conference, at which her military superiority on the battlefields would give her a dominant position. At the conference table she would be able to achieve her dream of world power, without the necessity of continuing the war. Further proof to bear out this interpretation of the peace initiative was provided by Germany's immediate launching of a new, military offensive. And on 1 February 1917, in contravention of all existing international agreements, she started an unlimited submarine war.

This step, which had been hotly debated in the German General Staff for a long time before the actual decision was taken, led not only to an intensification of the main antagonism of the war – that between Britain and Germany – but also to the entry into the war on the Allied side of a power that had so far stood apart from the two blocks, the United States of America.

The American attempts at mediation had not been dictated by idealistic motives but by harsh reality. German naval actions involved attacks on merchant shipping, and America found her freedom of navigation increasingly curtailed. By trying to mediate between the combatants, Wilson had hoped to prevent the American-German conflict from coming to a head. But as soon as Germany unleashed her submarine campaign, the United States broke off diplomatic relations, following this on 6 April 1917 by a declaration of war.

The appearance of the United States on the scene immensely strengthened the Allied cause. And the new situation gave grounds for hope that the Czech and Slovak problem might yet be satisfactorily solved. The danger of a 'peace without victory', which would have meant the maintenance of the *status quo* after the war, receded, and the Czechoslovak independence movement was able to continue its work.

Apart from Germany's action, another factor helped to bring the United States into the war. This was the first eruption, early in 1917, of the Russian revolution. The Tsar was deposed, and a provisional government led by Count Lvov set up. The new Government's work was strongly influenced by the revolutionary soviets of workers, peasants, and soldiers which were established at the same time. There were now, in effect, two governments in Russia, and in the months between the spring and autumn of 1917 events sped towards a climax, which was to be the victory of the proletarian revolution, a new type of revolution, quite distinct from anything the world had known before.

The explosion in the East soon began to alter the very nature of the war, the power struggle between the two camps ceasing to be the one and only issue in this great and costly conflict.

The Russian revolution brought a new protagonist on to the world stage – the popular masses who had borne the chief burden of the war. They now tried to find their own solution to the conflagration, irrespective of the interests of the great powers. It also gave a new direction to the war, its dynamic force pressing the world towards the solution of new problems in a thousand different, often scarcely discernible ways. The war began to assume a different character than it had had originally as a power struggle for world domination. The subconscious ideas of the millions dragged against their will into the machinery of war took on a tangible shape. The world's stability was shaken, old certainties no longer counted, the barriers were down, and the road was clear for new developments. Mankind began openly to attack its new economic, social and ethical problems, the problems of a new world, a new society, a new Europe.

The effect on the world of the Russian revolution was too profound and followed paths too intricate to allow any simple explanation. It would be naïve to try to trace that influence directly in the case of individual events, individual phenomena, or even individual demonstrations. Its influence went much deeper than that, and was therefore also more complicated. The revolution affected entire ways of thought, changing accepted ideas about life and the world. Its influence was felt even by those who viewed it with abhorrence and rejected it.

The Russian revolution had a decisive impact on the Czechoslovak question. Here again its influence found expression in a highly complex process that was intricately bound up with developments elsewhere in the world. While the strengthening of the Entente by the entry of America into the war had opened a new phase of the war, the Russian revolution gave the Czechoslovak cause a new and more concrete basis.

The lack of interest in Czechoslovak problems shown by France at the end of 1916 and beginning of 1917 was now somewhat less marked, though it still continued, by virtue of the growing desire of the Allies in general, and France in particular, to negotiate a separate peace treaty with Austria-Hungary.

It had by this time become evident that the Entente lacked the necessary means to bring about a defeat of the Central Powers as a bloc. German policy ruled out the possibility of any peaceful settlement with that country, and at the same time the Allies had to take into account a new factor – their fear of the consequences of the Russian revolution. This was clearly shown, for instance, by the fact that the U.S.A. only declared war on Germany after the outbreak of the revolution and as a direct reaction to it, to compensate for the disintegration of the Eastern front. All this determined the guide lines of Allied policy in 1917, when it became their intention to split Austria-Hungary off from her partner, Germany, and then sign a separate peace treaty with her. The Allies hoped that an isolated Germany would be unable to withstand their intensified onslaught and that the war could thus be brought to an early end. Another advantage would have been the retention of Austria-Hungary as a buffer state to prevent the spread of revolution.

In Austrian circles, too, there were many who favoured such a solution. Throughout 1917 and right up to the spring of the following year, secret talks were held incessantly, primarily between Austria and France, in the hope that a separate peace might be negotiated. The Americans did not at first declare war on Austria-Hungary for the same reason – in order to try to drive a wedge between her and Germany. War on Austria was only declared later, at the end of 1917.

In these circumstances it was not surprising that France no longer had the same interest in furthering the Czechoslovak cause as she had earlier. But as the situation remained uncertain she never entirely withdrew her support.

For the Czechoslovak National Council in Paris the events of 1917 meant a way out of a seemingly hopeless crisis. It, too, entered on a new phase of its work, trying on the one hand to regain full French support and on the other to thwart the negotiations with Vienna. The National Council therefore sought new allies, one of whom was Italy. The Council's activity throughout 1917, in Italy as well as in France, was concentrated on the foundation of an independent Czechoslovak Army which would be able to take part in the war and thus contribute to an Allied victory.

The Czechoslovak independence movement was, however, soon to receive much stronger support from another quarter, at the same time gaining an entirely new perspective.

Following the success of the Russian February revolution, the Entente, and with it the Czechoslovak leaders in exile, counted on Russia's renewed co-operation in the fight against the Central Powers.

Masaryk welcomed the fall of the Tsar's regime but was apprehensive from the very beginning of what the future might bring. As he put it, 'The first reports about the Russian revolution were vague and incredible: I feared it from the outset.' Over and over again he returned to the example provided by the Russo-Japanese War and the revolution of 1905.

On the other hand he took a hopeful view of the democratic changes that were obviously coming in Russia, finding the new regime politically congenial. The provisional Government included several friends of his, notably Professor Milyukov, the new Foreign Minister, whom he had last met in London in 1916, when they had talked at length about various European, and in particular Central European problems. It was to Milyukov that he sent a telegram immediately after the revolution, on 18 March 1917, in which he gave expression to the hopes he cherished about the outcome of the new Russian policies:

'On behalf of the National Council of the Czech lands, and I may say on behalf of the entire nation, we stand by you in the great work you are undertaking for the Slavs and for mankind as a whole. The solution of the problems of the Slavs is now assured . . . the unification of the Serbo-Croats with the Slovenes and the liberation of Bohemia and Slovakia will come to pass with the aid of a renascent Russia. . . . A free Russia represents the most terrible blow to Prussianism. A free Russia spells death to Austria-Hungary, that hypocritical and treacherous enemy of the Slavs, a free Russia will help strengthen the Entente, a free Russia together with France and England, who are also Asiatic powers, will resolve the old problem of the East, bringing about an organic unity in Europe, Asia and Africa. The great Eastern republic will join in this world policy, whose aim is the transformation of the world and of mankind.'

Masaryk's viewpoint reflected the traditional emotional Czech attitude to Russia which he had hitherto shunned because of his sceptical approach to the Tsarist regime. The new Russian Government was to him a personification of his endeavour to create a democratic society. His joy was all the greater for the crisis his movement had so recently undergone. He was well aware that this Russian solution of the Czechoslovak problem would be the most acceptable one in view of the political feelings of the popular masses in the Czech lands and in Slovakia.

The new Russian Government made it quite clear that it favoured the setting up of an independent Czechoslovak state. Thus Milyukov declared at the end of March: 'By the creation of a Czechoslovak state a barrier will be erected to prevent Germany from carrying out her aggressive plans against the Slav countries.'

Several days later he told journalists from the French newspaper *Temps* that 'their endeavours were only aimed at altering the map of South-Eastern Europe in such a way as to make these alterations permanent. This map presupposes a united and free Poland, the division of the Austro-Hungarian Empire, the creation of an independent Czechoslovak state, the unification of Serbian territories. . . .'

This was the first time that a representative of one of the Allies had come out unequivocally in favour of the procedure recommended by Masaryk's independence movement. Masaryk immediately went to Russia.

Masaryk's first and most important aim was to ascertain the political and military situation in the country, and then to act accordingly. He went to Russia on his own behalf and on that of the Czechoslovak independence movement, but as he was widely recognized as an expert on Russian affairs, his findings provided valuable information for both London and Paris. Both Britain and France were naturally anxious to know whether Russia intended to go on fighting or not. He was disappointed on his arrival in St Petersburg by the discovery that Milyukov was no longer Minister of Foreign Affairs, having been replaced by Kerensky. And he was further disturbed by the obvious growth of the revolutionary movement, which was becoming increasingly clamorous in its demands for an immediate end to the war. Russia was passing through a serious internal crisis, and peace was the only thing its war-weary people wanted.

At the end of May, Masaryk sent word to London that the situation in Russia being what it was, the Allies could no longer count on her further participation in the war.

Masaryk consequently changed his mind and ceased to look upon Russia as the power which would directly resolve the Czechoslovak problem, as the chief and decisive factor influencing his independence movement.

During his stay in Russia he therefore concentrated on trying to heal the rift in the movement caused by Dürich's action in setting up a separate Eastern resistance organization. Masaryk succeeded in this, his hand having been strengthened by the Russian revolution itself.

Dürich, whose activity had been supported by the Tsarist Government, had relied on the pro-Tsarist sections of the Czech and Slovak colony in Russia, on those groups which continued the tradition of Russophile Czech politics represented by Karel Kramář and by Dürich himself. The February revolution had removed these groups from their leading positions, their place being taken by *bourgeois* democratic representatives backing the provisional Government. Dürich was first of all deprived of his office and later expelled from the Czechoslovak National Council. Prisoners-of-war arriving from home were beginning to play a leading part in the organization of Czechoslovak *émigrés* in Russia.

A new organizational structure combining the Czech and Slovak movement in Russia with Masaryk's group in Paris was established at a congress held in Kiev in 1917. The Czechoslovak National Council presided over by Masaryk was proclaimed the supreme organ of the whole movement. It was to have a branch in Russia, to be led by whichever member of the Paris National Council happened to be in Russia at any time. The split in the independence movement was thus healed and organizational unity restored. Masaryk, who returned to Paris the day after the congress ended, was able to work on this basis and further strengthen the newly-achieved unity.

While in Russia he also had to deal with another difficult problem, the creation of armed units of Czechs and Slovaks who wished to fight against Austria-Hungary.

At the very beginning of the war, as early as August 1914, a volunteer force comprising members of the Czech and Slovak *émigré* colonies in Russia had been formed as part of the Russian Army. These men were not expected to fight but engaged in reconnaissance and propaganda. For this reason the force was organized in small units seconded to the various divisions and regiments of the Russian Third Army. An unsuccessful attempt was made at the beginning of 1915 to turn the force into a regular Czech and Slovak army. Instead, qualified industrial workers among Czech and Slovak prisoners-of-war were drafted into special units for work in Russian factories. In the meantime efforts continued to bring about the formation of a proper army, and in the summer of 1916 the Tsar's permission was obtained. This, however, provoked a sharp reaction from the Russian authorities who were opposed to such a step, and the Ministerial Council went so far as to stop the drafting of prisoners-of-war altogether.

The Russian Army had sufficient manpower, while on the other hand qualified workers were badly needed in industry. Apart from this, the military did not take kindly to the idea of building an army of some future Czechoslovak state. Should such a state come into being, they wanted it to be as a result of Russian military action alone. Furthermore, on political grounds the Tsarist authorities viewed with considerable suspicion this Czechoslovak independence movement, which had since the end of 1915 been closely linked with Masaryk's centre in Paris.

The provisional Government with which Masaryk negotiated after his arrival in Russia readily agreed to the formation of an independent Czech and Slovak Army Corps within the Russian forces. Organized on the lines of the French Army, its officers were to use Czech as well as Russian in issuing orders. Reinforced by a lightning recruiting campaign among prisoners-of-war, the newly-formed Corps was able to play its part by the summer of 1917, when it was used to bolster the crumbling Russian front. Its victory at Zborov on 2 July of that year provided an incentive for the further organization of the Czech army.

At the same time, in view of Masaryk's assessment of the Russian situation in May, attempts were made from the very outset to get part of the army transferred to the French front. France and Russia had in 1916 signed an agreement according to which the latter was to reinforce the Western front with its troops, but little had been done to implement that agreement. A mere 16,000 Russian soldiers arrived in France instead of the promised half million.

Masaryk was able to use this agreement in his talks in Paris, suggesting that Czechoslovak soldiers should be sent to France in place of Russians. After negotiations with Masaryk and French representatives in the summer of 1917, the provisional Government gave its consent to the scheme. 30,000 Czechs and Slovaks were to be transferred to France, and in November the first transport left via Archangel. Further contingents were to follow by way of Siberia, as that was a more tranquil route.

It was Masaryk's intention to get the greatest possible number of Czechoslovak soldiers away from Russia, where the situation remained highly unsettled. But before this could be achieved, a second revolution took place and triumphed. The October socialist revolution was to have strong repercussions on the further development and fate of the Czechoslovak Army in Russia.

The victory of the proletarian revolution gave rise to sharp political clashes among the Czechs and Slovaks in the country. The political situation was a most complex one.

We have seen how the February revolution had led to the unification of the Western and Eastern independence movements under Masaryk's leadership. But in spite of this there remained deep political divisions inside the movement which could not be healed by organizational measures alone. Already in the course of 1917 a part of the Czechoslovak Army which favoured the Tsar had defied the leadership and, forming the 'Kornilov battalion', together with specially selected Russian regiments under Kornilov's command, attempted a right-wing *putsch* in September 1917.

When the Russian Army disintegrated following the October revolution, the Czechoslovak legionary corps became even more important than before, with both sides attempting to win its support. This was reflected among the legionaries themselves. Right-wing tendencies grew stronger, and the adherents of the old, Tsarist policy found themselves allied with Tsarist officers in trying to overthrow the Soviet régime. Plans were put forward for the formation of a joint anti-Soviet front made up of former Czechoslovak, Rumanian, and Yugoslav prisoners-of-war. The Kornilov battalion took an active part in the fighting on the Don, by the side of a white army led first by General Kornilov and later by General Denikin.

The Soviet Government, too, tried to win the Czech legions over to its side, supported in this endeavour by the Communists on the left wing of the legions. A revolutionary Czechoslovak soviet of workers and soldiers was even set up in the Russian branch of the National Council, and in February 1918 it tried, unsuccessfully, to overthrow the existing leadership of the legions with a view to forging closer links with the Soviet Government. Following this abortive coup, the left-wing members of the legions started to organize Czechoslovak Red Army units to fight alongside the Soviets.

Masaryk, however, managed to retain his position at the head of the legions, and immediately after the October revolution he took steps to maintain their neutrality in the Russian civil war and to have all the Czechoslovak soldiers, and not only some as had been the intention previously, transported to France.

As a first step it was agreed that the Czechoslovaks could only be used to fight the foreign enemy, i.e. the German and Austro-Hungarian armies. In a letter dated 9 November, Masaryk informed all military authorities and Czechoslovak legion commanders of this agreement.

'On the basis of the agreement reached between the Czechoslovak National Council and the High Command and General Staff to the effect that Czechoslovak troops may not be used in internal Russian conflicts but solely to combat Russia's external enemies, I demand that Czechoslovak military formations should not in any way be involved in the present conflict between the parties.'

The Czechoslovak Army Corps thus proclaimed its neutrality in Russian home affairs.

During 1917 an independent Czechoslovak corps was formed in France as well as in Russia, forming part of the regular French Army.

Another important agreement between the legions and the Soviet government was concluded at the time when preparations were in progress for the Brest-Litovsk peace treaty. According to this agreement, the Czechoslovak legions ceased to be responsible to the Russian Army, becoming part of the newly-formed Czechoslovak Army in France instead. In this way they were in fact incorporated in the French services and were supposed to continue fighting against the Central Powers on the Western front. The Soviet Government agreed to this arrangement, and it was decided that the legionaries would travel by train to Vladivostok by way of Siberia, and thence by Allied ships to France. The Czechoslovak independence movement in Russia would thus cease to exist.

Early in 1918 the first Czechoslovak troop transports entrained for the East.

The decision to take the Czechoslovak legions out of Soviet Russia was in the main a political one. Masaryk's opposition to the socialist revolution was a logical consequence of his political views. As early as 1898, in his *The Social Question,* he had taken a firm and unequivocal stand against Marxism. It was therefore hardly surprising that he did not sympathize with a regime that gave practical expression to Marxist theory.

It was, however, considerations of international policy that were uppermost in his mind when he decided to withdraw the Czechoslovak Army from Russia, namely the negotiation and signing of the Brest-Litovsk separate peace treaty.

The new Soviet Government made every effort to bring the war to a close as quickly as possible, to avoid prolongation of the unimaginable misery suffered by the Russian people. The first measure adopted by the revolutionary government was the Peace Decree.

In it the Government appealed to all the warring states to put an immediate end to hostilities and start peace talks. The Soviet leaders were determined to take Russia out of the war even if they had to sign a separate peace treaty to do it. Revolutionary Russia found itself in a situation in which only such a step could prevent the complete collapse of the Eastern front, where Russian forces were in retreat before the Germans. Peace was essential if the proletarian revolution was to be carried to its successful conclusion throughout the vast expanse of Russia, which was far too busy with its internal problems to be able to continue fighting. That was why Lenin insisted on an immediate peace treaty, for he realized that, however harsh its conditions, only such a treaty could save his revolution.

Following dramatic negotiations, the peace treaty between revolutionary Russia and the Central Powers, Germany and Austria-Hungary, was signed at Brest-Litovsk on 3 March 1918. The treaty gave Germany all of Poland and the Baltic states, shifting her frontiers far to the East and bringing Finland and the Ukraine into her sphere of influence. The continued existence of Austria-Hungary was confirmed. The Central Powers had in fact secured victory on the Eastern front and become the masters of Eastern Europe. In these circumstances the Czechoslovak Army in Russia, fighting for the destruction of the Habsburg monarchy, lost its *raison d'être*. And so Masaryk set about evacuating it.

At the same time he realized that Soviet Russia could no longer be reckoned with as a world power supporting the Czechoslovak independence movement. He had no interest in the new Russia, and as soon as the Brest-Litovsk treaty was signed he left the country. On 7 March 1918 he started out on his long journey, the same as that to be taken by the departing legions – across Siberia to Vladivostok and then across the ocean. He now decided to seek support elsewhere for the creation of an independent Czechoslovakia, and he pinned his hopes on America.

The year 1917 had seen the failure of Masaryk's efforts in Russia, and the situation was not much better in Western

Europe. In France the exiles had achieved success by persuading the Government to approve the formation of an independent Czechoslovak Army, and the independence movement had grown considerably in size and influence. But the overall political situation was not favourable. In spite of the bloody battles on the Western front, the French and the British failed to break through the enemy lines. And, to make matters worse, the Central Powers pushed through successfully on the Italian front in the autumn.

Secret talks went on, chiefly with Austria-Hungary, in the hope that a separate peace might yet be negotiated. Austria tried other means as well to bring the war to an end, making use of the renewed activity of the Second International for the purpose. Through the Stockholm Congress she advocated the integrity of the Habsburg as well as the Turkish empire. The Stockholm Congress passed a resolution in favour of the signing of a peace treaty as soon as possible, to be negotiated on the principle of *status quo ante bellum.*

Yet another, completely different, political force took a stand to save the Habsburg monarchy. On 1 August 1917, Pope Benedict XV issued a note urging peace talks and a speedy end to the war on the basis of pre-war conditions. In so doing, the Vatican came out on the side of the 'most Catholic power' and the 'most Catholic dynasty', but by taking up arms on behalf of Austria-Hungary, the Vatican was also fighting its own battle, defending its whole Byzantine heritage.

In November 1917 Britain also started secret talks with Austria, which, if successful, would have meant the end of hostilities between the two countries and the survival of the Austro-Hungarian Empire after the war.

On 5 January 1918, speaking in the name of the Allies as well as of his own country, Lloyd George announced that the war could only end by a genuine victory over German militarism, but that the British Government had no intention of dividing up the territory of the Central Powers, preferring to grant the various nations of Austria-Hungary their old wish and give them autonomy based on democratic principles. Three days later President Wilson made public the finalized programme of the Allies in the famous fourteen points. The Wilson Plan was not

only a programme of Allied war aims, it was at the same time
conceived as a defence against the ideas of the Russian revolution. Accepting the attractive slogan of the October revolution
on the self-determination of nations, Wilson did his utmost to
prevent the further spread of the revolution itself, in particular
in Central, Eastern, and South-Eastern Europe where its
example was most likely to be followed.

Wilson's programme reflects the endeavour of the Entente to
maintain a stable power structure in that area in order to
prevent the spread of the revolution from its Russian centre. In
Point 10 it said: 'The nations of Austria-Hungary, whom we
wish to find their rightful place among the nations, ought to be
given the opportunity for an absolutely free, autonomous
development.'

Both these declarations – Lloyd George's and Woodrow
Wilson's – dealt a political blow to Masaryk's campaign, clearly
showing the intention of the Allies to maintain the Austro-
Hungarian monarchy intact after the war.

But just as the Russian revolution of 1917 had changed the
character of the war, which ceased to be merely a struggle
between two power blocs, so did these blocs no longer act
as the decisive force in determining the fate of Central,
Eastern, and South-Eastern Europe and of the Habsburg
monarchy.

Under the influence of the Russian revolution there came into
being here a political current independent of power politics, a
current which came to the forefront in the confusion of 1917. It
was created· by the revolutionary movement of the broadest
popular masses – the soldiers in the trenches, as well as the
peasants and workers at home. The Russian revolution was the
key which opened the floodgates.

This revolutionary current was lagging behind its Russian
exemplar, both in its pace and in its aims, but its strength grew
in keeping with the revolutionary wave in Russia. As a movement it demanded self-determination of nations, peace, and
land.

Since the heyday of the Russophile movement in the early
stages of the war the Czechs and Slovaks had experienced a
period of tough military dictatorship. Political opposition to the

monarchy took the form of silent passive resistance and of de-
sertion by Czech and Slovak soldiers to the enemy – the Russians,
Serbians, or Italians. There was a stifling atmosphere in the
country, some of whose leading politicians decided to collaborate
with the Habsburg monarchy, as was shown in January 1917 by
the completely pro-Austrian proclamation issued by the Czech
Union.

The Russian revolution of February 1917 marked a turning-
point in this development, dealing yet another and this time
final blow to the Russophiles. In prison, Kramář reacted to
news of the revolution by saying laconically, 'We're finished.'

The revolution, however, gave new strength to other Czech
political tendencies. The traditional pro-Russian feelings no
doubt played their part, but in a different guise. As far as the
ordinary man-in-the-street was concerned, Russia was still the
great Slav brother. And if this relation had now got rid of his
Tsar, this was considered a step worthy of imitation, the more
so as the Czechs and Slovaks were ruled by a foreign emperor.
The Russian revolution went to show that in the turmoil of war
such a thing was not impossible.

The Russian revolution rapidly intensified the anti-Habsburg
attitude of the Czechs and Slovaks. When the Austrian Government convened Parliament for 30 May, there was strong
popular pressure on the Czech representatives not to go against
the will of the nation any longer and to stop supporting the
monarchy. On 17 May 1917 Czech writers, on the initiative of
Jaroslav Kvapil, issued a manifesto protesting against the pro-
Habsburg policy of the Czech Union and urging the nation's
political representatives to act in accordance with the people's
wishes.

The newly-formed workers movement became a part of this
political current. Following the example of the Russian revolutionary soviets, Czech factory workers set up the first illegal
workers' council. The strike wave that had hit the country
throughout the spring culminated in a protest demonstration
held on the day of the opening of Parliament, 30 May. A resolution addressed to the Czech members of Parliament demanded
that they, 'in this historic hour work for the establishment . . . of
a Czechoslovak state, basing their claim on the great ideal of the

Russian revolution which speaks of every European nation's right to self-determination'.

The Prague police authorities reacted on 31 May with official proclamations posted at every street corner, announcing that at a time when 'our brothers are shedding their blood in the field for the homeland . . . any disorder or demonstrative gatherings in the streets and squares will no longer be tolerated and will, without further warning, be dispersed by force of arms'.

Military discipline was introduced in all steel works and coal mines. All workers between the ages of seventeen and fifty were proclaimed soldiers, forced to take an oath of allegiance to Austria, and placed under military law. This meant that anyone who complained about low wages was guilty of mutiny and treason.

Nevertheless the strikes continued. The movement acquired an increasingly political character and rapidly became a struggle for national independence. In August 1917 the military authorities reported on the situation in Bohemia in the following words: 'Silent forces are at work among the working population . . . which have a purely political character. . . . They take the form of meetings, predominantly in secret, and it would seem that their aim is to create more revolutionary ferment'.

On 9 November 1917, all Czech newspapers carried reports on the new revolution in Russia. Radio stations monitored the appeals sent from St Petersburg to all the armies, as well as the statement made by the military revolutionary council to the effect that 'the revolution of the workers and soldiers has triumphed in Petersburg'.

The press also reported on the programme of the new revolutionary Russian Government. On 26 November *Právo lidu* printed the official Soviet proclamation signed by Lenin and Stalin, which said:

'The November revolution was started in the name of universal liberation. We shall liberate the peasants from their estate-owning overlords. The right of land ownership no longer exists. We have abolished it.
'We have liberated the soldiers from autocratic generals. As from today, generals will be elected and can be removed.

'We shall put the factories under the workers' control and liberate the people, who are still suffering. . . .

'Freedom and sovereignty will be guaranteed to all the nations of Russia.

'Every nationality will have the right to form its own state, thus having the right of self-determination guaranteed.

'National and religious privileges and discrimination of every kind are to be abolished.

'National minorities are to have the right of completely free development.'

A few days later, on 30 November 1917, the Czech press printed the peace proposals put by the Soviet Government to all the nations concerned.

The socialist revolution acted as a catalyst in Bohemia, affecting Czech politics on two levels. First there was its consistently revolutionary, class programme, which appealed to the proletariat and provided it with the incentive to attempt a revolution of its own. The Soviet Government's decree concerning peace and land ownership signposted the way for the Czech working class.

The Soviet demand for the self-determination of nations also inspired Czech *bourgeois* politicians. Under revolutionary pressure from below and under the influence of the far-reaching programme of self-determination, Czech politics underwent a marked change as 1917 ended and 1918 began, turning away from the earlier fixation on Austria. The existence of an independent Czechoslovak state now became a distinct possibility, and Czech politicians adopted it as their programme. A similar situation arose in the other nations of the Austro-Hungarian monarchy.

The Austrian Government, troubled by difficult internal problems, welcomed the Soviet peace proposals, which were in harmony with its own efforts to bring the war to a close. That was seen as the only hope of saving the monarchy. On 30 November the Austrian Premier Seidler announced that, like the German Government, his administration accepted the Soviet invitation to start peace talks. On the other hand Seidler rejected the second part of the Soviet programme on the right of nations to self-determination. In this, however, he was opposed by Czech political circles, which had the support of Yugoslav leaders.

A conference under the historic title of 'The General Assembly of Deputies from the Czech Lands' was held in Prague on 6 January 1918. The conference adopted a declaration which, 'on behalf of the Czech people and the oppressed and politically silenced Slovaks in Hungary', read as follows:

'The new Russia, in her endeavour to bring about universal peace, has included in the peace terms the principle of the self-determination of nations, which means that the peoples should by their own choice decide if they wish to build an independent state of their own or form part of a bigger entity together with other nations. . . . Like all the democracies of the world, our nation desires universal and lasting peace. It is, however, fully aware of the truth that peace can only be lasting if it rights ancient injustices, the brutal power of arms superiority, as well as the domination of certain nations by others, a peace that will give nations great and small a chance to develop and will liberate those peoples which are still labouring under a foreign yoke.

'Our nation demands its independence, basing its claim on its historic rights and imbued by the desire, in free competition with other free nations, as a sovereign, democratic and socially just state built on the equality of all its citizens in the historic Czech lands and in Slovakia, to contribute to the great new progress of mankind on the basis of freedom and brotherhood, giving the national minorities in its state full minority rights. . . .'

With this declaration Czech politicians put forward their claim for an independent Czechoslovakia, laying the foundations for a political union between the Czech leaders at home and Masaryk's independence movement abroad.

Thus, at the end of 1917 and the beginning of 1918, primarily as a result of the October revolution in Russia, the war situation was rife with paradox.

The Allied great powers – Britain and America – fearing

the spread of revolution in Central, Eastern, and South-Eastern Europe, openly advocated the retention of the Austro-Hungarian monarchy. Masaryk left revolutionary Russia, in which he failed to find support for his movement. But the popular masses, acting on the inspiration of the Russian proletarian revolution, stood up to achieve national independence, sweeping the *bourgeoisie* along with them under the slogan of every nation's right to self-determination. And thus a large region adjacent to the Russian revolutionary centre – the region comprising Central, Eastern, and South-Eastern Europe – began to disintegrate.

## The Avalanche

On 11 January 1918 the Prague Vice-Regent, Count Coudenhove, wrote to his friend, the Austro-Hungarian Minister of Foreign Affairs, Count Czernin, who was at that time in Brest-Litovsk:

'I have no doubt that the Austrian Government has informed you how low are our stocks of grain, which will have to last until the next harvest. However, the impression I gained in Vienna leads me to believe that you are not aware of the whole truth, which is that we are faced with unavoidable catastrophe within the next few weeks unless we get help from abroad at the eleventh hour. The stocks in the Czech lands will last, at best, until the middle of April, and then only if it will not prove necessary to send anything to other countries. The situation is incomparably worse in the other Crown lands, where there are already grave shortages. Difficulties are beginning here in Bohemia, too, since the grain required for the normal rations is in short supply. In the last few days in Vienna I had the opportunity to discover how desperate the overall situation of the monarchy really is. The monarchy is receiving very little from Hungary. Another 10,000 truckloads are due from Rumania, which still leaves a deficit of 30,000 without which it will perish. Having found out the true state of affairs, I went to the Premier in order to discuss the situation with him. I asked him whether he was aware that as things stood at present, both the war industry and rail transport would come to a complete standstill in a matter of weeks, the army would not get its supplies and would collapse, this leading to the destruction not only of Austria but also of Hungary. To each of my questions he replied "Yes, I know about that", and told me that he was doing all he could to achieve some improvement as regards the markets and supplies. No one, not even the Emperor himself, had succeeded in doing anything about it. All that remained was to hope that some *deus ex machina* would at the last moment save the monarchy from the worst.'

But no *deus ex machina* appeared. On the contrary, as the year progressed, the spectre of famine and of the social, economic, political, and military collapse of the Danubian monarchy became a reality.

At the beginning of this train of events, by which the Austro-Hungarian Empire was plunged ever deeper into a crippling crisis, was the great, spontaneous January strike. Its immediate cause was the reduction of the flour ration, and the strike spread from the large industrial centres to affect all of Austria. Hungarian workers downed tools in sympathy with their Austrian colleagues. On the railways transport was brought to a standstill. What was originally intended as a protest demonstration soon grew into something far more significant. Revolutionary leaflets were distributed among the workers, calling for the immediate signing of a peace treaty. The leaflets urged the workers to unite under the red banner of the revolution, demanding that representatives of the Austrian proletariat take part in the peace talks with Soviet Russia. Workers' soviets were elected, and they demanded the release of imprisoned proletarian leaders, in particular of Viktor Adler. The movement found support in the revolutionary wave that swept neighbouring Germany, led by a group of revolutionaries from the Spartakus Union, which early in 1917 had centred around Karl Liebknecht and Rosa Luxemburg. The movement followed the same road as the proletarian revolution in Russia, its aim being a socialist revolution in Austria-Hungary and Germany.

'During recent strike action in Vienna,' said a report from the

Austrian Ministry of the Interior, 'it was ascertained that various agitators, mostly belonging to the young generation, tried particularly hard to spread among the workers revolutionary principles that correspond exactly to the views held at the present time by the Bolshevik Party in Russia.'

The Austrian Government succeeded in suppressing the January strike, but the damage was done: by its size and revolutionary goals it had shaken the very foundations of the Habsburg monarchy.

Shop stewards came from Austria to the Czech lands, urging Czech workers to follow the Austrian example. A general strike was declared in Bohemia on 22 January 1918, but it did not lead to the formulation of the same revolutionary aims as in Austria and Hungary. The workers' chief demands were the speedy negotiation of peace and the implementation of the nations' right to self-determination.

This strike was followed by the first military mutiny. On 1 February 1918, men of V Division of the Austro-Hungarian Navy, which was at anchor in Kotor Bay, hoisted the red flag of revolution on the masts of their ships. The sailors, among them many Czechs and Yugoslavs, demanded that the Government sign a peace treaty and acknowledge the nations' right to self-determination. However, they lacked the necessary political and organizational experience, and their mutiny was suppressed within three weeks. But it was the first manifestation of trouble inside the Austro-Hungarian armed forces. How important the mutiny really was can be judged from the way it was dealt with by the authorities. The Minister of Foreign Affairs, Count Czernin, took a personal part in the trial of the mutineers and demanded the execution of their leaders. The Austro-Hungarian Government in this instance, and in other cases until the autumn of 1918, resorted to brute force in order to set an example and intimidate the growing revolutionary movement. It was the last means at the Government's disposal in its desperate efforts to save the monarchy, but the brutality only led to further resistance, intensifying the existing conflicts within the state.

The spectre of famine had, by March 1918, become harsh reality, hastening the process of disintegration. In the second week of that month many households in Vienna did not receive any flour. On 16 March some twenty-five thousand people stood in a queue all night long in the market hall for the meagre meat ration. The black market flourished. At the end of March, Czech factory workers received a special bonus to enable them to buy the basic foodstuffs on the black market. By May the flour ration was available on paper only. 'What will we eat tomorrow?' was the question on everyone's lips. People were sick and weak. In the Ostrava coalmining region twenty per cent of the population had tuberculosis. The death rate went up alarmingly.

The despair felt by the people turned into a fierce hatred of the Austrian Government and the whole monarchy. At Vítkovice the mayor offered housewives groats in place of flour, receiving the reply, 'Keep them, we want peace and bread!' Strike after strike crippled the war effort, with the Government attempting to deal with the situation by sending in troops against the strikers.

The individual strikes soon became a flood, deluging whole regions of the country. Hungry strikers and their families went on the rampage, destroying and looting farms and mills. In vain the Government declared martial law and sent gendarmes to disperse the demonstrators. The protests went on, shops were broken into, warehouses looted or burned down, public buildings stoned. The starving masses started attacking trains carrying bacon from Hungary to Germany. The army fired on defenceless people, killing three and seriously wounding two in Pardubice, and killing six and wounding many in Pilsen.

When the Brest-Litovsk peace treaty was signed, prisoners-of-war began to return home, bringing eye-witness accounts of the revolution, about which the people still knew very little. The returning men spoke of a great revolution that had given unlimited rights to the workers, peasants, and soldiers.

An official report at the beginning of May 1918 stated that:

'The majority of the prisoners-of-war returning from Russian captivity experienced the revolution and have been exposed to revolutionary tendencies. These men have freedom of movement in their camps, they travel around the neighbouring villages telling the local inhabitants about the Russian revolution, and allegedly some of them go so far as to say that it would be a good thing if it happened here as well.'

The prisoners-of-war, who after a short leave were sent back to the war, also created unrest in the ranks of the Army, helping to hasten its decline. The number of desertions mounted until it turned into an avalanche. At first the authorities condemned deserters to death in accordance with the military law, but as their numbers increased the Government was forced to change its attitude, merely returning captured deserters to their units. But in some regions the men formed armed bands and resisted efforts to send them back to the front.

Whole Army units now mutinied, mostly those made up of members of the oppressed nations, Slovenes, Ukrainians, Czechs. On 21 May, the reserve battalion of VII Rifles at Rumburk, composed mainly of Czechs from the vicinity of Pilsen, rebelled, the mutiny sparked off by former Czech prisoners-of-war, many of whom were included in this battalion on their return from Russia.

The Prague Vice-Regent reported to the Austrian Minister of the Interior:

'The events which were reported to Your Excellency on the twenty-first of this month were so serious that I wish to return to them in more detail. For, despite the fact that they concerned chiefly the military, by affecting the civil population they are of grave consequence also for the civil administration.

'First of all there is an increasingly clearer connection with socio-revolutionary phenomena in Russia and their effect on the military and political conditions and events at home. It is scarcely necessary for me to point out the terrible dangers if they were to spread, especially in Bohemia. . . . As regards the events of 21 May, it is hardly necessary to enlarge on the danger they represent. It is only thanks to the lack of organization and leadership on the part of the mutineers, together with the quick, effective, and resolute action by the military and political organs and the gendarmerie that the mutiny was suppressed in a matter of hours without claiming any victims among the forces of law and order. Had the rebels succeeded in penetrating farther south and gaining – which possibility cannot be discounted – help and support from the local populace, we should today be faced with revolution in various parts of Bohemia.'

In view of the 'terribly grave situation and the possibility that a revolution may break out at any moment', the Vice-Regent asked for the most severe punishment of the mutineers, concluding his alarming report:

'I would not suggest this if the situation, further complicated by the catastrophic shortage of food, were not such that any procrastination, any sign of weakness, and any delay might well result in a complete breakdown of law and order.'

The revolutionary aspect of the independence movement inside Austria-Hungary gained great impetus from the activity of the returning prisoners-of-war who had seen the revolution in Russia, while at the same time friendly relations were established between Austrian, German, and Russian soldiers.

The Soviet Government also appealed for international revolutionary workers' solidarity, by means of leaflets.

'The German and Austrian revolutionary front must join the Russian revolutionary front. Your brothers in Russia are ready, they are waiting for you ... Brothers! The world social revolution is not the fortuitous rampaging of a band of murderers. It is clearing the way. It builds. It does not punish, it uplifts. It liberates. It redeems. Brothers, it can only succeed, you must not see merely the myriad individual details. You must see just the great result in which all these details become one. Brothers, in the name of pure reason, begin!'

As the year 1918 wore on, developments in Austria and Germany began increasingly to resemble those in pre-revolutionary Russia. The profound internal cisis of the monarchy was further exacerbated in April 1918 by the no less grave international crisis.

Throughout 1917 the Entente had been trying to split Austria-Hungary off from Germany and negotiate a separate peace with her. At first it was the French who had the greatest interest in these negotiations, but they failed to achieve their purpose. At the end of 1917 Georges Clemenceau came to the forefront of French political life, and he started to follow a tough anti-Austrian as well as anti-German policy. France's two allies, Britain and the United States, however, maintained their view that it was necessary to save the Austro-Hungarian Empire. Their resolve was certainly stiffened by the socialist revolution in Russia, and in February 1918 they issued their openly pro-Austrian proclamation.

The Austro-Hungarian Government also placed all its hopes in a separate peace with Britain, looking especially to President Wilson for help. The Emperor maintained direct contact with the President through a number of channels, in particular through the Spanish King Alfonso. In an endeavour to keep this as secret as possible, Woodrow Wilson personally typed out his reply to the Emperor Charles.

The Austrians tried to play up the differences that existed between the Allies. In his message to Wilson the Emperor emphasized that they must negotiate a peace treaty under which none of the belligerents would annex any foreign nation. Austria-Hungary, for her part, was determined to do everything in her power to persuade her allies to adhere to this principle. Wilson was asked to do likewise with the Entente. The Emperor's message left no doubt as to against whom this proposal was directed, saying that the sole obstacles to peace were the 'expansionist intentions of Italy and France. If President Wilson succeeds in making these countries abandon them, then the door to peace stands open.'

This was an obvious attempt to drive a wedge between the Allies, between the Americans and the British on the one hand, and the French and the Italians on the other. The very real difference of opinion in the Allied camp made this attempt all the more dangerous.

At the same time the Austro-Hungarian Government was able to draw some comfort from the actual battlefront situation. After the Brest-Litovsk peace treaty was signed, Germany was able to transfer a large part of her armed forces from the Eastern to the Western front. The German High Command was anxious to launch its offensive before the fresh and well-equipped American troops could take a hand in the fighting, and so the German spring offensive began on 21 March 1918. The Germans were winning. They broke through enemy lines and were advancing towards Paris.

Basing his speech on the certainty of a German victory, the Austrian Foreign Minister, Count Czernin, made a statement on 2 April which, in combination with the country's secret negotiations, was aimed at sowing discord in Allied ranks by discrediting and politically isolating the French. In his statement, in which he for the first time openly attacked the Czechoslovak independence movement in exile, referring to 'the poor, wretched Masaryk', Czernin hinted that Clemenceau had made secret approaches to Vienna with a view to negotiating a separate peace.

Paris took this attack as a challenge. Clemenceau knew all about the secret Austrian negotiations with President Wilson and he was fully aware of their anti-French character. Living up to his nickname of 'Tiger', the French Premier used Czernin's statement for a sharp counter-attack, declaring categorically that the Austrian Foreign Minister was lying.

There followed a controversy which greatly discredited the Austrian political leaders. Clemenceau published a facsimile of a letter in Emperor Charles's own handwriting, in which the latter agreed to French claims to Alsace-Lorraine. It became clear that the Emperor had lied, even to his own Foreign Minister, that the Empress was maintaining contacts with the enemy behind the backs of Austria's official representatives, and that Austrian foreign policy was unreliable and disloyal. She was being shifty in her dealings with the Entente, and plainly treacherous towards her German ally. The scandal brought about Czernin's resignation, and the crisis caused by it had serious political consequences which were to affect the further course of the war.

Germany and Austria signed an agreement on 12 May 1918, according to which these two powers entered into a long-term political and military treaty and tariff union designed to foster the economic unification of the signatories. At this decisive moment, when not only the first, but also the second German attempt in April to launch an offensive on the Western front had failed, Berlin gave up all pretence of equality between the two monarchies, asserting its authority over its Habsburg partner in every respect.

The crises that occurred in April and May destroyed all hope of a separate peace between the Allies and Austria-Hungary. In the Allied camp this signified a political victory for Clemenceau, as a result of which a joint military command was created, with the French General Foch as Generalissimo commanding all Allied forces. And once again, as at the beginning of the war, two clear-cut fronts faced each other, Germany assuming the leading role among the Central Powers and France among the Allies.

This change in international politics affected the Austro-Hungarian monarchy in a number of ways. It was now not only France followed closely by Italy, but also Britain and the United States who abandoned, at least officially, their efforts to keep the Austro-Hungarian Empire intact. In the circumstances, Britain saw no alternative to an all-out struggle against the Central Powers, and by April and May of 1918 British politicians had resigned themselves to the fact that this would mean the inevitable downfall of the Habsburg monarchy. Wilson, too, changed his mind on the subject, his view in May and June that 'all the members of the Slav race must be completely liberated from the Austrian yoke' being a far cry from his Fourteen Points, published in February.

And for all the reserve that is evident in the official proclamations of both the British and American Governments, there was no doubt that they had abandoned their earlier policy of trying to save the Austro-Hungarian Empire.

One consequence of this was the increased support given by the Allied powers to the independence movement of the oppressed nations. The first indication of this came at their congress, held at the height of the April crisis in Rome. Meeting

under Italian patronage, this was the first time that the representatives of the Czechs, Slovaks, Poles, Yugoslavs, and
Rumanians had come together. Their political leaders, who had
for years been striving in exile to win independence for their
people, had now pooled their resources and were enjoying the
official support of all the Allied governments.

The change in Allied policy towards Austria-Hungary, and
thus also towards the independence movement of the small
nations forming part of that Empire, was influenced by yet
another factor, which, although it did not enter openly into the
negotiations, none the less played an important and in some
respects even a decisive role.

This factor was the Russian revolution, which had so radically
altered the character of the war, and whose effect was beginning
to be felt in a number of other countries, in particular Germany
and Austria-Hungary. The growing revolutionary activity in
these two countries made them seem less important to the
Allies from the point of view of stemming the tide of European
revolution, and they, fearful of this tide, sought new means for
dealing with the new situation. These were found in the independence movements of the oppressed nations, which were
concerned with self-determination and national independence,
not with socialist revolution. The Allies sought to turn the
'self-determination' slogan of the Russian revolution to their
own advantage.

The conviction grew in the Allied camp that something
would have to be done soon to prevent the proletarian revolution from spreading any further. The first plans for an anti-
Soviet intervention were put forward. And it was in this connection that the Czechoslovak independence movement, with
its own army inside Russia, suddenly gained in importance.

The victory of Clemenceau's foreign policy, supported in the
Allied camp by Italy, had proved beneficial to the Czechoslovak movement, which again chose Paris as its headquarters.
Beneš had been there, busily working and drafting his memoranda throughout the long period of negotiation for a separate
peace with Austria – i.e. from the end of 1916 to the beginning
of 1918 – and when, in 1917, France and Italy gave their consent to the formation of an independent Czechoslovak Army,

unbroken contacts were maintained with the French and Italian Governments. Now the whole movement acquired a new significance.

The Allies were increasingly looking to the Czechoslovak forces in Russia for help in dealing with their problems. But they differed in their views on how to do this. France, fighting off the German spring offensive, needed more troops and wished to see the Czechoslovak Army, now grown to some fifty thousand men, on the hard-pressed Western front. Britain, on the other hand, still not wholeheartedly in favour of Czechoslovak independence, thought that if the Czechoslovak forces were to be used at all, it would be better to use them on the spot in Russia rather than transport them halfway round the world to France. This view was dictated, apart from a variety of other factors, by British reluctance to allow France to increase her influence in Europe after the war. The Americans adopted a similar standpoint, though they did not enter openly into the discussion.

At the beginning of April Britain put forward the first proposals on the role to be played by the Czechoslovak legions in Russia, suggesting that they occupy and defend Siberia in the vicinity of Omsk. Another possibility was to send them to Archangel and, stationing them on the North Sea coast, keep the way to Siberia open via Perm. A third alternative, considered the best by the British, was to send the Czechoslovak forces to the Baikal region to link up with counter-revolutionary units under the command of the White general, Semyonov.

France was at first opposed to this solution, having political as well as military reasons for wanting these troops transferred to France. These Czech legions, while autonomous, were nevertheless part of the French Army, and they were commanded by the French general, Janin. Franco-British talks on this subject continued throughout April, showing what importance the Allies attached to the Czechoslovak legions in Russia.

The Czechoslovak National Council in Paris was not united in its standpoint on the issue, its deliberations made more difficult by the absence of Masaryk and the lack of contact with Russia. Policy decisions at this time were virtually in the hands of two of its representatives, Beneš and Štefánik.

While Štefánik seemed more or less in favour of the Allied

plans, though even he changed his mind about it several times, Beneš adopted a more cautious attitude, resisting the idea that the Czechoslovak Army should be used to fight the Soviet regime. He saw only too clearly that the legions were pawns in a dangerous game, the intention being to make them do a risky job the Allies were none too keen to do themselves. At the same time Beneš realized that the legions had now become an important political factor, and that they greatly improved the standing of the entire Czechoslovak independence movement. 'The negotiations concerning our Army following the revolutionary outburst in Russia had strong repercussions and resulted in our talks with the Allies in Paris and London', wrote Beneš. 'From this moment we have become a force to be reckoned with among the Allies, both politically and as a power.'

On the other hand he was well aware that if the legions were destroyed in Russia – and this was an eventuality that could not be ruled out if they took a hand in fighting the regime – the Czechoslovak independence movement would lose a vital weapon.

In the middle of April, Masaryk himself took a hand in the negotiations. He was in Tokyo at the time, on his way to the United States. On 10 April he prepared a memorandum on the situation in Russia, which he had been asked to provide by the American Government. In it he summed up his views as follows:

'1. The Entente ought to recognize the Soviet Government.

'2. It should not support the various monarchist counter-revolutionary movements such as those led by Alexeyev and Kornilov, or at the present time by Semyonov.

'3. The Bolsheviks would stay in power longer than their opponents expected.

'4. He thought that later some form of coalition would come into existence, with the Russian Communist Party participating in it.

'5. All the small nations in the East ... need a strong Russia, or they will be left at the mercy of the Germans and the Austrians. The Allies must at all costs and by every means give their support to Russia. Should the Germans subjugate the East, they will go on to subjugate the West.'

Masaryk's point of view, which became known in France on 15 April, was most unfavourably received by the Allies, who were now quite clearly preparing to intervene against the Soviets.

The final decision on the part the Czechoslovak legions were to play in the anti-Soviet front was taken at the end of that month. At a meeting of the Supreme War Council at Abbeville on 2 May, attended by all the leading Allied representatives including Clemenceau, Pichon, Foch, Pétain, Lloyd George, and Bliss, it was decided to incorporate the Czech and Slovak legionaries in the intervention campaign. They were to change their route, only those units which happened to be east of Omsk continuing their journey to Vladivostok, as had been originally agreed with Masaryk. There they would be engaged in 'assisting the Allies in their campaign in Siberia'. The trains west of Omsk were to take a different route, to the northern ports of Murmansk and Archangel. The soldiers they were carrying were 'prior to embarkation to be effectively used for the defence of the ports of Archangel and Murmansk, as well as for the guarding and defence of the Murmansk railway'.

This decision came at a time when Japanese and American troops were being sent to the Far East and British and French forces were coming ashore at Murmansk and Archangel. The Czechoslovak legions were to be added to these interventionist armies.

The talks on the subject were held, and the ultimate decision taken, without consultation with the Czechoslovak National Council in Paris, whose members only took an indirect part in the negotiations. They were not asked to participate in the Allied talks, even though the question was of such vital importance to them.

In these circumstances they were powerless to oppose the decision, and the Council tried, on the one hand, to make use of the new role of the legions for the strengthening of the independence movement and, on the other, to save the legions and speed up their departure from Russia. That was why, on instructions from Paris, the Russian branch of the National Council was constantly negotiating with the Soviet Government in an effort to get the legionary trains moving more quickly on their long journey across Russia.

French representatives approached the Soviet authorities on the proposed alteration of the route to be taken by the Czechoslovak legions and on the question of dividing them up into an Eastern and a Western group. The Soviet Government gave its consent, since it was in its own interest to get this foreign army out of the country as quickly as possible. But as the Allied intervention got under way the Soviets realized that the Czechoslovak legions were to be used against them. The Soviet Government therefore tried, as early as April, to delay the legions in their trek to the East. Germany was also bringing pressure to bear in this connection, hoping to slow down the transport of troops who were intended to reinforce the French Army on the Western front.

The People's Commissar Chicherin issued his first order regarding the legions on 21 April: 'The Czechoslovak units must not be moved to the East.'

Once the intervention had been launched, the Soviet Government insisted that the legions be disarmed. On 23 May the head of the Operations Department of the Army Commissariat, Aralov, issued an order to the Red Army, in which he said: 'Confirming an earlier order, I instruct you to take immediate measures for the stopping, disarming, and disbanding of all trains and units of the Czechoslovak Army Corps. . . .'

The whole business was further complicated by the confused situation inside Russia. Communications between the Central Government and local revolutionary organs left a great deal to be desired, so that the latter frequently took individual action, sometimes without reference to the Government, which was itself not united on the best course to adopt. While Lenin was in favour of seeking an amicable settlement with the Czechs, Trotsky advocated a hard, relentless struggle.

Thus it was that the relations between the Government and the Czechoslovak legions, originally extremely good as a result of the victory in a joint action against the Germans at Bakhmach and the comradeship established in the fight against Germany, rapidly deteriorated. By early May they had reached a state of crisis.

The Entente was doing its utmost to bring the legions into the fray on the side of the intervention, and express instructions were issued to this effect. The legions formed part of the French Army, and this in itself made it incumbent on them to obey the Allies. And moreover, they could not leave Russia without the help of Allied ships.

As soon as the intervention started, the legions became an enemy army as far as the Soviet Government was concerned, and the authorities had no alternative but to try and cripple their striking power and liquidate them. The branch of the Czechoslovak National Council in Russia entered into nego-tiations with the Soviet Government in the hope of reaching an agreement, giving its approval to the voluntary disarming of the legions. The Council's representatives, Prokop Maxa and B. Čermák, tried very hard to avoid an open conflict and so avert the mutual slaughter of Soviet and Czechoslovak soldiers. Their efforts culminated on 20 May in an order to the legionaries that they were to surrender their arms to the local soviets under the threat that failure to comply would be treated as treason.

At this point the legions themselves took a hand. The majority of the legionaries were neither anti-Soviet nor pro-Soviet, supporting Masaryk's ruling on the neutrality of the legions, his decision to withdraw them from Russia and send them to the Western front. But although this was the majority view, there were two dissenting factions. One of these factions supported the revolution, and was all for quitting the legions to form Czechoslovak Red Guards. Even though they represented only a minority, these men had a strong influence within the legions. At the same time, following Masaryk's departure, a diametri-cally opposed group began to assert itself. Its political attitude was dictated by old pro-Tsarist sympathies, which now found new adherents among the legion's officers, who maintained close contact with various Russian anti-Soviet groups. These officers were hostile to the Soviet Government and wanted the legions to fight against it.

They soon came into conflict with the National Council representatives attempting to reach an agreement with the Soviets. In some instances members of the Council were actually turned out of the army trains in which they were attending a meeting or discussion. The Soviet Government knew of the activity of these officer groups, and this worsened relations with the legions still further, the mutual distrust affecting even rank-and-file legionaries.

The order by which the legions were split up and their route altered brought the situation to a head. The legionaries were not properly informed and did not realize that it was an Allied decision which had been accepted by the leaders of the independence movement. Indeed, a French representative in Moscow had expressly ordered the Czechoslovak National Council to keep this a secret. Disgruntled by a number of earlier incidents, by the halting of the transports, as well as by the Soviet demands for their disarmament, the legionaries thought it was the Soviet Government which was responsible. Their anger turned against the Soviets and against the National Council representatives who were negotiating with the Soviet Government.

In this tense situation an incident took place on 14 May at Chelyabinsk, a town in the foothills of the Urals, which was to have far-reaching repercussions.

From a train carrying German and Hungarian prisoners-of-war to the West, someone threw a stone at a group of Czechoslovak legionaries who were standing by their own train, hitting one of the Czechs. Pandemonium broke out as the legionaries stopped the prisoner-of-war train, identified the culprit, and 'executed' him on the spot.

The Chelyabinsk soviet started investigating the incident, and ten of the legionaries who had forced the prisoners-of-war to alight and had been present at the killing were arrested. So was a delegation which was sent to the authorities with a request for the release of the imprisoned Czechs. Upon this, Czechoslovak units, which numbered some 8,400 men, invaded the town, placing guards at all crossroads, disarming the Russian sentries and some of the Red Army men in the town, surrounded the soviet headquarters, and secured the release of their compatriots. Then they returned to their trains. From that day there was a state of war between the Czechoslovak soldiers, who held the railway station, and the local soviet, which administered the town. Both sides were on constant alert, posted sentries, and sent out patrols against each other.

In itself the Chelyabinsk incident was of no great consequence; many similar clashes had occurred throughout Russia at the beginning of the civil war. But it was made use of by the officers' group inside the legions for their own purposes. As it happened, the Czechoslovak legions were holding their first congress in Chelyabinsk at that very time, and the Congress decided against the legions travelling north. Instead, they would continue on their way east, to Vladivostok. The Congress also refused to obey the order issued by the Czechoslovak National Council in Russia that the legionaries should surrender their arms, for this was 'against the wishes of the legions, which therefore do not consider it binding'.

At the same time another important decision was taken.

'The Congress of the Czechoslovak Army Corps declares that the troop transports on their way to Vladivostok are no longer in the competence of the Russian branch of the Czechoslovak National Council. The Congress has elected instead a Provisional Executive Committee, which alone is empowered to issue all necessary orders while the transports are on their way to Vladivostok. Any instructions issued by the Russian branch of the Czechoslovak National Council are invalid.'

The Congress had given a clear answer to both questions: it refused to negotiate with the Soviet Government and to obey the existing leadership. This meant that in those critical days of May 1918 Czechoslovak politics in Russia were, for the second time, taken out of the hands of Masaryk's independence movement.

An officers' *putsch* followed, with a triumvirate being formed by members of the Provisional Executive Committee elected at the Congress – Gajda, Čeček, and Vojcechovský. Couriers were sent to all legionary units, which were then scattered all the way from Penza, via Chelyabinsk and Irkutsk, to the Amur railway. Shots rang out along the way, heralding the outbreak of an armed confrontation between the Soviet Government and the Czechoslovak legions in Russia.

At the outset, in the summer of 1918, the legionaries scored one victory after another, occupying the entire Siberian railway, which was an unexpected triumph in view of their relatively

small numbers. This gave them military, political, as well as
economic control over the whole of Siberia.

The action taken by the legions led to a number of anti-
Soviet revolts, and it received some support from the Allied
forces in Russia. But the main brunt of the intervention was
still borne by the Czechoslovak legionaries, who were equally
successful on the European Volga front. Here their advance
culminated in the taking of Kazan, where they captured the
Russian state gold treasure worth 600 million roubles.

However, the legions proved to be a meteor in the anti-
Soviet sky, which faded as swiftly as it had flared up. The first
defeats came at the end of August, followed by retreat before
the reorganized Red Army on the Volga front. These military
failures were accompanied by the first signs of political disintegration within the legions. The legionaries were growing increasingly impatient with the influence exerted by reactionary
officers, and they refused to support a White counter-revolution.
The Allies had promised to give considerable aid to the legions,
but these promises remained on paper, and the legionaries'
wrath turned against the Allies. The worst fears of the Czechoslovak representatives in Paris, and especially of Beneš, were
now realized: the legions in Siberia were left to their own
devices.

By the end of the year, the conflict with the Soviet Government, waged in the immense expanse of Russia, justified the
name given to it by some of those who took part, 'the Siberian
hell'. It was only due to a number of fortunate coincidences that
the Czechoslovak legions did in the end succeed in reaching
home, although the conflict was not officially ended until much
later, in February 1920.

In the situation prevailing in 1918, however, the legions were
of great importance. Their fame spread throughout the world,
and their military achievements impressed the Allied powers.
All this helped to strengthen the political position of the Czechoslovak National Council in Paris, despite the fact that the conflict had taken place contrary to its wishes and efforts. It played
its part in bringing the Czechoslovak National Council speedy
recognition by France, Britain and the United States as the
Provisional Czechoslovak Government.

## Preparing for the Future

In the summer of 1918 it became clear that the defeat of the Central Powers was imminent. The first intimation of this came with the collapse of both German spring offensives, which the German Government, encouraged by initial success, had hoped would end in final victory. In the summer the German Army attempted yet another offensive on a broad front, trying on three occasions to push ahead, but falling back each time. The Austrian front in Italy on the river Piave had already crumbled in June, and in July the Allies launched *their* offensive along the entire Western front. This concerted effort proved too much for the Germans. On 8 August, the battle of Amiens began, with British tanks breaking through the German front. This 'black day' for the German Army was the beginning of the end. A turning-point had at last been reached in the Great War.

The defeats suffered by the Central Powers on all fronts in the summer of 1918 hurtled the Austro-Hungarian Empire towards complete disintegration. The monarchy was in its death throes.

The various nations comprising the centuries-old Danubian Empire began to prepare for their independent future.

In the middle of April, in direct reply to Czernin's speech of the 2nd, in which he had condemned Masaryk's independence movement in exile, the representatives of Czech public life met to take the following solemn oath:

'Firmly convinced that our sacred rights will finally prevail, having indomitable faith in the victory of justice, in the triumph of right over force, liberty over oppression, democracy over privilege, and truth over deception, at this great watershed of history we raise our hands in the dear memory of our forefathers, before the eyes of our resurrected nation, and over the graves of those who fell in the struggle and, in the mighty unison of our souls, we swear today and for all time: We shall remain faithful in work, in battle, in suffering, as far as the grave! We shall not desist until we have won! We shall not desist until we achieve the independence of our nation! Long live the Czechoslovak people! May it remain a budding branch, may its time draw near! May it grow and develop and prosper in freedom and independence, as one of the great, fraternal family of nations, for its own happiness and the welfare of all liberated mankind!'

But political reality was much more prosaic than this rhetorical solemn oath. The ground was being prepared for the creation of an independent state, and this brought into sharp relief the divergences of opinion within the Czech political camp.

There were, to all intents and purposes, three distinct schools of thought, the first represented by the Kramář group, the second by those who were in favour of Masaryk and his movement in exile, and the third, revolutionary one, led by Bohumír Šmeral. This was practically the same political grouping as had existed before the war, with the exception that the Catholics gradually identified themselves with Kramář, who was backed by the newly-formed Czech Democratic Party.

In the second group, the National Socialist Party entered into co-operation with the new leadership of the Social Democrats, which had dropped Šmeral and was now headed by Soukup and Němec. Part of the Mafia also joined up with this group, whose programme was partly the old Social Democrat programme and partly a new one, drafted for the National Socialists by Franke and adopted on 1 April 1918 by the Party Congress. It radically altered the entire party policy, emphasizing not only the struggle for national independence but also the socialist character of the future Czechoslovak state. The collaboration between these two parties created in Czech political life a socialist bloc which supported Masaryk's policies.

Masaryk himself had outlined his political views in the course of 1917, strongly influenced by the revolutionary events in Russia. These views were published in the *Czechoslovak Daily*, a Czech paper issued in Russia, between January and April 1918. Masaryk drafted the final version of his political programme on his way to the United States, publishing it in Washington in October under the title *The New Europe*.

As the title indicated, it dealt with the wider issues of a

European renascence after the war, with Masaryk attempting to define Czechoslovakia's place in the new Europe. As far as internal matters were concerned, Czechoslovakia was to be a republic and to carry out various far-reaching reforms, in particular land reform. This programme, as we shall see, was adopted in the course of 1918 as the official programme of the entire Czechoslovak independence movement in exile.

Apart from these groups, aiming to set up an independent state but differing widely in their ideas on its political form and structure, there existed yet another, dissident group, led by Bohumír Šmeral. It might be as well at this point to look a little more closely at Šmeral's political standpoint, which was to become the subject of a great deal of controversy.

Šmeral had right from the start expressed doubts on the advisability of creating an independent Czechoslovak state, thinking it not only next to impossible but also undesirable that such a state should come into existence. Already before the war he had stated quite categorically:

'... should, by some miracle, the historic Czech state be reconstituted overnight, how could it hope to survive with a full third of its inhabitants being Germans? Such an attempt to renew Czech national independence could very easily become a highly risky gamble with the very existence of the Czech people....'

Looked at with the hindsight of more than half a century, this assessment of the situation and these misgivings can be seen to have some justification. Masaryk himself, and many others, had held similar views at the turn of the century. But at a time when a growing, ruthless pan-German movement threatened to destroy the Czech nation, such an assessment was bound to come into conflict with the nation's desire to defend itself.

Šmeral, however, held on to his beliefs. He refused to co-operate with the Mafia, and was the first of the three leading Czech politicians who, in January 1917, disavowed the Czechoslovak movement in exile, adopting a firmly pro-Austrian attitude.

There was growing opposition to Šmeral inside the Social

Democratic Party, an opposition whose fires were fanned
vigorously from below. The congress of the Second International held in Stockholm in 1917 considerably affected the
course of events. Not by what went on at the actual conference,
for, as we have seen, this ended with a demand for peace on the
basis of a *status quo ante bellum*, but for quite a different reason.
While in Stockholm, the leaders of the Social Democratic
Party – Němec, Habrman, and Šmeral – made personal contact with Professor Maxa, a representative of Masaryk's *émigré*
movement. While earlier contacts between that movement and
the politicians in Prague had been more of an informative
nature, here for the first time serious political discussions were
held. And Šmeral, unlike his two colleagues who came out fully
in support of Masaryk, maintained his sceptical attitude regarding the possibility of Czechoslovak independence.

The Stockholm conference exacerbated the political conflict
within the Social Democratic Party, and in September 1917 an
important political change took place. Faced by a strong opposition, Šmeral resigned as the Party chairman, and leadership of
the Party was assumed by a group which joined Masaryk's
movement in the struggle for an independent Czechoslovakia.

Šmeral's political aims remained the same as they had been –
to preserve the Austrian Empire and effect a political transformation in it. The victory of the Russian proletarian revolution
opened up new vistas and presented Šmeral with new ideas. He
was in close touch with the left wing of the Austrian Social
Democrats, who in turn had strong links with the left-wing
Spartakus movement in Germany. They were all working for a
socialist revolution in the two countries of the Central Powers, a
revolution that in conjunction with Soviet Russia was intended
to solve all existing problems and conflicts.

But Šmeral did not manage to gain sufficient support among
Czechoslovak workers, who were at this stage chiefly interested
in the question of self-determination. This caused a rift between
the Czechoslovak and Austrian workers, which first came into
the open during the January strike in 1918, and then in a
number of other revolutionary situations. The Czech workers
under their new leadership did not join in a strike movement
aimed at achieving the goals of the proletarian revolution.

All this contributed to the weakness of Šmeral's group in the summer of 1918 and prevented it from playing any significant role in Czech political life, which was dominated by the groups led by Kramář and Masaryk.

By May 1918 both these groups were working for the establishment of a Czechoslovak state, though Kramář proceeded very cautiously, the more so because no one expected the monarchy to crumble as soon as it did. On the other hand the pro-Masaryk group, egged on by Beneš from Paris, became increasingly more active, organizing both the April oath and a gathering which was intended to be a follow-up to a congress of the oppressed nations of the Austro-Hungarian Empire held earlier in Rome.

On the occasion of the fiftieth anniversary of the laying of the foundation-stone to the Prague National Theatre, a theatre festival was held in the Czech capital in the middle of May, attended by Czechs, Slovaks, Serbians, Croats, Rumanians, Poles, and Italians. Together with the Rome congress it highlighted the crisis of the Empire and gave added force to those in the Allied camp who argued that Austria-Hungary must be broken up.

Political life now began to revive in Slovakia too. That country, as part of Hungary, had been much worse off than the Czech lands, the relentless Magyarization practised by the authorities making even the most fundamental national and political development impossible. There were no Slovak secondary or technical schools, much less universities, and consequently the intellectual community was very small. The working class and all the other sections of the population were also very weak. The Hungarians did not permit the existence of independent Slovak political parties, deliberately stifling the political life of the nation.

The events of the war years inevitably left their mark on Slovakia, however, just as on the other parts of the Empire. By the end of 1917 regular contacts had been established between the Czech Mafia and Slovak political representatives. And 1 May 1918 saw the awakening of Slovak political life, when a Social Democratic demonstration was held at Liptovský Svätý Mikuláš. Those present passed a resolution, which stated:

'The world war which has now been raging for four years has exacted from all the nations of the world, including the Hungarian branch of the Czechoslovak people, a fearful toll of property, blood, and human life . . . we demand: 1. That the governments seize every opportunity for the conclusion of a just and permanent peace based on an honest solution of all international and internal political problems, a peace that will prevent the outbreak of further wars, bringing the desired calm and freedom to all the nations of Europe. 2. As a natural consequence of this freedom, we demand the unconditional recognition of the right of all nations to self-determination, not only beyond the borders of our monarchy but also of the nations of Austria-Hungary, including the Hungarian branch of the Czechoslovak people. . . .'

The resolution further demanded the introduction of universal suffrage, freedom of speech and of the press, an eight-hour working day, and the end of exploitation.

The first of May gave the necessary impetus to further developments. Slovak politicians began discussing the future of the nation. The younger generation was in favour of a joint Czechoslovak state, advocating a programme of political and cultural unity – the same programme as had been adopted by the Masaryk group in exile.

But there were at the same time those who doubted the wisdom of such a solution, older Slovaks fearing that it would lead to a loss of Slovak national identity. They were also apprehensive of the economic effects if Slovakia were to be linked with the much more highly industrialized Czech lands. These fears were, however, overcome by strong pressure from below as the Slovak people fought against the oppressive measures of the Budapest Government.

Andrej Hlinka put it into words at a conference of the Slovak National Party at Turčanský Svätý Martin on 24 May 1918: 'Our thousand-year-old marriage with the Hungarians has failed. There must be a divorce.'

At this conference too a resolution was adopted, stating:

'The Slovak National Party insists on the Slovak nation's inalienable right to self-determination, claiming for it the right to form an independent state together with Bohemia, Moravia, and Silesia. Matúš Dula will inform the Czech representative in Prague accordingly.'

Slovakia was represented at the Prague theatre festival by Vavro Šrobár. The persecution and imprisonment that followed were characteristic of the harsh measures used by the Hungarians to suppress political opposition.

Thus in the middle of May 1918 Slovakia too had its political movement aiming at the creation of an independent Czecho-slovak state.

The following months brought increasing political activity to both the Czech lands and Slovakia. In July, at the instigation of the Czechoslovak exiles in Paris and the pro-Masaryk group at home, a new representative political body came into being in Prague, setting itself the aim of building an independent Czecho-slovak state. The National Committee, as it was called, re-presented a new spirit in Czechoslovak politics, replacing the Czech Union, which was compromised by its loyalty to the monarchy. Much heart searching had preceded this step, which was only taken after the Czechoslovak National Council in Paris was recognized by the French Government, on 29 June 1918, as the provisional Czechoslovak Government. It was also at a time of a mighty Allied offensive, at a time when the suc-cesses achieved by the Czechoslovak legions in Russia gave rise to the illusion that, with Czechoslovak help, the Soviet Govern-ment might be brought down and the old regime returned to power, restoring the traditional bulwark of Czech conservative politics.

All this undoubtedly played its part in the establishment of the National Committee, which had Karel Kramář for its chairman, Antonín Švehla and V. J. Klofáč as vice-chairmen, and František Soukup as secretary.

The Committee was set up shortly before the final military crisis of September and October 1918. The Austro-Hungarian front had collapsed completely, the soldiers deserting the trenches and the army becoming incapable of any further action. The Germans had been driven back by the Allied offensive and were in retreat all along the Western front. And revolution was gathering force inside both Germany and Austria-Hungary, where workers and soldiers followed the Russian example by forming soviets and trying to overthrow the Government.

The Generals Hindenburg and Ludendorff, representing the Prussian military clique which was the chief exponent of German militarism, demanded an immediate armistice as the only way to avert a revolution, and so on 4 October both the Central Powers asked for a ceasefire.

Simultaneously, the Austro-Hungarian Government made one last attempt to save the Empire, turning to President Wilson with a request that he convene a peace conference on the basis of his Fourteen Points of February 1918, according to which the continued existence of the Empire would be guaranteed. Wilson refused. On 17 October the Austrian Emperor Charles issued a manifesto addressed to all the nations of his monarchy, promising to carry out the federalization of the Empire, but again in vain. The offer was rejected, and Hungary seceded from Austria-Hungary, declaring itself an independent state.

On 27 October the Austrian Government, in a note signed by Andrássy, accepted Wilson's peace conditions, and on 3 November the armistice was signed. Eight days later, on 11 November an armistice was signed in the Compiègne Forest between the Allies and Germany. The war was over.

The last days of the war coincided with the last phase of the Czechoslovak struggle for national independence, a struggle that was now closely linked with efforts to shape the internal structure of the new state and define its international standing. It was conducted in four major political centres – in Prague, throughout Slovakia, in Paris, and in Washington.

Events followed one another thick and fast in that autumn of 1918, the situation changing every day, every hour. Although the end of the war was at hand, no one really expected it to come quite so soon. There was still the possibility of a decisive battle in the spring of 1919, with the end of the conflict some time in the autumn of that year.

The Hungarian Government sought ways and means to loosen its association with Austria and thus avert the approaching catastrophe. But in this respect, too, things took a faster and different turn than that which the Budapest Government desired. A Slovak National Council was formed in mid October, Deputy Juriga making an official announcement on the subject in the Budapest parliament on the nineteenth. In his speech he asserted the Slovak nation's right to self-determination, saying that the Hungarian parliament had no right to make decisions on behalf of the Slovaks. Together with the Rumanians and the Croats, the people of Slovakia stood up in opposition to the Budapest administration.

Ever since the end of August the Czechoslovak National Council in Paris had been receiving reports from Prague about the new peace offensive planned by the Entente, reports that spoke of secret nocturnal meetings in Vienna to discuss the possibility of preserving the Austro-Hungarian Empire intact by means of a separate peace, and political reform on the basis of federalization. Plans for the constitutional reform of the state were submitted by the Austrian Government to representatives of the Czech aristocracy, who were asked for their approval. Austrian governmental circles were showing an increasing interest in reaching an agreement with Czech politicians, the growth of the revolutionary movement providing them with an added incentive.

The representatives of the Czechoslovak independence movement in Paris were most apprehensive of any such agreement with the Austrians. Ample evidence of this is provided by the reports and instructions sent from Paris to Prague at this time, their *leitmotif* being the reiterated request that the Czech politicians should enter into no negotiations with the Austrian Government. That would have made further activity of the movement impossible and led to its eventual liquidation. 'Our position would be most seriously undermined, there would be a crisis in our army, and we should be forced either to resign or to liquidate the movement.'

Similar sentences recurred in Beneš's reports from Paris throughout September and October 1918, proving that there was a real danger of some kind of agreement between the Czech political representatives and the Austrian Government.

A conflict now arose within the National Committee in Prague, with the members of the Kramář group deciding in

September to hold separate meetings to discuss their future course of action. They were preparing to take over the government in Prague as soon as Austria-Hungary capitulated. This group was distrustful of the independence movement in exile, chiefly on political grounds but also for reasons of personal prestige. Kramář and his followers were not so wholeheartedly optimistic about the situation as was Beneš in his messages from Paris, and they therefore kept their options open to the last minute as regards possible negotiations with the Austrian Government. At the same time they were taking steps independently of their colleagues on the Committee, to enable members of the group to assume key positions in the new state.

These efforts were intensified the moment the National Council in Paris became the provisional Czechoslovak Government, following its recognition by France on 29 June, Britain on 9 August, the United States on 2 September, Japan on 9 September, and Italy on 3 October. Trying to dispel their fears, Beneš repeatedly assured the Prague politicians that this was only a part of the Government, which would be supplemented by its Prague members as soon as it was set up.

The movement abroad helped considerably to strengthen the position of the National Committee, but at the same time it severely restricted its political sovereignty. An important role in all this was doubtless played by the pre-war political and personal disputes between Masaryk and Kramář, as well as by the fact that Beneš was an unknown quantity as far as the Czech politicians at home were concerned.

These differences of opinion led to an open conflict, and on 6 September 1918 a new body, the Socialist Council, was formed, a coalition of Social Democrats, National Socialists, and anarchists. Their suspicions aroused by the secret talks conducted by the leadership of the National Committee, they began to plan action of their own.

One of the members of this Socialist Council was Bohumír Šmeral, who gave its work a revolutionary character that its creators had not intended. He acted as the spokesman of the revolutionary proletariat, whose activity in the Czech lands was at that time rapidly becoming a force to be reckoned with.

It was due to the influence of the Socialist Council that an attempt was made on 14 October to end the cautious and hesitant attitude of the National Committee and go over to radical revolutionary action.

The Socialist Council was of the opinion that 'the decision to establish an independent state has already been taken', and that, abroad, the Czechoslovak Republic was already a fact. It therefore wished to carry out a takeover of power at home and proclaim the Republic in Prague itself. Having organized a strike in protest against the export of food from 'our Czechoslovak Republic', the Socialist Council tried to take this opportunity for a *putsch*, giving the following instructions:

> 'Let the speakers, in the name of the sovereignty of the socialist working people which forms the majority of our nation, proclaim our independence, directly as the independence of a sovereign Czechoslovak Republic. Let them emphasize that democratic principles will be adhered to and important socialist problems solved in our state.'

The appeal by the Socialist Council was heeded in a number of places, a socialist Czechoslovak Republic being proclaimed in Písek, Pilsen, Třebíč, Stará Boleslav, Strakonice, and Moravská Ostrava. The assembled populace began to remove the symbols of Austrian sovereignty.

But the campaign had not been properly organized, and when the members of the National Committee learned of the Socialist Council's plan, they realized that it was an attempt to defeat their own political concept. They therefore took immediate precautions against any such action in the country's political centre, Prague. The Austrian authorities also acted against the demonstrators, and so this attempt to proclaim a socialist Czechoslovakia ended in failure. The immediate consequence was the expulsion of Šmeral from the Socialist Council, which was forced to accept the authority of the National Committee, the latter thus acquiring a leading role in Czech affairs at the decisive moment.

On the same day as the abortive attempt to create a socialist republic at home, the Czechoslovak Republic was officially proclaimed abroad, the provisional Czechoslovak Government being named in Paris on 14 October. Masaryk became its President, Premier, and Finance Minister, Beneš was appointed Minister of Interior and of Foreign Affairs; and Štefánik became Minister of War. The provisional Government also appointed its official diplomatic representatives in London, Paris, Rome, Washington, and Omsk, the seat of Kolchak's Siberian government.

The Government drafted its political programme. Masaryk was the author, and it was officially announced on 18 October as the Washington Declaration, in which Czechoslovak independence was proclaimed.

The Washington Declaration was not only the programme of the provisional Czechoslovak Government in Paris but also Masaryk's blueprint for the international role and internal system of the new Czechoslovakia. It stated unequivocally that it was to be a republic, at the same time announcing a number of far-reaching economic, social, and political reforms.

'The Czechoslovak state will be a republic. Aiming at constant progress, it will guarantee absolute freedom of conscience, religion, and science, literature and art, freedom of speech, of the press, of assembly and petition. The Church is to be independent of the state. Our democracy will be based on universal suffrage: women will have political, social, as well as cultural equality with men. The rights of minorities will be safeguarded by proportionate representation; national minorities will enjoy equal rights. The Government will be of a parliamentary form, working on the principles of initiative and referendum. A militia will take the place of a regular army.

'The Czechoslovak people will carry out far-reaching social and economic reforms; large estates will be expropriated and distributed to small farmers, aristocratic privileges will be abolished. Our nation will take over its part of the pre-war Austro-Hungarian national debt, leaving the war debts to those who are responsible for them.

'In its foreign policy the Czechoslovak nation will accept its full share of responsibility for the reorganization of Eastern

Europe. It unreservedly accepts the democratic and social principle of nationalities, and it supports the theory that all treaties and agreements should be negotiated openly and in all sincerity, without resort to secret diplomacy.

'Our constitution will ensure effective, reasonable, and just government, which will rule out any special privileges and prevent legislation favouring any particular class.'

The proclamation of the Czechoslovak Republic in Paris, the setting up of the provisional Government, and the declaration of its programme were the first steps towards the actual creation of the new state.

While all this was taking place, in the middle of October, the Austrian authorities made one last attempt to save the Empire. On 15 October the Emperor Charles signed his manifesto on the federalization of the monarchy, which was made public two days later. It was no secret to the Allies that it was in preparation, and was indeed one of the factors which hastened the establishment of the Czechoslovak Government in Paris and the publication of its programme, which had originally been scheduled for 8 November 1918, the anniversary of the Battle of the White Mountain, which in 1620 brought to an end the attempt by the Czech nobility to regain independence from the Habsburgs. By federalizing the Empire, the Austrian Government hoped to bring unity to Czech politics in a reorganized state. For this reason it permitted Czech politicians to go to Geneva for talks with the representatives of the provisional Czechoslovak Government in Paris. It was still counting on a separate peace with the Allies, who would then, it was hoped, refuse to recognize the Czechoslovak Government in exile, thus leaving the National Committee in Prague in exclusive control. The Austrians counted on being able to come to an agreement with the Committee on the federalization of the Empire and on the position of the Czech lands in the new federation.

None of this was to be fulfilled, however, the talks in Geneva having a completely different outcome from that expected by the Austrian Government. In spite of all its efforts, the talks produced a united front of Czech politicians under the leadership of Masaryk's group. The talks were held between 28 and

31 October 1918, the Czechoslovak independence movement in exile being represented by Eduard Beneš, the Prague politicians by Kramář and Klofáč. They negotiated without having any knowledge of what was happening at home. The presence in Geneva of Kramář, Klofáč, and other members of the National Committee showed that the Committee had not expected events there to reach a climax so soon.

These discussions in Geneva centred on two major issues: the establishment, existence, and international position of an independent Czechoslovak state on the one hand, and its inner structure on the other. The movement in exile had the advantage of clear-cut ideas on both these issues, based on factual documents and a carefully prepared programme, whereas Kramář's group was uncertain how to carry out its aims. The detailed report given by Beneš on the foreign situation and the standing of the provisional Government in Paris was followed by full approval of the Government's actions by the National Committee representatives. There was also an exhaustive discussion of the internal structure of the new Czechoslovakia. Kramář advocated a monarchy on the British model, his old pro-Russian sympathies and the success of the Czechoslovak legions in Russia making him think in terms of some Russian nobleman related to the Romanovs, who he was convinced were going to return to the throne. But the majority of the delegates, though at first lacking unity, unhesitatingly accepted the political programme of the Washington Declaration, which presupposed a republican form of government.

The proclamation issued at the end of the Geneva talks meant that the provisional Government in Paris was recognized as the political representative of Czechoslovakia. Unity had been achieved between Czechoslovak politicians in exile and at home under the aegis of Masaryk's ideas, and it had been achieved at the precise moment that the independent Czechoslovak state was being born in Prague and when, in America, Masaryk himself was conducting far-reaching political negotiations.

Masaryk departed for the U.S.A. on 7 March 1918. Reaching his destination in May, Masaryk stayed in America until the end of November. His chief aim was to work for the destruction of the Austro-Hungarian monarchy and thus for the establishment of an independent Czechoslovak state. Following Wilson's actions in 1917 and at the beginning of 1918, Masaryk realized that it was the U.S.A. who now played the decisive role in Allied politics, and he therefore turned to America for support. At the same time he knew that she sharply differentiated between the two leading Central Powers, being irreconcilably opposed to Germany, whose expansionist aims and naval warfare brought her into direct conflict with American interests. America, however, did not wish to see the collapse of the Austro-Hungarian Empire but was, on the contrary, trying to separate it from its German ally. Wilson's Fourteen Points of February 1918 gave official backing to this attitude, while the President's secret negotiations with Emperor Charles provided unofficial proof.

Masaryk came to America with the intention of starting a propaganda campaign to convince the Americans of the unity that existed between Austrian and German policies, hoping thereby to weaken the pro-Austrian stand of the U.S.A. This was his chief concern during his political campaign on the other side of the Atlantic. But before he ever reached the shores of the U.S.A., American ruling circles were taking an interest in Masaryk for quite a different reason. This was the revolution in Russia and its aftermath.

The American Government regarded Masaryk as an expert on Russian affairs, on the strength of his pre-war book. His information and views on the present situation in Russia, where he had just spent ten months as the socialist revolution gathered force and triumphed, were of first-rate importance. Apart from this, he stood at the head of an army of 50,000 men inside Russia. And so, when he reached Japan en route to the U.S.A. Masaryk was welcomed by the American Ambassador to Tokyo and asked, on behalf of the American Government, to give his views on the events in Russia.

Masaryk then wrote his memorandum of 10 April 1918, in which he recommended recognition of the Soviet Government and the establishment of economic and political relations with it. Published in the middle of April, the memorandum was ill-received by Allied governmental representatives, who were at that time already considering their anti-Soviet intervention. And Masaryk's avowed intention of getting the legions out of Russia lessened American interest in his views.

After his arrival in America, Masaryk officially submitted his memorandum to the American Government on 9 May, together with a second document in which he explained what lay behind his political campaign, a memorandum on the prevailing conditions in Austria-Hungary. In this Masaryk analysed the Central European problem, saying that it was one of the major problems of the war and demanding its democratic solution in the spirit of the nations' right to self-determination.

The Americans, however, were still averse to disintegration of the Austro-Hungarian Empire, although their attitude was somewhat weakened as a result of the political crisis in April and May 1918 which brought discredit to the Austrian government. But the change in American thinking did not go further than the approval given by the United States to the congress of the oppressed nations in Rome, which was mentioned earlier. In his memoirs Masaryk emphasizes the strongly pro-Austrian attitude of leading Americans, including President Wilson himself.

Masaryk devoted all his efforts to changing that attitude. All his interviews, lectures, and public speeches had the sole aim of convincing America that, 'the first thing the Allies ought to understand is that the destruction of Austria-Hungary is the first step to victory. As soon as it is removed, the fate of Germany will be sealed. But as long as Austria-Hungary exists, Germany is invincible.' In this connection Masaryk set to work organizing Czech and Slovak, Croatian and Slovene *émigré* colonies in America, trying to persuade them to take a stand against Austria-Hungary and in favour of the establishment of an independent Czechoslovakia and Yugoslavia. His efforts in this direction resulted in the Pittsburgh Agreement of 30 May 1918, an agreement signed by the representatives of the Slovak League and the Czech National Union, and demanding that the two nations be brought together in an independent Czechoslovak state. In his position as Chairman of the Czechoslovak National Council in Paris, Masaryk was a co-signatory, thus underlining its political relevance to the American public.

Yet, for all the undoubted success achieved by Masaryk in the United States, his activity remained outside the sphere of America's main interest. The American Government was, however, showing an ever increasing concern about events in Russia. That country, and particularly its Asian parts, seemed to present America with fresh economic and thus also political opportunities. And it was in this connection – indeed, *only* in this connection – that America started taking more interest in Czechoslovak affairs. And this was chiefly due to the Czechoslovak legions, which in the latter part of May and early June were becoming the decisive political and military force in Siberia.

As a result, on 19 June Masaryk had his first personal meeting with Woodrow Wilson. The very different aims of the two men can be judged from the way Masaryk, in his introductory speech, tried to focus the President's attention on conditions in Austria-Hungary and the liberation struggle of the oppressed nations, while Wilson, assuring Masaryk of his 'sincere interest', pointed out to him that he wished to discuss 'the grave situation' in Russia.

The two men spent three-quarters of an hour together, most of which time Wilson sounded the expert on Russian affairs on the use to which the Czechoslovak legions could be put, and on the possibilities of trade relations with Siberia. Masaryk refused to commit the legions on the side of the intervention and asked Wilson to help in getting them transferred to the Western front. He again returned to what he considered the most important problem: the necessity of the dismemberment of Austria-Hungary. But President Wilson remained non-committal on the subject.

The continuing success of the legions in the first phase of their intervention and the consequent popularity they enjoyed in America forced Masaryk to reconsider the whole situation. At a time when the legions were fighting the Soviet régime, out of Masaryk's control, his political activity in the U.S.A. increased in scope.

Better than anyone else, Masaryk knew that their fight against the Soviet Government could well end in a tragic blood-bath, and he therefore persevered in his efforts to withdraw the legions from Russia. The Entente, however, did everything to prevent this, for instance by failing to send the ships necessary to transport the legions to France. Masaryk was well aware that the U.S.A. had a vested interest in the legions remaining in Siberia, hoping that with their aid it would be able to gain influence there.

In his endeavour to withdraw the legions Masaryk tried to establish contacts with the Soviet Government, but he encountered determined opposition on the part of the American Government and also of the legions themselves. This being so, Masaryk tried at least to help the legions in their struggle, urging the Americans to send their troops to Siberia and create a broad interventionist front with the participation of other Allied forces. The Czechoslovak legions would then not have had to do other people's dirty work for them. But again his efforts were not rewarded with success. All he achieved was the decision taken by the American Government on 3 August that arms and ammunition were to be sent to the Czechoslovak legions. No real military aid was forthcoming.

By the beginning of September reports began to come in of the legions' first defeats and of the first signs of dissension within their ranks. This led Masaryk to renew his efforts to get the legions out of the country. On 29 October 1918 he sent a cable to Paris, which contained his first instructions to the newly-formed Czechoslovak state: 'If possible, start negotiations with Lenin on sending our army in Russia home; in that case it would travel via Galicia, or even across the Black Sea, provided Turkey surrenders in time.'

Independently of this move, dictated by his anxiety to save the legions from annihilation, Masaryk made political capital out of their successful anti-Soviet intervention, using the part played by the legions in Russia as his argument in trying to persuade the American Government to give recognition to the Czechoslovak National Council as the political representative of the future Czechoslovak state. The Americans, however, showed great unwillingness to do so, as it would have implied, *via facti*, the dismemberment of Austria. It was after the Central Powers were driven back along the entire Western front in August 1918, and after France, Britain, and Italy had officially

recognized the Czechoslovak National Council, the Czechoslovak legions now being fully in command not only of the Volga
front but of the whole of Siberia, that the United States at last
agreed to grant the recognition it had for so long withheld. The
American announcement, made on 3 September, was the first
real success Masaryk's political work in America had brought
him; but even this did not by any means signify complete
victory.

As we have already seen, armistice negotiations between the
Allies and the Central Powers were in progress in September
and October 1918. And it was when, on 4 October, Germany
and Austria laid their joint request before President Wilson,
that the last stage of Masaryk's political struggle really began.

In his reply of 8 October, Woodrow Wilson turned sharply
against one of the defeated Central Powers – against Germany.
A dialogue followed between Washington and Berlin, with
Austria standing quietly on the sidelines, hoping that she might
yet succeed in concluding a separate peace that would impose
less harsh conditions and would, above all, preserve the Empire
intact. That this was still a possibility was borne out by the
cancellation of the congress of the oppressed nations of the
monarchy, which had originally been scheduled to meet in
Paris on 15 October. Hopes of the continued existence of
Austria-Hungary grew considerably stronger.

This danger provided the chief and most urgent reason for
the speedy formation of the provisional Czechoslovak Government in Paris on 14 October 1918. It remains an open question
to what extent it affected the decision of the Socialist Council to
try that same day to proclaim Czechoslovakia's independence
in Prague.

At this critical juncture Masaryk brought political pressure to
bear on President Wilson by solemnly handing over to him, in
person, the 'Declaration of the Independence of the Czechoslovak People by its Provisional Government' – the Washington
Declaration, which was also the political programme of the
Provisional Government in Paris.

The effect the Declaration had was reflected in Wilson's reply
to the Austrian Government of 18 October. The President said
he was 'no longer able to accept the mere autonomy of these

nations [Czechoslovakia and Yugoslavia] as a basis for peace, but must insist that they, and not I, should judge what action on the part of the Austro-Hungarian Government will satisfy the aspirations and views of the nations on their rights and their place as members of the family of nations'.

In this note Wilson openly and publicly refused to play any further part in the attempts to save the Habsburg monarchy. Yet it still did not give clear confirmation of any intention to dismember the Austro-Hungarian Empire. On the contrary, the note once again stressed the necessity of separate negotiations, the solution of the problem of the Empire's internal organization being left to the Austrian Government.

Masaryk therefore did not slacken his efforts, intensifying his pressure on the American Government. At the same time he was laying the foundations, not only of the Czechoslovak state but of a much larger federation to replace the old Danubian monarchy.

The Democratic Middle-European Union, with Masaryk at its head, was formed at a conference of the representatives of the small nations at the beginning of October, specifying the following aims:

'1. To create a continuous barrier of free, democratic nations co-operating with one another, from the Balkans to the Mediterranean, as a bulwark of freedom and world peace against imperialist aggression.

'2. To dismember Austria-Hungary.

'3. To help organize and strengthen the new states and bring about the cultural and economic reorganization of Europe.'

A congress of the oppressed nations of Central, Eastern, and South-Eastern Europe was held at the Union's suggestion in Philadelphia between 23 and 26 October, attended by the representatives of Czechoslovakia, as well as by Poles, Yugoslavs Ukrainians, Lithuanians, Rumanians, Italians, Greeks, Albanians, Jews, and Armenians. Presiding over the congress in the historic Independence Hall, Masaryk sat in the same chair in which, in 1776, George Hancock, Benjamin Franklin, and Thomas Jefferson signed the declaration announcing the birth of the new American State.

The Congress adopted a declaration on the common interests of the nations of Central, Eastern, and South-Eastern Europe, which was seen as the beginning of their new co-operation, 'the beginning of a union which will act to promote prosperity and peace throughout the world'.

Masaryk was here beginning to implement his great concept for the creation of a new, democratic Central, Eastern, and South-Eastern Europe, whose ideals he set out in his book, *The New Europe*, written during his trip to America across Siberia and the Pacific. At a moment when the struggle for the creation of new independent states was culminating in Europe, Masaryk was trying to forge new links between them, having in mind a similar instance – the birth of the United States of America one and a half centuries earlier.

But it was not to be. The Middle-European Union in America began to disintegrate as soon as the independent national states came into existence. Masaryk's plan for their federalization encountered insurmountable obstacles, and the new countries themselves resisted it. As a result, Masaryk's concept never became reality.

## The Decision

On the morning of 28 October 1918 Austria made public the reply sent by her Foreign Minister Andrássy to President Wilson's note of the eighteenth. The nation, weary of war and suffering, read the following words:

> '. . . as regards the President's decision to negotiate separately with Austria-Hungary on the questions of an armistice and peace, the Austro-Hungarian Government has the honour to declare that, just as it agreed with his earlier pronouncements, it is in agreement with his view, contained in his last Note, regarding the rights of the nations of Austria-Hungary, in particular the rights of the Czechoslovaks and Yugoslavs.'

None of those who read the statement paid any attention to the careful diplomatic wording of the note, which made it clear that Austria wanted a separate peace treaty, but which was far less clear about the rights of the peoples of Czechoslovakia and Yugoslavia. The nations concerned interpreted the note quite unambiguously to the effect that Austria had been defeated. The door had been thrown open for them to leave the Danubian Empire, the day of long-awaited liberation was at hand. With thoughts such as these, the people poured into the streets in order to put the finishing touches to the overthrow of the centuries-old monarchy.

Red-and-white flags and red-white-and-blue tricolours were hoisted in Prague. Soldiers tore the hated 'Charlies' (badges with the Habsburg sceptre and the Emperor's initials, symbolizing the Austrian state power) from their forage-caps, signs with the two-headed Austrian eagle were removed from public buildings, singing and cheering crowds tearing them down and throwing them in the river. Cries of 'long live independent Czechoslovakia!' were heard everywhere.

Now, and only now, the National Committee decided to put into operation its plan for a political coup. The leading role was played by 'the men of 28 October' – Rašín, Švehla, Soukup, Stříbrný, and Vavro Šrobár, who came to Prague that day from Slovakia.

In the morning the National Committee took charge of the key economic centre, the Corn Exchange, taking over the public and military administration in the course of the day. In the evening hours the National Committee issued its first public proclamation:

> 'To the Czechoslovak people. Your age-old dream has become reality. This day the independent Czechoslovak state has taken its place among the free, civilized states of the world.'

At the same time the National Committee assumed the function of a provisional government, promulgated the first law of the new republic, and took precautions to prevent the popular movement from going over to revolutionary activity not in line with its own political programme.

That afternoon the first reports of the coup spread to other Czech towns and villages. Officially, it was announced by the

National Committee in a 'round robin' telegram, with which went the text of the first law of the Republic, proclaiming the founding of an independent Czechoslovak state. In the course of the following two days – 29 and 30 October – local national committees were set up throughout Bohemia and Moravia, and they put into practice the instructions sent out by the National Committee in Prague.

Slovakia joined in on 30 October, when representatives of Slovak national and political life met at Turčanský Svätý Martin on the initiative of the Slovak National Council. The Hungarian Government had virtually cut Slovakia off from the rest of the world, so that those taking part in the conference knew nothing of Andrássy's note, nor did they have any inkling of what had taken place in Prague. Outside the windows lay the stacked rifles of Hungarian soldiers, who had orders to suppress any public demonstrations.

It was in this sombre atmosphere that the Martin conference was held, to consider the future of the Slovak people. In spite of the circumstances under which they met, the delegates expressed their joy at the approaching end of the war, referring in their speeches to the disintegration of Austria-Hungary.

The conference elected a twelve-member National Council to be the sole authorized spokesman of the Slovak nation. The twelve included representatives of three different political groups: the nationalists, the Catholics, and the Social Democrats, Matúš Dula being elected Chairman.

A resolution known as the Martin Declaration was adopted at the close of the conference:

'The National Council ... declares: 1. The Slovaks are part of the united Czecho-Slovak nation, both from a linguistic and a cultural-historical point of view. . . .

'2. We, too, demand for this Czechoslovak nation the right of self-determination on the basis of complete independence. . . .'

The Martin Declaration was of decisive importance for Slovakia's political development. Though it did not speak in so many words about the establishment of a sovereign Czechoslovak state, and although the National Council took no practical steps to seize power, the Slovaks were left in no doubt as to the meaning of the Declaration, seeing in it their liberation from the harsh Hungarian rule and their freedom in a new, independent Czechoslovak state. The Martin Declaration was not only published in the press, it was also read from church pulpits, in front of town halls, in the squares. It became the foundation-stone of the newly-formed state.

Just as did the Czechs and Slovaks, so the people of other nations formerly belonging to the Austro-Hungarian Empire decided their future in those last days of October. On 29 October the 'National Council of the Slovenes, Croats, and Serbians' took over all power in the new Yugoslavia. An independent Poland and Great Rumania came into being, a new German Austria – *Deutsch-Österreich* – was constituted, Hungary withdrew from the federation, splitting apart in the process. The Ottoman Empire on the Bosporus collapsed, Germany disintegrated. The whole of Central, Eastern, and South-Eastern Europe was on the move.

The war and the defeat of the Central Powers, together with the effects of the revolution in Russia, combined to create the chaos out of which, in November and December 1918, the contours of the new states gradually emerged.

As the machinery of war ground to a halt, industry came to a standstill, and there was no force capable of starting the wheels rolling on peacetime production. All the participants were exhausted; there was an acute shortage of food, clothing, and coal, and winter was coming. Central, Eastern, and South-Eastern Europe was a region of confusion and hunger.

The governments of the newly-born countries had no means of asserting their authority, possessing neither an army nor as yet a police force, and being left with a defunct state administration. The old frontiers were gone and new ones had not yet been drawn up. Hundreds of thousands of armed men were returning from the fronts. A region inhabited by over 100 million people had become completely unstable.

The general chaos naturally left its mark on the first days of the Czechoslovak Republic. The orders issued by the National Committee in Prague remained mostly in the realm of fiction, and in the middle of November it seemed indeed as if they were never going to be translated into reality.

The Germans living in the border regions refused to become part of the new state, and the situation in Slovakia was extremely complicated.

When the independent Czechoslovak state was proclaimed in Prague on 28 October 1918, all the German deputies from the Czech lands were hastily summoned to Vienna. Meeting there on the following day, they announced the formation of an independent German-speaking province in North-West Bohemia, which they named Deutschböhmen. A constitution was immediately drafted, a provincial parliament established in Liberec, and an independent provincial government set up, with Deputy Pacher at its head. A few days later he was replaced by Lodgman von Auen, a liberal German politician. On 30 October the Austrian provisional National Assembly gave its approval to the creation of Deutschböhmen, proclaiming it to be part of German Austria and promising it full support. Further German provinces sprang up in rapid succession in the first half of November: Sudetenland in north-eastern Bohemia and northern Moravia, Deutschsüdmähren in southern Moravia, and Böhmerwaldgau in southern Bohemia and the Šumava region.

Leadership of this movement was assumed by extreme nationalist *bourgeois* groups of a pan-German character, and Lodgman von Auen, who went over from his pre-war liberal standpoint to an extreme nationalist position, became their spokesman. The movement then joined forces with the German Social Democrats led by Josef Seliger.

The struggle for the establishment of a German Bohemia was part and parcel of a much broader political endeavour, aiming at the creation of one large German state consisting of Germany, German Austria, and German Bohemia. It was only feasible in this context, which made it a great threat to the newly-established independent Czechoslovakia.

The Prague National Committee was well aware of this danger. Also Masaryk, in his first instructions from Washington on 29 October, emphasized the need for an agreement with the representatives of the German population in the Czech lands. And at the Geneva talks at the end of October, an understanding was reached between Beneš and the National Committee representatives that the Germans would appoint one minister to the newly-formed Czechoslovak Government.

The Czechoslovak representatives had very sound political reasons for wanting the Germans to be represented in their Government, knowing that this would mean the recognition of Czechoslovakia by her German inhabitants. The position of the new state would then have been much easier, both from the international and internal points of view. And so the representatives of the National Committee lost no time, inviting Lodgman von Auen to hold talks with them as early as 28 October.

The first meeting between Lodgman von Auen and the Czech leaders Švehla, Stříbrný, and Soukup took place on 30 October, this being followed by another meeting of the Czechs with Josef Seliger. In both cases the National Committee representatives offered the Germans participation both in their Committee and in the provisional National Assembly, promising to ensure proper food supplies to the German regions, which were cut off from the rest of the country and were suffering from acute shortages, hunger, and economic chaos.

But the German representatives saw things in a completely different light. Having as their aim the creation of a German Bohemia, to be linked with Germany and Austria, they were not interested in membership of the Czech National Committee and parliament. To accept would have meant *de facto* recognition of Czechoslovakia, which was not in keeping with their own plans.

The change had come too suddenly for the German population of the Czech lands, for so long influenced by pan-German ideas on the superiority of the German race over the Slav nations. The war had seemed to them an opportunity to give practical expression to this superiority and at the same time to partake of the fruits of Germany's efforts to gain world domination. It was in the German regions of Bohemia and Moravia that this nationalist movement was at its strongest, embracing even the German working class by linking extreme nationalist demands with the social aspirations of the workers. And the young generation, to which belonged men such as Rutha, Sebekowski, Henlein, and others, had formed the finest volunteer units of the Austro-Hungarian Army.

The more grandiose the plans of 1914, the more bitter the realities of 1918. Having dreamt of world power, the German politicians found it hard to reconcile themselves to defeat and to the position of a minority in the new Czechoslovak state. That they deigned even to negotiate with the Prague National Committee was only due to the cruel facts of their situation, to hunger in the German-speaking provinces, economic disruption, and the increasingly revolutionary mood of the people.

In their talks with the National Committee, the German representatives insisted on the independence of the German regions, demanding that they be treated as equal, politically independent partners of the Czech politicians taking part in the meeting. They refused to recognize the National Committee in any shape or form, and Seliger wanted the discussion of legal relationships to be left to the peace conference. On the other hand they asked the National Committee to help consolidate conditions in the Sudeten regions and to take over responsibility for food supplies.

This meant that by creating independent German provinces they were trying to destroy the unity of the Czech lands and thus prevent the establishment of the Czechoslovak state, while on the other hand requesting help from Prague for the maintenance of those provinces, which could not exist on their own. It was a foregone conclusion that no agreement was possible on those lines. But there was more to it than that.

Early in November the Austrian Government, and with it the representatives of Deutschböhmen, embarked on an international political campaign for the creation of a large German state. In these circumstances it was not in their interest to come to an understanding with Prague; they, on the contrary, needed arguments against such an agreement, with which to support their demands for the secession of the German provinces. For propaganda purposes they had to put the blame for the failure of the talks on the Czechoslovak representatives in order to be able to justify their own tactics to their compatriots.

That was why Seliger, when giving an account of his negotiations with the Prague National Committee at a mass rally in Teplice, made no mention of the invitation extended by the Czechs for them to send their representatives to the Prague

Government, telling his audience instead that he had been greeted with the words, 'We don't negotiate with rebels'. And he went on to spell out his political programme, aimed at an *anschluss* with Republican Germany.

German and Czech political aspirations were irreconcilable, and no one found this more unwelcome than the Czechoslovak Government, which was faced with extremely grave complications. It therefore made several more attempts to start negotiations and reach an agreement, but all to no avail.

On 12 November the provisional National Assembly in Vienna passed an Act declaring the foundation of the Austrian Republic. In the second paragraph the Act said: 'German Austria is an indivisible part of the German Republic.'

Negotiations with a view to carrying out the *anschluss* began in Berlin and Weimar. Simultaneously the Austrian Government appealed to the parties of the Second International, the Vatican, and President Wilson, invoking the right of nations to self-determination and asking that Austria be given the right to annex the German regions of Bohemia and Moravia. Attempts were made at this time to arm the German-speaking population in the Czech lands. The Hungarians made similar moves with regard to Slovakia, no doubt having agreed with the Austrians to co-ordinate their actions.

The new Károlyi Government, which on 12 November proclaimed the establishment of the Hungarian Republic, succeeded the following day in getting the French representative in Belgrade to agree that Slovakia, together with certain other parts of what used to be the Hungarian half of Austria-Hungary, should for the time being remain under Hungarian administration. This separate treaty, signed in Belgrade, helped the Károlyi Government to strengthen its position in Slovakia. Hungarian officials were in charge of the state apparatus, Hungarian transport workers ran the railways, and in the latter half of November the Hungarian army occupied the whole of the country.

The Austrian declaration of the *anschluss* and the Belgrade agreement presented serious problems for the Czechoslovak Government. Beneš emphasized that the struggle over Slovakia 'was very serious from the legal point of view, politically difficult and dangerous. . . . The question of the occupation and even the annexation of Slovakia now became a problem that occupied the minds even of many of our own people.'

The very existence of the newly-born Czechoslovak state was at stake.

The struggle that followed was conducted on two different levels. There was an armed conflict in Czechoslovakia itself, and diplomatic talks conducted in an international forum.

In Czechoslovakia the new state enhanced its political and legal position when, on 14 November, the National Committee was replaced by the first real Czechoslovak Government, composed of members of the Committee and of the provisional Government in Paris. Kramář became Prime Minister. The Habsburgs were ousted, and the country declared a republic, with Masaryk as its first President. The Government put forward fresh proposals to the German population, but at the same time it resolved to assert its sovereignty by force.

The German regions were in a state of utter confusion and chaos. There was an acute shortage of food, and a growing revolutionary movement. The German territories grew smaller in size every day, the Czech inhabitants forming local national committees which took over the administration. In the second half of November Czechoslovak troops started occupying the German provinces.

The weak Czechoslovak Army, consisting of members of the Sokol gymnastic movement and of legionaries who had fought in Italy and France, met with next to no resistance, and by the end of the year had occupied all the German border regions, with scarcely a shot fired. The representatives of the German Regional Government in Deutschböhmen, Lodgman and Seliger, fled the country, and the other regional governments ceased to exist.

Even more important from the Czech point of view, the local representatives of the Prague Government managed to improve relations with the German population, who started to cooperate with the authorities.

All this was accompanied by diplomatic moves. Following a protest by Beneš in Paris, the French Government, in a special note of 21 December 1918, rejected all attempts at separating the German provinces from the Czech lands, confirming that it was necessary to retain the historic frontiers until such a time as a peace treaty was concluded. Similar views – though after far more arduous diplomatic negotiation – were also expressed by Britain, Italy, and finally the United States. In this way the action of the Czechoslovak Government was endorsed by the major powers.

The situation in Slovakia also resolved itself. Having enthusiastically received the Martin Declaration, which proclaimed its national rights, the Slovak people now began to make increasing demands for social justice. Throughout the country there occurred violent demonstrations in protest against the shortage of food. In the villages people rose up against black marketeer traders, whose warehouses were stocked with food, against large estate owners who exploited the rural poor, against notaries who made unjust requisitions, and against the Hungarian authorities in general. The Hungarian authorities and the Hungarian Army were becoming increasingly helpless in the face of this spontaneous movement, the more so as they received no support and no reinforcements from Hungary, where a revolution was also in the offing. Cases of brutal action against the demonstrators by the soldiers and by the special *bourgeois* 'national guards' were becoming ever more frequent, and Slovaks demanding their national and social liberation were fired on by the troops.

The Prague Government was all this time waging a struggle against the Hungarian political and military rule in Slovakia. On the diplomatic front, the Belgrade armistice was annulled in Paris, and at the end of November the Hungarian Government was ordered to pull out of Slovakia. In early December Vavro Šrobár, as Minister Plenipotentiary for Slovak Affairs, was instructed by the Prague Government to do everything he could 'for the maintenance of law and order, the consolidation of conditions, and the safeguarding of normal life'. By 20 January 1919 all Hungarian troops had been driven out of Slovakia, the Czech lands and Slovakia at last being joined together in fact as well as on paper.

It was only now, at the beginning of 1919, with the Czechoslovak Government fully in power both in the Czech lands and in Slovakia, that the new Czechoslovak state really came into being.

In that same period a similar process of consolidation took place in the other new states of Central, Eastern, and South-Eastern Europe. The popular movement had succeeded in breaking up the four ancient states that had hitherto dominated this region. A power vacuum was created, with a number of new nation states replacing the former Russian, German, Austro-Hungarian, and Turkish empires. The socio-political structure of the region was altered at the same time, the most dramatic example being the transformation of Russia from a Tsarist monarchy into a Soviet republic, with a brief spell of *bourgeois* republicanism in between. Central and Eastern Europe saw the rise of the German, Polish, Czechoslovak, Austrian, and Hungarian *bourgeois* republics, while in South-Eastern Europe new states were established, which, though retaining the monarchical system of government, nevertheless also underwent far-reaching social and political changes.

Out of the hard political, economic, and social struggle that followed the Great War there emerged a new map of Europe. Its central, eastern, and south-eastern parts were not unlike the cracked earth that is to be found in the vicinity of a volcanic crater. The Europe of 1918 was born.

## CHAPTER II

# *REVOLUTION AND COUNTER-REVOLUTION*

~~~~~~~~~~~~~~~~~~~~~~~~~~~~~~~~~~~~~~~~~~~~~~~~~~~~

### Moscow – Paris

The war was over and the world, united by suffering, brutality, and cynicism, lay in ruins. Those who survived were uprooted, transformed by their experience. Either they had become exceptionally sensitive to all inhumanity and injustice, or their moral sense had been numbed and they were indifferent to violence and death. Everyone, however, was trying to replace the certainties of the past, now irretrievably lost, with new ones, with new human and social values. Now that the conflict was over, people embarked on a search for peace. Caught up in the holocaust of war, millions of men and women the world over had come to treasure their human dignity, to realize their human and social rights. They were conscious as never before of the power they wielded by virtue of their numbers, and in the name of those who died and of their own suffering they demanded the right to have a say in the building of the new, post-war world. The Russian revolution had given tangible form to these demands in the shape of the Soviet State.

This movement, which had led to the collapse of the battle-fronts in the closing stages of the war, exploded into violent action now that the war was over, taking a variety of forms according to the level of development, and according to the requirements and aspirations of individuals, nations, countries, and indeed whole continents.

In the meantime, efforts were made in Soviet Russia to organize this movement and define its concrete aims. The Third

Communist International, which was to act as an organizational centre and political headquarters of the world revolutionary movement, was set up in Moscow on Lenin's suggestion at the beginning of March 1919. It was made up of representatives of the revolutionary proletariat of Soviet Russia, Germany, Austria, Hungary, Sweden, Switzerland, America, the Balkan federation, Poland, the Baltic states, and the French left wing. Czechoslovakia did not take part in the congress, despite the fact that a Czechoslovak Communist Party had been formed in Russia as early as May 1918.

The Third International had as its chief aim the organization of the working class, as the most progressive element of the world revolutionary movement, in a close-knit, united vanguard. With the aid of soviets composed of workers, poor peasants, and soldiers, this vanguard was meant to trigger off the revolutionary transformation of the world. The movement intended to carry out a world revolution which would destroy the society that had led mankind to the horrors of the Great War, to destroy it in whatever form it might exist, whether as a monarchy or as a *bourgeois* democracy. A new, socialist society was to be built on the ruins of the old order, a society in which there would be no exploiters and no exploited, no rich and no poor. They would construct a society free from hunger and hate, from national animosities and the suffering of war. The world was to be united in a World Federation of Soviet Republics and ruled by a proletarian dictatorship.

Lenin's broadly-based revolutionary concept grew out of the past experience of the European working class. Taking into account the revolutionary situation in Europe, it nevertheless went a step further by plotting a world revolution that was not to be confined to Europe alone. In his final speech at the first congress of the Communist International, Lenin could justly claim:

'The fact that we have succeeded . . . in a short space of time in making important decisions on all the highly topical problems of the present revolutionary epoch, is due to the proletarian masses throughout the world, which have placed these problems on the agenda and have taken the first practical steps towards their solution. . . . The triumph of proletarian revolution all over the world is assured. We shall soon see the foundation of an international Soviet Republic.'

The events immediately following the Congress certainly bore out this conviction. Revolutions broke out in three European countries which, together with Russia, were the most important founder members of the Communist International – in Germany, Austria, and Hungary.

Although an attempted rising in Berlin in early March 1919 was brutally put down by the army, the revolutionary movement spread to Württemberg and Saxony, and on 7 April a Soviet Republic was proclaimed in Bavaria. In the middle of that month an abortive attack was made on the building of the Parliament in Vienna, which was intended to serve as a signal for a general rising. In Hungary a Soviet Republic had already been set up on 21 March. The revolutionary proletariat was convinced, to quote the *Rovnost* newspaper in Brno, 'that we are on the threshold of a world-wide social revolution'.

But, with the sole exception of the Hungarian Soviet Republic, the revolutionary front created inside the countries of the defeated Central Powers did not, as it turned out, spread beyond their frontiers. The individual foci of revolution were snuffed out, one by one, and the revolutionary flood was held in check by the Versailles peace treaties. While Moscow had become the headquarters of world revolution, Paris was now the centre of anti-revolutionary activity. And at the same time it was in Paris that ways and means were sought to resolve the crisis caused by the war.

The Peace Conference held its first session in the Versailles Hall of Mirrors on 18 January 1919, the victorious nations of the Entente meeting together to discuss the peace that was to terminate the Great War, to give new shape to the world emerging from the holocaust, and to prevent further revolutionary change. The conference was attended by delegates of the Big Powers, 'states with common interests'. France was represented by 'Tiger' Clemenceau, Britain by the Liberal politician Lloyd George, the United States by President Wilson, Italy by her Prime Minister Orlando, and Japan by Makino. Then there were the delegations of the smaller countries which had fought against the Central Powers on various fronts, which were given the status of 'states with limited interests', and as such participated in the negotiations on specific problems. They included delegations from the newly-formed succession states, one of which was Czechoslovakia. It was here that the new Czechoslovak Republic first appeared on the international stage in order to assert its right to existence, but also to sit in judgment over the defeated enemy and to help create the post-war capitalist world. The defeated countries were excluded from the talks and were only to be called in after the victors had agreed on what was to be done. Soviet Russia was also missing at the conference table, but its very existence exerted a powerful influence on the proceedings.

Apart from the official delegations, hundreds of expert advisers, journalists, and observers came to Paris for the conference, which became a glittering social occasion in a city only recently delivered from the nightmare of war. However, the actual talks did not by any means live up to the external pomp. From the very beginning they ran into difficulties and were plagued by disagreement. It was no easy task to divide up the world, and it was made all the more difficult by the widespread chaos on one side and the growing Communist movement on the other. How, in these circumstances, were the delegates to find an answer to the urgent question of the day: 'What now?'

There were, in effect, two different plans – Wilson's and Clemenceau's – before the conference, which soon concentrated its deliberations into discussions between the three major Powers, France, Britain, and the United States. Each of these plans reflected the outlook of the country submitting it, and as a result they contained quite irreconcilable views.

America had come out of the war greatly strengthened, her position as a leading world power secured by her great control of capital. Moreover, she had not been directly concerned with the main conflict of the war, and although in the end she had fought on the side of the Allies, her attitude towards the Central Powers was never one of bitter hostility. This was apparent at the end of 1916, when the Americans acted as mediators between the two sides, tending to support the Central Powers rather than the Entente. True, this standpoint later underwent a certain change, but this was due to the ruthless German naval policy which posed a threat to shipping and trade, rather than to any feelings of enmity towards Germany. And as regards Austria-Hungary, we have already seen that Woodrow Wilson championed the cause of the Empire right up to October 1918.

All these considerations naturally affected the plan President Wilson laid before the Peace Conference. And there were others. There was, first and foremost, the model of American society which Wilson used as his yardstick, as well as the various trends of European development since the latter half of the nineteenth century, aiming at the co-ordination of various aspects of international relations. And in a number of ways Wilson's programme was directly influenced by the October Revolution in Russia, by its new principles such as the abolition of secret diplomacy and the right of the nations of the world to self-determination. At the same time, however, Wilson did his best to prevent revolutionary change. He tried to do this by a profound reform of capitalism and by weakening the revolutionary activity of the Communist movement, as well as by initiating co-operation with the Soviet Government.

All these diverse and even contradictory influences found expression in Wilson's far-reaching plan for a new world order based on unity, which led him to propose the creation of the League of Nations. All the countries of the world, irrespective of which side they were on in the war, were to become its members. All countries, big and small, old or recently established, underdeveloped, capitalist, or the new Soviet State. The League would, according to Wilson's plan, discuss all the problems arising out of the war and the armistice, the problems of the new organization of the world, as well as all problems that might arise in the future. But when Wilson put forward his plan at the Paris conference, he came up against harsh reality. It was one thing to suggest it, and quite another to carry it out. His grandiose plan presupposed that the victors and the vanquished would sit down at one table and unite in trying to solve all these problems. And Clemenceau's reaction to the Wilson plan was an unqualified '*Non!*'

While Wilson's plan was idealistic, the French proposals were

D.D.—4*

firmly rooted in post-war, and in particular European, reality. France was well aware of the dynamic power of the revolutionary movement and reacted to it by organizing an anti-Soviet front intended to stamp out the fires of the revolution in Russia. France at the same time kept in mind her own historical experience, knowing that there existed in Europe strong forces of destruction, concentrated especially in German militarism. She therefore did not trust Germany, whose generals were hastily building a new army and scheming to breach the armistice and launch a new offensive. France had not conducted a war lasting four years in order to come to an amicable arrangement with her German foe. Consequently she came to the Peace Conference armed with a detailed and very concrete programme for the division of the spoils of war and the safeguarding of the fruits of the Allied victory over the Central Powers in the years to come. Only after this was France willing to talk about Wilson's plan for a League of Nations.

The incompatibility of the plans put forward by Wilson and Clemenceau was obvious, and it paralysed the Paris peace talks, which reached a stalemate in the second half of March 1919. Clemenceau threatened to resign, while Wilson ostentatiously summoned to France the ship that was to take him home across the ocean. It seemed that the victors' peace talks were about to break down.

However, at this critical stage came the offensive of the revolutionary Communist movement, which was seen as a threat by all the participants. Lloyd George, in his conciliatory 'Fontainebleau Document', warned against a continuation of disagreement at a time when 'anarchy and Bolshevism threaten the whole of Europe'. He urged Wilson and Clemenceau to settle their differencies, at the same time insisting that Germany be offered an acceptable peace. The agreement reached in the first week of April brought victory to the French conception. The peace treaty with Germany, signed at Versailles on 28 June 1919, was followed by similar treaties with Austria in September, with Hungary in June of the following year, and with Turkey in August.

These treaties confirmed the victory of the Entente over the Central Powers, as well as putting the seal on the new map of the world created at the end of the war. They confirmed the profound changes that had taken place in the political power structure of Central, Eastern and South-Eastern Europe, where a number of new countries had come into existence. In this respect they closely concerned Czechoslovakia, which was one of the signatories on the victorious Allied side, for they confirmed and assured the country's new statehood.

The creation of the so-called Versailles system codified the results of the war, and at the same time Wilson's proposal was put into practice by the foundation of the League of Nations with its headquarters in neutral Geneva. Czechoslovakia was one of its founder members, welcoming the new institution as one more guarantor of her own existence.

## Revolution in Central Europe

The newly-created Versailles bloc at once took steps to safeguard Europe against the forces of revolution, striking a blow at the revolutionary centres in Central Europe. The Bavarian Soviet Republic was suppressed by the German Army before the peace treaty was actually signed. The revolution in Hungary was put down by Allied forces, although not without a clash of French and Italian interests, and by the forces of the succession states bordering on Hungary.

Rumania took the initiative in the struggle against the Hungarian Soviet Republic, her armed forces crossing the Hungarian-Rumanian demarcation line in the middle of April 1919. The Hungarian Army retreated along the entire front. In the latter half of April Czechoslovak units, commanded by French officers, joined in, occupying the territory evacuated by the Hungarians. First they advanced as far as the demarcation line, the drawing up of which had caused the Károlyi Government to resign and hand over power to a revolutionary body, and then beyond the line. But in the meantime the revolutionary government in Hungary had consolidated its army, and on 20 May it launched a successful counter-offensive.

The Hungarian Red Army broke through the advancing Czechoslovak front, penetrating deep inside the country and occupying the whole of eastern Slovakia, where there was a large Hungarian population. By the middle of June it had reached the Polish border in its attempt to link revolutionary Hungary with Soviet Russia. This situation led to an intensification of revolutionary activity in eastern Slovakia. As the Hungarian Red Army advanced, welcomed by the Hungarian inhabitants of the region as their liberators, the first Slovak soviets were formed. And on 16 June 1919 the Slovak Soviet Republic was proclaimed at a mass rally in Prešov, electing a provisional revolutionary council, which transferred its headquarters to Košice. Meeting there on 20 June, it set up the Slovak Revolutionary Soviet Government numbering twenty 'People's Commissars', and headed by Antonín Janoušek, a Communist from the Czech mining town of Kladno.

The Prešov rally also adopted a resolution addressed to 'The proletarians of the whole world', which stated:

'The victorious revolution, whose advance cannot be halted, has crowned its previous successes with yet another great triumph. An independent, Soviet Republic has today been established on Slovak territory, liberated from imperialism. Freed from the yoke of Czech imperialism, the proletariat, in its first subconscious, instinctive act has put into practice the theory of self-determination, so volubly preached by the oppressors who, in actual fact, falsify it. By so suddenly taking power, Slovak workers, soldiers, and peasants are joining the revolutionary front created by the Russian and Hungarian Soviet Republics, winning over a new region for the great idea of soviets the world over.

'The newly-born Slovak Soviet Republic considers its victorious brothers, the Russian and Hungarian Soviet Republics, to be its natural allies, and it seeks the protection of the entire world proletariat and its united workers' International. Its first greetings go to its Czech proletarian brothers, who are still oppressed by imperialism. . . .'

This new Slovak Soviet Republic immediately took various revolutionary measures, nationalizing all factories with more than twenty employees, all banks, and agricultural estates. It carried out a number of social reforms and struck against black market operators and speculators. With its creation and the advance of the Hungarian Army, Czechoslovakia was faced with a grave international, as well as internal, political crisis.

These events could well have led to a break-up of the new Republic, since the revolutionary Hungarian Government was seeking to re-establish the old Hungarian State. The question of frontiers had indeed been the actual cause of its formation. When, on 20 March 1919, the new Czechoslovak-Hungarian frontier was drawn up, Károlyi's *bourgeois* democratic government refused to accept the line of demarcation and resigned, handing over authority to the revolutionary government, which was formed on the following day under Béla Kun. This new Hungarian Government proclaimed the integrity of Hungary, basing its claim on the now annulled Belgrade armistice of 13 November 1918. The Slovak Soviet Republic came into being on the same legal premise, thus seriously infringing the integrity of the new Czechoslovakia.

The creation of the Slovak Soviet Republic sparked off Communist activity aimed at destroying the *bourgeois* character of the Czechoslovak Republic. The political crisis that ensued both on the home and the international front led to a clash between the Communists and the other considerably disunited political groups in Czechoslovakia.

The nationalists, led by the foremost Czech politician of the pre-war era, Karel Kramář, and his National Democratic Party, strove to create a 'national state', in other words a state guaranteeing exclusive and decisive rights to the Czechs and Slovaks as opposed to inhabitants of other nationalities, in particular the Germans. This became the sole criterion in their political work, the form of government and the political structure of the state being considered questions of secondary importance. Kramář himself was a monarchist who would have liked to see the structure and administration of the country taken over unchanged from the Austro-Hungarian monarchy. As regards foreign policy, this group remained Russophile in outlook, Kramář playing an active part in the various international plans for the restoration of Tsarism in Russia, which he considered a necessary pre-condition for his own political action.

Another clearly defined political trend was that represented by the workers movement, which placed the greatest emphasis on social problems. The socialist bloc was formed by two political parties – the Social Democrats and the Czech Socialists. They planned to carry out a complete transformation of society, hoping to create a socialist state by evolutionary means. This bloc had no clear foreign policy of its own, limiting itself to co-operation with similar movements in other European countries, notably the parties belonging to the Second International. On the home front the socialist bloc acted as a political base for Masaryk.

Masaryk returned to Prague from abroad on 21 December 1918, and while accepting the political support of the bloc, pursued his own policies, his programme covering both internal and international affairs. In 1918 it was the most concrete, detailed, and consistent political platform in the country, which was why, having the added advantage of Masaryk's personal authority behind it, this programme was adopted as the official policy of the new Czechoslovak state. It was aimed at turning Czechoslovakia into a democratic republic on West European and American lines. It was intended to carry out a reform of society on the principle of maximum individual freedom for each citizen. In this way, by creating a new, democratic society, Masaryk hoped to solve the vexed social and nationality problems that existed in Czechoslovakia.

He saw that nationalism, exacerbated and intensified by the war, could not lead to a peaceful solution of the problem of nationalities. He believed that calls for national unity and separation must necessarily result in still fiercer nationalism and eventually in the disintegration of society and the state. Masaryk likewise rejected policies that were concerned solely with social problems, convinced that their isolated solution would aggravate the class war. That was why he attempted to resolve the two most urgent problems of the time, the rights of nationalities and the demands for social reform, not by giving rights and privileges to individual national groups as a whole or individual social groups or classes as a whole, but by assuring every citizen, irrespective of nationality or social position, a maximum of individual liberty. Masaryk was convinced that only by the greatest possible national, religious, and political tolerance and freedom could the new state achieve the happiness and co-operation of its citizens.

In order to carry out his programme, Masaryk formed a special group of politicians and intellectuals which came to be known as the 'Castle Group'. One of its two elements was composed chiefly of democratic intellectuals of all nationalities – Czech, Slovak, as well as German, organized in various political parties, as well as those who owed allegiance to none. Drawn from a variety of professions, they included economists, administrators, scientists, writers, and artists, and formed, as a group, a kind of horizontal cross-section of the population – a brains trust under Masaryk's leadership, whose purpose was to ensure that the best advice was always available in dealing with the problems of State and Government. It also helped to overcome party political and national differences in the country.

In contrast to this element of the Castle Group, the second had a distinctly political character and represented a vertical cross-section of Czechoslovak society. It secured the necessary mass support for Masaryk's programme, without which this could not have been put into practice. Its members came chiefly from the various socialist parties, again regardless of nationality. These parties included the Czech and the Slovak Social Democrats, and after 1920 the German Social Democratic Party, and the Czechoslovak Socialists, as well as the democratic groups within all the other Czech, Slovak, and German parties in the country. Masaryk also tried, not without a measure of success, to reach a working understanding with the internationalist Communist Party.

This political group was instrumental in broadening and modifying Masaryk's original political programme. In his book, *World Revolution*, Masaryk gave new, wider, and far more precise definition to the demand for not only political but also economic and social democracy which he had voiced earlier, and in more general terms in the Washington Declaration, as 'the need for a far-reaching social and economic reform'. In this respect Masaryk went further than the democratic societies in Western Europe and the United States, which had served as his model. In his foreign policy, aimed at securing the independence of the new Republic, Masaryk used the same principles that he applied in domestic matters.

Masaryk's Castle Group held that Czechoslovakia's existence was inextricably bound up with the structure of the new Europe that came into being in 1918, and in particular of Central, Eastern, and South-Eastern Europe. Though aware of the complexities and faults of this structure, they were of the opinion that these could be removed by negotiation between the countries concerned, and as a result they tried to achieve the greatest possible stability in this part of the world.

The adoption of Masaryk's programme as the official policy of the new Czechoslovak State naturally did not take place without conflict with political groups holding different views. His ideas of national and social tolerance met with fierce opposition in the highly emotional post-war atmosphere. He first came into conflict with the nationalists, both of the Czech and the German variety, led by Karel Kramář and Lodgman von Auen respectively. Both these clashes resulted in Masaryk's victory, Kramář's nationalist group suffering a decisive defeat in the course of 1919 and being forced to take a back seat in the new Czechoslovakia. In the German camp, however, despite Lodgman's weakened position, the nationalists were by no means put out of the running. They remained a strong political force in the years that followed.

Simultaneously, in the latter part of 1918 and the beginning of 1919, the revolutionary workers' movement rapidly developed into a political factor to be reckoned with, gradually dissociating itself from the official leadership of the Social Democratic Party. The movement took 14 October 1918 as its starting-point, and it was further strengthened by Communists among the Czech and Slovak prisoners-of-war returning from Russia. These men led the revolutionary opposition inside the Social Democratic Party, and throughout the country Communist ideological and organizational centres were formed in the industrial regions and around the many workers' newspapers and magazines.

A number of young representatives came to the fore in this movement, which found its leader in Bohumír Šmeral, an experienced politician of European stature. The first issue of

*Sociální Demokrat*, a paper founded by the left-wing opposition in February 1919 on Šmeral's initiative, carried an editorial which stated:

'For us the achievement of Czech independence does not mean the end of history. We consider it essential that the proletariat should continue the revolutionary development over the heads of the propertied classes, going beyond their goals. We welcome the creation of the Czechoslovak Republic, but our aim is not merely a *bourgeois*-democratic republic, we want a socialist republic.'

In this way Šmeral logically linked his endeavours with his pre-war and wartime programme.

The emerging left wing knew what it wanted: a socialist state. But it had no real idea how it was to achieve its aims, knowing very little about the experience of Soviet Russia, which was at that time cut off from the rest of Europe by an economic and military blockade, and the only information was that brought by the former prisoners-of-war. As they returned home, the Communists among them told of their experiences in Russia, of the work of the Czechoslovak Communist Party founded in May 1918, of the Red Guards, and of Soviet Russia in general. They also brought with them the first Soviet printed matter – the speeches of Lenin and other leaders, newspapers, books, booklets, and leaflets. Yet all this was not enough to enable the left wing to provide the revolutionary movement with the necessary tactics. The left wing itself was only just being formed, and it was numerically weak and split up into a number of centres, all of which were trying to find their bearings. And to act meant to part company with the new republic, which was no easy undertaking.

The revolutionary movement gained great impetus from the formation of the Hungarian and Slovak, and also the Bavarian, Soviet Republics. The revolutionaries in Kladno, led by the former prisoner-of-war Alois Muna and by Antonín Zápotocký, were in direct contact with the Hungarian Soviet Republic and its leader, Béla Kun. The birth of Czechoslovakia had not severed the old links between the Austrian and Czech proletariat, and the setting up of the Bavarian Soviet Republic had especially encouraged the German workers in Czechoslovakia.

As the revolution made headway in Central Europe, the popular masses in the Republic grew increasingly more radical, the difficult economic situation playing its part in making them adopt such an attitude. Food, coal, clothing, and all other necessities were in short supply, prices soared, and as a result the black market and profiteering flourished. Not even their joy at victory could overcome the dissatisfaction felt by the ordinary people. Between 22 and 27 May 1919, spontaneous protest demonstrations and strikes occurred, turning to violence in a number of places.

These demonstrations against rising prices and hunger first broke out in Prague, where industrial workers marched to the city centre carrying mock gallows with the inscription, 'Death to Profiteers'. But what started as an orderly demonstration led to attacks on shops, which were taken over by the demonstrators, who sold everything in them at one-tenth of the price or gave the goods away free. They repeated this the next day, and similar action was taken in various other towns.

In Kladno, the official in charge of food supplies for the district was forced to flee, and his job was given to a workers' council. 'People's courts' tried usurers, shopkeepers and tradesmen in the Kladno area, which was the only part of the country where members of the Marxist left wing assumed control of the spontaneous outburst of popular feeling.

The strength of this spontaneous revolutionary workers' movement at this time was such that the government did not dare take any action against the demonstrators. The disturbances were brought to an end by Social Democratic shop stewards, who persuaded the workers to disperse.

As a direct result of the demonstrations, the Government introduced measures to curb further price rises. People's price tribunals were set up to prevent excessive pricing of goods and to prosecute usurers. These tribunals were interesting in that they came into being through pressure from below, and resembled similar measures taken by the Soviet Government in Russia.

With the arrival of the Hungarian Red Army in Slovakia on 20 May 1919, the revolutionary crisis in that part of the country also came to a head.

The Slovaks, whose more radical aspirations had been held in check by the inclusion of Slovakia in the Republic and by Vavro Šrobár's precautions, reacted most sensitively to events in neighbouring Hungary. Here, again, there were a thousand ties with the past; Slovakia had for centuries been part of Hungary. The *Red News*, the Slovak-language Communist newspaper in Hungary, and revolutionary leaflets, informed both Slovak and Hungarian workers in Slovakia about the Hungarian revolution and its aims. The Red Regiment included among its members both Slovaks and Hungarians living in Slovakia. All this could not but have a strong effect on the people, especially those of Hungarian origin.

In turn, the establishment of the Slovak Soviet Republic and the action taken by it undoubtedly had its effect on the revolutionary-minded proletariat in the whole country, which was in favour of it because it threatened the position of the *bourgeoisie*. But there was another aspect which militated against the Slovak Soviet Republic. Being part of Hungary, it posed a threat to the Czechoslovak State, which in June and July 1919 stood on the brink of disintegration. Political and military action was taken against the Slovak Soviet Republic and against the revolutionary movement in Czechoslovakia as a whole, martial law was proclaimed, freedom of assembly annulled, freedom of the press curtailed, and a number of revolutionaries, including Alois Muna, were arrested.

A military dictatorship was set up in Slovakia, and an order was issued by the Minister Plenipotentiary on 5 June stating that 'the Army will assume supreme power over public administration and thus also over the civil service. . . . In his area each military commander is the highest state organ. . . . He is responsible for maintaining law and order in his area, and may use any means he sees fit to do so.' At the same time the French General Pellé, who was Commander-in-Chief of the Czechoslovak Army, took measures for the 'maintenance of order' in the armed forces, setting up military courts to try anyone who refused to fight against the Hungarian Red Army or the Slovak Soviet Republic.

The democratic front led by Masaryk, in which the Social Democrats closely collaborated with the Agrarian Party, took

steps to safeguard the Republic politically. The workers' movement led by the Social Democrats formed armed units made up
of members of the Workers' Physical Training Organization
(DTJ) and these, together with the Sokols, legionaries, and
regular Army units, took part in the fighting in Slovakia.

Even the left wing, whose most radical Kladno group led by
Muna had been isolated, stood up in defence of the Republic.
While in sympathy with the revolutionary movement, it could
not close its eyes to the strong chauvinistic tendencies in the
Hungarian Soviet Republic, and its Red Army, which was
staffed by many former Hungarian officers. And it had to take
account of the strong nationalistic feeling in the Czech lands,
where people wished to save the newly-formed Czechoslovak
Republic. And so the left wing, under Šmeral's leadership,
declared itself neutral in the revolutionary conflict, thus in fact
helping to defend the Republic.

However, the fate of the Hungarian and Slovak Soviet
Republics was decided on an international forum. The same
agreement between Wilson and Clemenceau which had made
it possible to sign the peace treaties, now served as a basis for
the suppression of the Hungarian revolution. In the middle of
June a definitive line of demarcation between Czechoslovakia
and Hungary was drawn up in Paris. The Hungarian revolutionary government was given an ultimatum to evacuate the
territory on the Czechoslovak side of the frontier, being told
that failure to comply would result in a broadly-based Allied
intervention. The Hungarian Red Army consequently withdrew from eastern Slovakia, and with it went the Slovak
revolutionary units and the Government of the Slovak Soviet
Republic.

June 1919 marked the first victory of Czechoslovak *bourgeois*
democracy over the revolutionary Communist movement.
The state was reunified, with Ruthenia added to the former
Czechoslovak territory, and its internal regime was strengthened.

The Versailles system had given existence to Czechoslovakia
in a capitalist Europe, and in June 1919 the powers which had
created that system helped Czechoslovakia fight the revolutionary movement in Central Europe in general and inside the
country in particular. In so doing they saved Czechoslovakia

from disintegration and helped to save and fortify her *bourgeois* democratic character. These were the reasons why, throughout the next twenty years, Czechoslovakia was closely linked with the Versailles system, staunchly defending the conditions it had established at the end of the war.

## A Revolution in the Making

The calm bestowed on post-war Europe by the Versailles treaties was the first mild symptom of a temporary relaxation of tension. The brief respite also brought at least a partial lowering of the temperature between the Entente and Soviet Russia. At the beginning of 1920, after the complete failure of the second campaign of intervention, the military and economic blockade of Russia was lifted, and tentative steps were made to establish the first contacts. However, a few months later these signs of stabilization gave way to another, deeper, and more stormy crisis. Both sides had used the brief interlude from the middle of 1919 to the summer of the following year to garner their resources and prepare for the new clash.

On the basis of the peace treaties the countries of Europe began to normalize their mutual relations, establishing a system of treaties which were to guarantee the new frontiers, and Czechoslovakia was among the first to enter into these negotiations.

Again it was Masaryk's foreign policy that the new state adopted as its own official line. This policy recognized the fact that Czechoslovakia was part of Europe and inevitably exposed to the conflict of interests of the major European powers. Dr Beneš expressed the thinking behind Czechoslovakia's foreign policy in a speech made after the signing of the Versailles treaty:

'It so happens that our country will always be at the crossroads of three important influences: western, German, and Russian (Slav). We must of necessity try and create out of them a *milieu* in which we shall never become the instrument of any one of them, in which we shall be able to maintain our highly important position, to create our own political thought, a high culture, and to remain genuinely ourselves. We must be aware of these three influences and our European, or perhaps I should say world situation.'

It was along these lines that the Czech leaders saw Czechoslovakia's international role in subsequent years.

To counter the chief danger – that coming from Germany – they tried to establish and improve contacts with democratic German politicians of the Weimar Republic. And, in order to bolster their defences against any possible resurgence of German aggressiveness, they turned to France, whose protection helped guarantee Czechoslovakia's continued existence within the framework of a capitalist world. But at the same time, in keeping with Czech political tradition, co-operation with yet another European power, Russia, was contemplated. As we have seen already, Masaryk was adamant in his political opposition to the Soviet regime. He was, however, in favour of negotiating with the Bolshevik Government while it was in power, expecting it to fall sooner or later. Once it did so, the new, 'resurrected Russia' would, in his view, become Czechoslovakia's proper partner and the pillar on which to build Czechoslovak international relations. However, despite Masaryk's political reservations, Russia and relations with it represented the second main factor in his foreign policy.

The third was the endeavour to forge closer ties with the rest of Central, Eastern, and South-Eastern Europe, closely linked to the new Czechoslovakia by the very facts of its origin.

Co-operation with the countries in this area was not guided by national considerations, such as the Slavonic policy whose re-introduction was urged by Kramář, but rather by purely political considerations, the basic idea behind Czechoslovak foreign policy in this part of the world being the strengthening of peace and security on democratic principles.

As a whole, this foreign policy as devised by Masaryk and Beneš was in sharp conflict with that of Karel Kramář. His was a distinctly nationalist policy, rejecting all negotiations with Germany and Austria, demanding tough measures against Poland, and advocating, as its chief aim, active Czechoslovak participation in the overthrow of the Soviet Government and the restoration of Tsarism in Russia.

While these two conceptions clashed on every single aspect of policy, it was Masaryk's European concept that was systematically applied in practice.

The first treaty to be negotiated by Czechoslovakia, to the astonishment of contemporary Europe, was signed in January 1920 with Austria, and was partly due to the efforts of the Austrian Chancellor and Foreign Minister, Karl Renner. The two countries had in 1918 become *bourgeois* democratic republics and they had a great deal in common, both in their political and social structure and in their political interests. The treaty paved the way for close co-operation between them in the years that followed.

Relations between Czechoslovakia and the Weimar Republic were normalized on the basis of the peace treaties, and economic and political contacts were established between the two countries.

When he had visited Paris as President of the American-born Democratic Middle-European Union, Masaryk had held talks on the creation of a similar organization embracing a larger part of Europe. He had discussed the subject with the Rumanian politician Take Ionesco, with Venizelos of Greece, and Dmówski of Poland, as well as with Yugoslav representatives. Although these plans for the federalization of Poland, Rumania, Yugoslavia, and Greece came to nothing, just as the Democratic Middle-European Union in America soon disintegrated, they gave rise to closer co-operation at least between Czechoslovakia, Yugoslavia, and Rumania. With the foundations laid at the Paris talks during the war, the official treaties were signed in the summer of 1920. Pejoratively dubbed as 'the Little Entente', the new grouping was in later years to adopt the title officially.

The Little Entente was based on the same principles as those that had given birth to the League of Nations, and was meant to contribute to European collective security. Despite considerable opposition in the early stages, this conception was later accepted as its *raison d'être*, and it was registered with the League in 1922 on these terms.

Czechoslovak-Polish relations remained unsatisfactory as the two countries laid rival claims to the industrial Těšín region.

This, however, was only part of the problem. The rivalry between them went much deeper and concerned hegemony in Central and Eastern Europe. It was this basic conflict which, though at times it grew less fierce and was even replaced by a considerable degree of co-operation, determined the tenor of Czechoslovak-Polish relations in the inter-war period.

As for relations with Hungary, these remained consistently hostile. It was not until the signing of the Trianon Treaty in June 1920 that the Hungarian Government finally accepted the frontiers drawn up in Paris. Incidents on the Czechoslovak-Hungarian border, including the assassination of Czechoslovak border guards, were a daily occurrence. But even after Trianon, the Hungarian Government did not relinquish its claims to Slovakia, just as it persisted in claiming Transylvania from Rumania, the Voivodine from Yugoslavia, and Burgenland from Austria. All this naturally gave rise to enmity and distrust. The Little Entente, with Austrian support, made mutual protection against Hungarian revisionism its chief aim.

Again, the conflict between Hungary and Czechoslovakia had deeper roots and was not concerned solely with the question of frontiers.

After the fall of the Hungarian Soviet Republic, the country veered sharply to the Right, with Admiral Horthy taking power at the head of various military and semi-military formations. Political assassination, anti-Semitism, the burning of books, and theories on the superiority of the Magyar race were typical manifestations of the reign of terror in the country. Various organizations, such as Gömbös's 'Resurrected Hungary', set up secret cells in Slovakia in their attempt to regain its territory for the Hungarian State.

Budapest became the main centre of a new, fierce European counter-revolution seeking to renew the pre-war conditions in Central, Eastern, and South-Eastern Europe and to bring about a restoration of the monarchies and of militarism. These developments, jeopardizing as they did the existence of Czechoslovakia as a state and as a democracy, were the true cause of the hostility that continued to exist between Czechoslovakia and Hungary.

Early in 1920 Bavaria joined Hungary as a counter-revolutionary centre. Following the abortive attempt at a military, monarchist coup in Berlin in March 1920, which was foiled by the German working class, its originators found asylum in Munich, where representatives of German reaction began to gather after the fall of the Bavarian Soviet Republic. Fanatics belonging to a host of military and semi-military organizations, such as Orka and Orgesh, were spoiling for a fight. Led by the former imperial General Ludendorff, they began to weave an intricate and highly dangerous web of conspiracy and counter-revolution, their immediate aim being the destruction of the Versailles system. Their network spread as far as the high command of the German Reichswehr on the one hand and, through the Budapest centre, into Eastern Europe on the other. Hand in hand with them went an underground movement supporting the return of the Habsburgs to the Austrian and Hungarian throne, of the Hohenzollern to Berlin, and the Wittelsbachs to Munich. An important part was played here by Russian exiles wishing to bring the Romanovs back to Moscow. And the successes of the anti-Soviet intervention encircling Moscow in the autumn of 1919 with Denikin's forces to the south, Yudenich's to the north, and Kolchak's in Siberia encouraged the counter-revolutionaries.

Emanating from the same centres as those of the revolution a year earlier, this movement represented a serious threat to Czechoslovakia, which stood in its way. The systematic forging of international links with Czechoslovakia on the basis of the Versailles system was aimed directly against those who hoped for the restoration of pre-war conditions in Central and Eastern Europe.

The new Czechoslovak Government coalition, led since the middle of 1919 by the Social Democrat Vlastimil Tusar, was at the same time working under Masaryk's personal guidance for the strengthening of democracy in the country, preparing for the decisive political confrontation that was to come in the first parliamentary elections in April of the following year.

These elections had a decisive effect on Czechoslovak political development in a number of respects. They brought about the defeat of the Right, led by the former Premier Karel Kramář,

whose National Democratic Party – and in particular he himself – was no longer to have any real say in policy-making. The
elections were a triumph for the Social Democrats, who became
the strongest single party in the country, having polled more
than one and a half million votes, representing 37·4 per cent of
the total. No other party was to achieve so marked a victory in
the next twenty years. Far behind the Social Democrats were
two *bourgeois* parties – the People's Party with 700,000 votes
(16·4 per cent), and the Agrarian Party with 604,000 (14·2
per cent). The National Socialists gained 500,000 votes (12 per
cent). The Social Democratic Party also won in the German-
speaking regions, but in Slovakia it had to be content with
sharing the honours with Hlinka's People's Party.

The victory of the Social Democratic Party, however, sowed
the seeds of a serious political crisis. Its electoral success was not
merely the triumph of its official leadership but rather the
victory of the Marxist Left and the revolutionary movement as
a whole. It provided tangible evidence of the growth of revolutionary forces in the country.

The Left had come a long way, in its ideology and its organization, since its beginnings in the spring of 1919, and it had also
gained valuable allies among the intellectuals. In July the
writers and poets S. K. Neumann, Josef Hora, Helena Malířová,
Ivan Olbracht, Fráňa Šrámek, and Antonín Sova founded the
Socialist Council of Soviet Workers, issuing a manifesto in
which they promised to 'fight for a socialist republic'. Another
newcomer to the ranks of the Left was Professor Zdeněk Nejedlý,
who brought with him some of the university students belonging to the Realistic Club.

On 5 October 1919 the left wing made its first public appearance as a group, criticizing the Party leadership at a meeting of
Social Democratic representatives. In a separate proclamation
it pointed out that the Party's role in the Government did very
little to achieve the demands of the proletariat and that, on the
contrary, by compromising with the *bourgeoisie* the Party was
helping it to strengthen its position. The left wingers demanded
the adoption of an independent, truly revolutionary policy
which would prepare the proletariat for the takeover of power
in the state. The proclamation said: 'Our goal is a socialist

republic, and this cannot be achieved otherwise than by means of an uncompromising class struggle against the *bourgeoisie*.'

At the end of the year the Left constituted itself as an independent group within the Social Democratic Party. At a special conference on 27 December, it adopted as its official title the name, 'The Marxist Left', and announced its own programme which was to help attain its aims by the formation of workers' councils. The programme emphasized that 'socialization can only be achieved by taking over power in the state. . . . Present experience of the proletarian struggle shows that its fight for power cannot be waged by the existing organizations alone. The present revolutionary era has created its own organs in the system of workers' councils. It is the duty of the Party to make these organs the instrument on the road to the liberation of the proletariat.'

Lenin's directives on the setting up of soviets as a new revolutionary force were now being put into practice in the Czechoslovak revolutionary movement.

The results of the parliamentary elections and the sweeping victory of the Left hastened the growth of the revolutionary movement. Those Social Democratic members of Parliament who sympathized with the Left issued a proclamation, sharply criticizing the Party policy and Tusar's new government, and appealing to the workers to 'prepare openly for the takeover of power and start setting up workers' councils as the organs of a new social system'. These councils were actually being established throughout the country, and in particular in its industrial regions. Delegates of the revolutionary centre in Kladno travelled to Pilsen, Ostrava, Oslavany, Brno, and to industrial centres in Slovakia and Ruthenia, where, in May and June 1920, they organized elections to workers' councils. In this way a strong opposition began to form, not only against the right-wing nationalist faction but also against Masaryk's group. The revolutionary opposition, made up of the proletariat with the Marxist Left at its head, started to prepare for a revolutionary overthrow of the Government.

It was at this stage that events in Czechoslovakia were influenced by the crisis of the revolution throughout Europe.

## The Summer of 1920

In the unsettled Europe of the post-war years, in which the dynamic revolutionary movement came into conflict with the endeavour to achieve stability under the Versailles system, with both of these protagonists opposed by the Munich-Budapest monarcho-military front, France and Poland took a step that was to ignite the powder keg.

In the middle of April 1920 the Polish Army, equipped by France and commanded by French generals, launched a new anti-Soviet intervention campaign. More realistic European forces, which included Britain as well as Czechoslovakia, opposed the Franco-Polish action, condemning it as an irresponsible adventure.

Despite some initial successes, their fears proved to be well-founded. In early June the Soviet Red Army started a counter-offensive, its units advancing victoriously into the heart of Poland. By the middle of August they were standing outside Warsaw. The *bourgeois* Government in Poland was expected to fall at any moment. At the same time the revolutionary movement, especially in the new states of Central, Eastern, and South-Eastern Europe, went into action with renewed energy, threatening to overthrow the existing regimes and set up soviet republics. The revolutionary crisis shook the Versailles system to its very foundations.

At this moment a hand was taken in the struggle by the counter-revolutionaries, who had already proved themselves in combating the revolutionary movement. The German militarists came forward with an offer of help, the newly armed and now well organized Reichswehr being ready, in the words of its boss, General Seeckt, to build 'a bulwark against Bolshevism', on the German frontier. In return he asked capitalist Europe to lift all restrictions on the further development of the German Army.

The counter-revolutionaries organized in the Munich and Budapest centres also wanted to help. General Ludendorff drafted a comprehensive plan of campaign aimed at rescuing Poland, while the Hungarian Army stood on the borders with Czechoslovakia, ready to march northwards across the country.

And again there were demands for a revision of the Versailles system, with Hungary reiterating her claim to Slovakia, the annexation of which would give her a common frontier with Poland. The Versailles system, and with it the new Czechoslovak Republic, was undergoing a profound crisis.

Czechoslovakia was well prepared for this contingency. Her leaders had no doubts about the seriousness of the situation, and as early as February 1920 Dr Beneš said in the Foreign Affairs Committee that Czechoslovakia 'must overcome it by her own resources, for she will have no one to turn to for help'. Czechoslovakia therefore chose her own tactics and used her own methods in dealing with the crisis.

First and foremost she had to achieve inner stability if she wished to cope with the international situation. Here the Czechoslovak Government concentrated on two major issues, which were not unconnected: she wanted to halt the growth of the revolutionary movement, and she wanted to keep Slovakia and Ruthenia in the Republic.

The revolutionary movement which, as we have seen, was getting ready for an attempt to overthrow the Government, was not united on a course of action. The more radical revolutionaries, centred on Kladno and supported by the German Left led by Karel Kreibich, demanded immediate revolution, whereas Šmeral advocated a more cautious approach. He rejected the idea that Czechoslovakia should act on her own, demanding thorough co-ordination with the revolutionary movements in the neighbouring states, with whose representatives he had close personal contacts. His views did not altogether conform with the policy of the Communist International, Šmeral's reserve being due mainly to the fact that he expected Germany to become the second country to carry out a socialist revolution. And in the decisive moments of the summer of 1920, faced with the anti-Versailles reaction of the monarchists and militarists in Germany and Hungary, who were about to invade Czechoslovakia, Šmeral came out in defence of the Republic. As a result, despite its size and strength, the revolutionary movement in the Czech lands under Šmeral's leadership did not make any real attempt to take over power in the land.

The situation was quite different in Slovakia, where the main internal struggle was fought out. In the summer of 1920 the Slovak revolutionary movement began quite openly to make its bid to wrest power from the *bourgeoisie*. A strike on the main Košice-Bohumín railway line at the beginning of July cut off the chief means of communication between the Czech lands, Slovakia, and Ruthenia. Slovak and Ruthenian workers started to take over the factories, and large agricultural estates were confiscated. Partisan units began to form in the forests.

At the same time Horthy's Hungary, through a special 'Committee for the Upper Land' – *Felvidéki komité* – was preparing a counter-revolutionary *putsch* in Slovakia. Contacts with Hungarian groups in the country were renewed and intensified. The Hungarians counted on Slovakia being weakened by her own internal revolutionary struggle, their final aim being the return of Slovakia to the Hungarian fold. The *putsch* was to break out as Hungarian forces marched into the country, on their way to assist the Polish intervention.

The defence of Slovakia became the primary problem of Czechoslovak home policy in the summer of 1920. Martial law was declared in Slovakia and Ruthenia, and large military contingents were sent there from the Czech lands. In Slovakia itself a broad political front was created for the defence of the Republic, composed of all the Slovak parties from the Social Democrats to Hlinka's Catholic People's Party. Taking a firm stand in support of the integrity of Czechoslovakia and against Horthyite revisionism, the front crippled the counter-revolutionary centres in Slovakia. At the same time, however, it also opposed the revolutionary movement represented by the International Socialist Party, which thus found itself completely isolated. The spontaneous, unorganized character of the Slovak and Ruthenian revolutionary movement made it possible for it to be put down as early as the latter half of July 1920, that is before the general crisis of the revolution in the rest of Europe.

Tusar's Government now found itself in a stronger position, both in Czech lands and in Slovakia, upholding the principles of the *bourgeois* democratic republic and making it possible for Czechoslovakia to conduct a large-scale, independent international political campaign.

Czechoslovakia first of all firmly rejected all suggestions made by France, which was later joined in exerting pressure on Czechoslovakia by Britain and America, to give military support to the anti-Soviet front in Poland. At the same time, Czechoslovakia refused to allow the passage of Hungarian troops over Czechoslovak territory. The Polish as well as the Hungarian frontier was fortified, and on 9 August 1920 Czechoslovakia proclaimed her neutrality in the Polish-Soviet conflict.

Czechoslovakia hurriedly concluded negotiations with Rumania and Yugoslavia, signing the treaties that gave life to the Little Entente. With Austria closely linked by the terms of the Czechoslovak-Austrian treaty, a strong bloc of Central and Eastern European succession states came into being, dedicated to the preservation of the Versailles *status quo*. The initiative for this defensive pact, formed in the summer of 1920, came from Czechoslovakia. The bloc served a twofold purpose, providing protection against the forces of Hungarian and Bavarian counter-revolution on the one hand, and against the revolutionary proletarian movement on the other.

The success of this bloc depended on the attitude of a single Central European power, Germany. The question was, which of the four strong political currents in that country would determine its future policy: the rapidly growing proletarian movement about to launch its revolution; the counter-revolutionary centre in Bavaria, preparing to march on Berlin; the Reichswehr; or the official government of the *bourgeois* democratic Weimar Republic which was in power at the time?

It was the latter, the Weimar coalition, which came out on top after a dramatic conflict. Germany declared her neutrality in the fighting between Poland and the Soviet Union, so that Germany, Austria, and the countries of the Little Entente now formed a vast bulwark intended to preserve the *status quo*, a bulwark reaching from the North Sea to the Mediterranean. Neutralizing the counter-revolutionary centres in its midst, it at the same time held back the forces of proletarian revolution, keeping them from taking over the unstable Central, Eastern, and South-Eastern Europe.

The Polish intervention was thus safeguarded against an attack from the rear and could be reinforced and armed by the Allies, with the result that the Red Army was defeated in the decisive battle outside Warsaw on 15–19 August 1920 and forced to withdraw from Poland.

The bloc defending the Versailles *status quo*, in which Czechoslovakia at this time played the most active role, was the first among the capitalist countries to normalize relations with the Soviet Union. Czechoslovak-Soviet talks, opened at the beginning of 1920, ended in the summer with the normalization of mutual relations. Red Cross missions were exchanged by the two countries to facilitate the transfer of prisoners-of-war, and also to pave the way for the establishment of trade, and later diplomatic relations. The European crisis of 1920 was over.

## Defeat of the Revolution

Throughout the second half of the year Czechoslovakia underwent a process of internal consolidation. Efforts were made to weaken the extreme right-wing nationalist tendencies in the Czech and German political camp on the one hand, and to prevent the further spread of the Marxist Left and avert a socialist revolution on the other. A broad political front was formed for this purpose under Masaryk's leadership, working on the platform of the new caretaker government of Premier Černý, which took office on 15 September 1920. It covered a wide political spectrum of Czech, Slovak, as well as German parties, from the Social Democrats on the left to the Catholic parties on the right. Czech-Slovak co-operation was based on the political coalition created in the summer for the defence of Slovakia. In the autumn this coalition was considerably strengthened by Hlinka's People's Party giving its support to the Černý Government, which they welcomed as 'the saviour of the new State'. The Government, in its turn, showed itself willing to accede to the demands put forward by the People's Party for greater Slovak autonomy, for using the land reform to the Party's economic and political advantage, and for strengthening the influence of the Catholic Church in Slovakia.

Hlinka conducted negotiations with various Czech and Slovak political groups, and co-operation with his party culminated in the signing by Hlinka in April 1921 of the con-

Dr Karel Kramář, Czech nationalist leader and Masaryk's chief opponent

1b  Dr Edvard Beneš, Secretary General of the Czechoslovak National Council in Paris

Milan R. Štefánik, leading Slovak member he Czechoslovak National Council in Paris. eral in the French Air Force, and the first Czechoslovak Minister of War

1d  Deputy Josef Dürich, leader of the Czech independence movement in Russia until the February Revolution in 1917: Masaryk's opponent

2a   London headquarters of the Czech Committee in Piccadilly. With the support of Professor S Watson and H. Wickham Steed, Masaryk launched *The New Europe*, a review devoted to the of 'freedom and self-determination for all nations'

2b   Following the revolution in Russia in February 1917, Masaryk succeeded in wresting the co of the Czech independence movement in Russia from the right-wing nationalists led by Dürich reunited it with his Paris group

In May 1918 the 70,000 Czechoslovak legionaries in Russia decided to fight their way to the Pacific; in a few months they won control of the entire Trans-Siberian Railway

Meanwhile in Bohemia, the reserve battalion of the 7th Rifles mutinied on 21 May 1918, led by Czech P.O.W.s who had returned from Russia. Fearing more trouble elsewhere, the Austrian cities swiftly crushed the mutiny. Ten ringleaders were shot on 29 May, and 560 soldiers went to gaol

4a    Professor Masaryk signing the Declaration of the Congress of the Oppressed Nations in Philadel
Independence Hall, 26 October 1918. As its Chairman, Masaryk saw the Congress as a first
towards a Central European federation with a structure similar to that of the United States

4b    News of the Austrian foreign minister's note to Wilson on 28 October 1918 became a signal fo
proclamation of a Czechoslovak state by the National Committee in Prague

ong after the armistice in Europe the Czech Legion played a big role in Soviet Union affairs.
:lf-styled ruler of Siberia, Admiral Kolchak, at a banquet in Yekaterinburg, 19 February 1919,
Czech General Gajda on his right, and the Allied C-in-C, General Maurice Janin, on his left.
e extreme left in the picture is General Jan Syrový, who was to become Czech premier at the
height of the 1938 crisis. *VHU Prague*

nfluenced by Masaryk's teaching of co-operation between national groups, Czech and German
Democrats worked well together in the twenties. This mixed meeting of workers in support of a
48-hour week was held under a bi-lingual banner in April 1924

6a  At the same time, the Sudeten German National Socialists were busy building up their str
after the setback suffered as a result of the defeat in 1923 of Hitler's Munich *putsch*

6b  Dr Beneš as a member of the Council of the League of Nations in September 1926. Left to
Vittorio Sciajola, Aristide Briand, Beneš, Sir Austen Chamberlain, Emile Vandervelde
Viscount Ishii

Until 1931, Nazi politicians from Germany were free to come and address subversive political meetings in Czechoslovakia. On 3 February 1930, Dr Josef Goebbels spoke to German university students in Prague. A Czech policeman can be seen on the right taking notes

'Who needs security in the South-East?' asks this German propaganda postcard, showing the alleged threat to Germany from a Czech military build-up

8a   Conference of the Permanent Council of the Little Entente in Sinaia (Rumania), 30 and 31 M
1933. The main point on the agenda was the Four Power Pact. In the front from left to right: Nico
Titulescu (Rumanian Foreign Minister), Dr Beneš, Dr B. Jevtič (Yugoslav Foreign Minister)

8b   Anthony Eden at Prague airport with Beneš, the Foreign Minister. The main topic of the meeti
was the revival by Hitler of conscription (16 March 1935) for compulsory military service. *Ka*
*Hájek, Prague*

While Britain and France pursued the policies of appeasement, Soviet Russia and Czechoslovakia
being drawn closer together by the Nazi threat. Here is Marshal Voroshilov with General Luža
d other high-ranking Czechoslovak officers during manoeuvres in Russia in 1936. *VHU Prague*

The VIIth Congress of the Comintern in the summer of 1935 adopted the principles of co-operation
other anti-fascist parties and groups. Left to right (standing): O. W. Kuusinen, Klement Gottwald,
ch Communist leader), Wilhelm Pieck from Germany, D. Manuilsky; (sitting): Georgi Dimitrov,
Palmiro Togliatti, Wilhelm Florin, and Ch'en Shao-yü

10a  After Hitler's takeover in Germany, Prague became the asylum for many leading Ger∎ intellectuals. This photograph shows Thomas Mann and his wife in the flat of another aut∎ Heinrich Mann (his brother), surrounded by their Czech friends: Professor O. Fischer; Ambass∎ Z. Fierlinger; Dr Weigner, rector of Prague University; Minister Nečas and Professors Kozák ∎ Matějček. Thomas Mann had then become a Czechoslovak citizen

10b  President Masaryk abdicated in December 1935, naming Dr Beneš as his chosen successor. right-wing opponents were taken by surprise and their attempts to secure the election of their candidate ended in failure

President Beneš receiving Lord Runciman on his arrival in Prague as the British mediator, 3 August 1938. *Karel Hájek, Prague*

One of the principal forts in the chain of fortifications built by the Czechs along the border with Germany. *VHU Prague*

12a    Leader of the S.d.P. (Sudeten German Party), Konrad Henlein, posing with
his gun to inspire his followers

12b    'Wir wollen heim ins Reich!' In many demonstrations the
Sudeten Germans demanded annexation by Germany

stitutional laws of the Republic, People's Party deputies publicly proclaiming their allegiance to a united Czechoslovak State.

Thus the Černý caretaker Government became the basis of closer political ties between the Czech lands and Slovakia, helping to strengthen the foundations of the new Republic.

Important new departures were also to be seen in the policies of the German camp. While Lodgman, in his role as chairman of the regional government of Deutschböhmen in his Viennese exile, continued to work against Czechoslovakia, the representatives of German economic and political life who had remained in the republic showed that they were willing to co-operate with the Czechoslovak authorities.

By the signing of the Saint-Germain peace treaty the campaign for secession of the German regions suffered total defeat and Lodgman's regional government was officially abolished. But the German nationalists did not give up the fight, setting up a front organization called the *Hilfsverein für Böhmen und Mähren* (Relief Organization for Bohemia and Moravia) in place of the regional government to carry on their activity in Austria and Germany. This association maintained contacts with the pan-German movement and with the various centres of German counter-revolution. Setting out their aims in a programme declaration called *Ziele und Wege* (Ways and Means), they wrote:

> 'Deutschböhmen and Sudetenland, Südmähren and Böhmerwaldgau, situated as they are in the geographical heart of the Central European area containing eighty million Germans, cannot for ever remain severed from the body of this great nation. . . . The eternal law: One God, one nation, one empire must also be valid for the German people. . . . The enslaved Deutschböhmen, Sudetenland and Südmähren must, for political, national, economic, as well as strategic reasons, become the lever of a future war that will decide the existence of the Germans in Europe. . . .'

Having returned to Czechoslovakia after the Government had declared an amnesty, Lodgman tried to achieve these aims from within the country. His arrival was accompanied by violent nationalist demonstrations intended at all costs to prevent any agreement between the Czechs and the Germans in Czechoslovakia. Lodgman's extreme nationalist standpoint, insisting that 'for the Sudeten Germans the Czechoslovak Republic is not the country of their choice', found support among the German-speaking population, thus hampering the efforts of the German Social Democratic Party, the Agrarian Party, and the Christian Socialist Party to come to terms with the Czechoslovak Government.

Lodgman's nationalism, which refused to recognize and respect Czechoslovak laws and the Czechoslovak State in general, goaded the Czech nationalists, who found their spokesman in Kramář's National Democratic Party. This group opposed Masaryk's policy of tolerance, demanding strict measures against the obvious provocations of Lodgman's supporters. Masaryk refused, and Kramář's group tried to get its way by other means.

In November 1920 the National Democrats incited a fierce nationalist campaign which led to riots and to clashes between the Army and the German inhabitants, resulting in deaths and injuries. The campaign was meant to bring about Masaryk's political downfall, but once again, as on other occasions in the past three years, the extreme right wing of the Czech *bourgeoisie* suffered a defeat. Moreover, in conjunction with the isolation of Lodgman's group in the German political camp, it made possible a broader Czech-German rapprochement, the German Agrarian and Christian-Socialist parties joining the Social Democrats in supporting the Černý Government and its policies.

At this point, with the Marxist Left unable to play any real part in political developments, it came to a show-down between the revolutionary proletariat on the one hand and the Social Democratic leadership and the Černý Government on the other.

The Left led by Šmeral gradually gained a majority inside the Social Democratic Party. This was borne out by the parliamentary elections, by the various strikes and demonstrations, by talks within the Party, as well as by opinion polls organized by a leadership preparing with great apprehension for the Thirteenth Party Congress, to be held between 25 and 28 September 1920. Fearing that the Party would inevitably swing to the Left, it decided to postpone the Congress, at the same time expelling the left-wing members from the Party on the grounds that 'those who support the Communist line cannot remain members of the Social Democratic Party and cannot, above all, have any say in its future destiny'.

The left wing, however, held the Congress on its own, and with 64 per cent of the elected delegates present, enabled them to make it the official Thirteenth Congress of the Social Democratic Party of Czechoslovakia. The Congress adopted the Party statutes, and in particular a political action programme based on the principles of the Third Communist International. At the Congress the left wing assumed leadership of the Party, proclaiming itself to be the Czechoslovak Workers Social Democratic Party (left wing).

In Slovakia the right wing of the Social Democrats virtually ceased to exist, whereas in the German-speaking regions it was, on the contrary, the left that found itself in a minority at the Party congress in Liberec.

In this highly charged atmosphere, the left and right wing of the Party in Prague became involved in a dispute over the Party's property. While the left wing pointed to the results of the Congress, which expressed the opinions of the rank-and-file, the right wing insisted on its legal rights, taking the case to court. The court ruled that the occupation of the People's House and the *Právo lidu* printing-house in Prague by the left wing was illegal, as it deprived the rightful owners of their property. On the strength of this court decision the People's House was cleared by the police and gendarmes and handed back to the right-wing leadership of the Party.

This action by the authorities caused great indignation in Prague factories, with workers marching to protect the People's House from being taken over. On 10 December 1920 the left-wing executive called a general strike in protest against the measures taken by the Government and the right wing of the Social Democratic Party. The executive also put forward a number of new demands, including a halt to the persecution

of workers belonging to the revolutionary movement, the release of those already arrested, the resignation of the Černý
Government, no more confiscations, the implementation of full
civic freedoms, the introduction of workers' control in the large
factories and on large agricultural estates, a 30 per cent increase in wages, the setting up of workers' committees to super-
vise the distribution of food, and the confiscation of superfluous
premises to house the homeless. This was followed by a nation-
wide strike of unprecedented dimensions, almost a million
industrial and farm workers taking part. In some places the
strike led to actual attempts at a revolutionary takeover of
power.

The mining town of Kladno spearheaded the December
strikes, the Central Revolutionary Committee formed here
under the leadership of Antonín Zápotocký directing the operations as workers occupied the factories, offices, and estates.
They even occupied the President's country residence at Lány.
Recruiting for the Red Guards took place in some working-
class villages. In Moravia the revolutionary centres were in the
Rosice-Oslavany coal-mining region, in Brno, and in Hodonín.
At Oslavany the workers seized the power station which
supplied Brno with its electricity.

In Slovakia, too, the strike was widespread, affecting all
centres of industry and in a number of places being joined by
farm workers as well. At Vrútky, Spišská Nová Ves, Zvolen,
and elsewhere workers occupied all post and telegraph offices.
At Gelnice, where revolutionary fervour ran highest, they took
over the police court, post office, and railway station, releasing
all political prisoners from jail. At Vráble the revolutionary
committee made an attempt to take over the municipal administration, and three workers were killed in the ensuing clash
with the gendarmes. At other trouble spots, too, the police
fired 'on striking workers. There were fatalities in Prague,
Most, and Oslavany.

In an endeavour completely to destroy the revolutionary
movement, the Černý administration resorted to a number of
extraordinary measures, which it announced in a special
governmental declaration on 14 December. A decree issued on
the same day curtailed personal freedom and abolished secrecy

of the mail in those districts where the movement was particulary strong. In Slovakia and Ruthenia the martial law proclaimed in the summer was still in force. All over the country the leaders and most active representatives of the revolutionary proletariat were placed under arrest. All the attempts of the left wing to enter into negotiations, which Šmeral especially was eager to do, were rejected both by the Government and by President Masaryk himself. As the strike progressed it became clear that the Marxist Left was immature and unprepared, and that its influence on the Czechoslovak workers as a whole was limited.

The strike, though declared to be a general strike, was in fact confined only to the most militant workers. The Czechoslovak Socialists and the Czech and German Social Democrats reacted by issuing anti-strike declarations, which considerably weakened the workers' unity of action. Only a minority of farm workers joined in the strike. Most agricultural workers supported the Agrarian Party and its policy of land reform, disassociating themselves from the revolutionary struggle of the working class. The middle classes, too, would have nothing to do with the strike, taking a hostile attitude to the strikers and supporting the Government in its efforts to bring them to heel.

The revolutionary movement abroad having passed its zenith, the Czechoslovak revolutionary proletariat was, moreover, deprived of international support. The Czechoslovak revolutionaries had insufficient contacts with similar movements in other, and in particular the neighbouring capitalist countries and therefore had to fight a lonely battle. Efforts to link up with the revolutionary movements of the whole of Central Europe, which Šmeral had so assiduously worked for, had come to nothing. This proved a great drawback for the revolutionary movement. Waging its struggle of December 1920, the Czechoslovak revolutionary proletariat found itself completely isolated, both on the home and the international front.

All these circumstances made it possible for the authorities to bring the strike to a relatively early end. A mere five days after it had started, on 15 December 1920, the strike was broken in the most important industrial centres. That day the left-wing executive issued a proclamation officially lifting the strike. And although the struggle went on for a few days in some places – especially in Slovakia and Ruthenia – these were only minor skirmishes. The war had already been lost. Thus in December 1920 the decisive battle between the *bourgeois* democratic regime and the Communist revolutionary movement ended with the defeat of the revolution.

# CHAPTER III

# *SEEKING A WAY AHEAD*

## Whither Europe?

The Versailles bloc had succeeded in warding off a frontal attack by the proletarian revolution in Europe, at the same time paralysing the counter-revolutionary centres. It thus preserved Europe as it was constituted in 1918. But in doing so, it gave rise to new problems. What would be the future development of the continent? Which path would Europe choose? How would it overcome the disruption caused by the war? All these questions required an answer.

Diversity, instability, and disunity were the characteristic features of the Europe of the inter-war period. The disunity was especially marked in its socio-political structure. In the twenties four different types of society developed which were in constant conflict with one another, the intensity of that conflict varying from time to time.

There was, first and foremost, the *bourgeois* democratic model as an expression of the mature and highly differentiated capitalist society as it had developed in Western Europe in the course of the nineteenth century. But even before the war this type of society had shown signs of crisis. The rise of political parties broadened its democratic base, but at the same time anti-democratic forces were born in the form of internal oligarchies within the parties. These forces, growing stronger all the time, imperilled the very democracy that was the greatest achievement of these regimes. It was this dialectical process that caused the 'crisis of democracy' which came to a head in the twenties. The crisis was accompanied, and indeed partly caused, by the decline of the Social Democratic parties of the Second International. Their crisis, too, had begun to reveal itself before the war, culminating in the disintegration of the parties after the end of hostilities because of the emergence of the revolutionary Communist movement within them. These parties, after 1918 the chief propagators of the *bourgeois* democratic model of society, were unable in any decisive way, and for any length of time, to put into practice their ideas for reforming this model.

The principles of Western European *bourgeois* democracy, however, came into their own immediately after the war in the region in which the war had destroyed the old, semi-feudal monarchist regimes, in Germany and throughout Central, Eastern, and South-Eastern Europe. In this area they were synonymous with freedom and progress. Some of the countries in this part of the world – Germany, Austria, Czechoslovakia, and Poland – became *bourgeois* democratic republics modelled on the Western democracies. Others introduced various democratic measures while retaining their monarchic system of government.

The spread of *bourgeois* democracy was due partly to the increased interest of European nations in the principles of freedom, equality, and brotherhood, and partly to the victory of the *bourgeois* democratic Allied powers in the war in general and the new role of France, that classic home of *bourgeois* democracy, as a world power in particular. Many of these countries, however, were only just entering the modern capitalist stage of development, and thus lacked the political experience that had given rise to the *bourgeois* democratic form of society. In consequence, the model adopted from Western European countries did not really work in the entirely different conditions prevailing in the majority of these states. Whatever the cause, whether the political developments in Germany or the very low economic, social, and political standards of most of the Balkan countries, the result was the same: in the course of the twenties democracy in all these countries was seriously weakened as their politics moved inexorably to the Right. Here again power considerations played their part, as Germany, led since 1925 by the old imperial general, Hindenburg, exerted its influence on the region, reviving and extending its pre-war connections with it.

A second type of social organization was represented by the monarchies, typical of Eastern Europe prior to the World War. The fall of the Russian, Habsburg, and Turkish empires had dealt them a serious political blow and ended their former status as world powers. Nevertheless, monarchies still existed in a number of the succession states, such as Hungary, Rumania, Yugoslavia, Bulgaria, and Greece. As we have seen, this monarchist movement also served as one of the pillars of European underground counter-revolution. The forces behind the monarchic system and the regimes themselves underwent a marked change in the twenties, moving away from democracy and towards greater authoritarianism. Constitutional monarchies were replaced by various shades of absolutist monarchist-military regimes.

In opposition to the *bourgeois* democratic and monarchic models of society a new social order came into being in Eastern Europe in 1917 in the shape of the Soviet Socialist Republic. It cut short capitalist development in Russia, and built a unified socialist society based on the dictatorship of the proletariat in place of the class society of capitalism. For Soviet society, too, the twenties were a time of search and experiment. The Soviet Government had repulsed three waves of intervention and had safeguarded its existence, saving the centre of world revolution from extinction. But there was to be no world revolution in the foreseeable future, the Versailles bloc having successfully checked the spread of the proletarian revolutionary movement. The Soviet Government was faced with the problem of normalizing its relations with the capitalist world.

At the Russian Communist Party Congress in March 1921 Lenin stressed the necessity of 'changing our relations with the capitalist countries from those of war to peace and trade relations'. The disruption caused by seven years of war and foreign intervention forced Russia to adopt this attitude and led to the introduction of the New Economic Policy (NEP) which revived for a time small-scale private enterprise.

The Soviet revolutionary movement also adopted new tactics. Speaking of the changed situation in Europe at the Third

Congress of the Communist International in the summer of 1921, Lenin stated that instead of an immediate revolutionary offensive it was necessary systematically to prepare for revolution by gaining the majority of the workers for the idea of a revolutionary struggle.

Lenin's departure from political life in the spring of 1922 brought new changes to Soviet policies and the general line of the Communist International. These took place under the leadership of Stalin, who in April 1922 became General Secretary of the Soviet Communist Party. The NEP policy was abandoned, and in the summer of that year the first political trial was held in the Soviet Union, when thirty-four leading Social Revolutionaries were tried and fourteen sentenced to death. A new policy was propounded at the autumn meeting of the Communist International executive, a policy aimed at setting up governments composed of workers and peasants in preparation for a revolution.

The workers' revolutionary movement was going through a very complex phase of its post-war development, as was Soviet Russia itself. It was only at the end of the twenties that the two were able to evolve a joint policy. At the Sixth Congress of the Communist International in 1928 the speedy preparation of a world proletarian revolution was demanded; and revolutionary nuclei were formed inside the individual Communist parties which were ready to undertake this task and expedite revolutionary action.

The Soviet model of society, even though confined to the Soviet Union, had a very strong influence on European and world developments, affecting them directly through the individual Communist parties.

Yet another type of society, the Fascist model, evolved in the twenties in opposition to Socialism and Communism, but also in opposition to *bourgeois* democracy. It aimed at abolishing the class system by creating a national corporative state run by a dictatorship. As an exemplar it attracted a variety of European military and monarchist organizations and regimes. It seemed a promising experiment even to some of the more conservative elements in the *bourgeois* democracies of the West, which were seeking a way out of the crisis, and feared the further growth of the Communist movement. But Fascism also attracted the middle classes and a part of the working class, which provided the movement with its mass following.

The year 1922 saw the first Fascist *putsch*, in Italy following Mussolini's march on Rome. A number of more or less successful attempts at Fascist coups took place soon afterwards: the installation of Cankov's dictatorship in Bulgaria, Primo de Rivera's in Spain, and the temporary strengthening of Gömbös's Fascist organizations in Hungary. Hitler's attempt to take power in Bavaria in 1923 ended in failure. Fascist movements were founded and grew in every European country. Hand in hand with these new forms of society went the search for new economic methods, the nineteenth-century Western European principles of free enterprise also having reached a crisis stage.

These principles were rejected most consistently and radically in the Soviet Union, by its socialist planned economy. But forces clamouring for new economic methods were also gathering strength within capitalist society itself following the grave post-war crisis in the early twenties. Attempts to curb capitalist free enterprise and impose some order on the existing economic anarchy were made not only by cartels and trusts, but also by economists, who put forward various plans for the establishment of state capitalism. The Fascists followed similar aims.

Attempts were also being made at this time to create new relations between states, the war having given rise to new ideas on this subject as well as on social organization. As opposed to the pre-war policy of big power alliances, the conviction had taken root that even small nations had a right to voice their opinions and take a hand in shaping their own destinies.

The Soviet proletarian revolution gave the most concrete and general expression to these views. In its declaration on the rights of nations 'big and small, advanced and backward, European nations as well as those living in distant lands overseas', the Soviet Government officially proclaimed this right for all. The principle of the right of nations to self-determination, propounded by the October Revolution, had become one of the basic principles in the political programme of the growing world Communist movement. Just as equality of individuals was to be achieved by the creation of a new, socialist society, so this same society was supposed to guarantee the equality and free development of all nations.

These principles of the Russian revolution had a strong influence on many *bourgeois* politicians, even though they were opposed to the revolution itself. They had been directly responsible for the Allied programme formulated by President Wilson and found expression in his plan to establish an organization that would bring together all the nations of the world – the League of Nations.

Its foundation stone was laid by the signing of the Versailles peace treaty. International disputes were henceforth to be settled, not by force but by negotiation, the small and the weak being able to state their case at the conference table, whereas before they would have gone unheard, as the big powers competed for supremacy among themselves.

The League of Nations was also meant to provide guarantees of the small nations' rights and existence, its guiding principle being collective security. Based on the conviction that world peace was indivisible, this collective security against any possible aggressors was meant to protect all nations, including the small and the newly-created states, and to save Europe and the world as a whole from another terrible war. The political forces which created the League of Nations were identical with those which, in the years between the wars, sought to implement the *bourgeois* democratic model of society.

The principles behind the League of Nations naturally found ready adherents in all the small nations of the world, who saw the League as an organization primarily set up to protect them. As for the capitalist powers, their opinion was sharply divided about its usefulness, the democratically-minded politicians in each of these countries giving their support while the more conservative ones saw it as an unwelcome innovation designed to limit their sovereignty. But from the very outset, the League of Nations foundered on its own basic shortcomings. The crisis of *bourgeois* democracy was very much its own crisis as well.

In the first place, the League did not possess the necessary means to put its principles fully into practice. The small countries were not strong enough to do the job, and the democratic forces within the individual big powers did not succeed in realizing their aims in their own countries, much less on an international scale. They grew progressively weaker and were steadily replaced by more conservative elements.

It was no coincidence that it was these conservative *bourgeois* elements, which came to the fore in European politics in the mid-twenties, who dealt the first blow to the authority of the League. At the end of 1924 the newly-formed British Conservative Government of Stanley Baldwin refused to support the Geneva Protocol on the principles of collective security which had been warmly received by the Assembly. Under the aegis of this Conservative Government Britain, for the first time since the war, introduced into European politics the principle of the decisive role of the big powers in determining political developments. Instead of agreement between all concerned, whether large or small, it was the four European powers, Britain, France, Germany, and Italy, who made the decisions at the conference table at Locarno in 1925. To the sound of bells there was talk of new guarantees of European security and peace, these guarantees being the co-operation of the big powers. Only when the decision had been taken did the subject come up for discussion at the League of Nations, which was increasingly becoming a mere tool of the great powers.

At the same time strenuous efforts were being made to change the *status quo* in Europe by revising the Versailles system. The peace treaties, which formed its basis by legalizing the great changes effected at the end of the World War, were unpopular with many, and were themselves full of inconsistencies. The revision demanded by those who opposed the Versailles treaties concerned the region where the most far-reaching changes had taken place: Central, Eastern, and South-Eastern Europe.

Mention has already been made of the counter-revolutionary centres in Munich and Budapest, which sought a return to pre-war conditions in this part of the world. When this movement made its first open attempt to reverse the outcome of Versailles in 1920, it suffered a defeat, but it was by no means destroyed. Throughout the 1920s the Horthy Government continued its frantic revisionist efforts to wrest Slovakia from Czechoslovakia, Transylvania from Rumania, Voivodine from Yugoslavia, and Burgenland from Austria. It twice attempted to restore the

Habsburgs to the throne in 1921, and it was only thanks to determined opposition by the Little Entente, with Czechoslovakia and Yugoslavia going so far as to mobilize, that this danger was finally overcome.

However, the revisionist attempts by Horthy's Hungary found support not only in Fascist Italy, but also among British Conservatives, which was particularly ominous for the future of the entire region. An unbridled propaganda campaign, constant border incidents, Hungary's attempt to disrupt the economies of her neighbours with counterfeit money, arms smuggling, espionage and subversive organizations, and the constant threat of armed conflict – all this maintained tension and unrest in the whole of Central, Eastern, and South-Eastern Europe.

Nor had the Bavarian centre given up its endeavours to have the peace treaties revised. Undergoing many complex changes, it gave birth to a new, specific form of Fascist reaction in the guise of Hitler's National Socialism. Apart from the characteristics it shared with other Fascist movements, it combined the brutality of pan-German counter-revolution with the despair and desperate resolve of people uprooted and dehumanized by war, the mentality engendered by centuries of German militarism with the fanatical chauvinism of the Sudeten Germans from the borderlands. By the late twenties German National Socialism, with Hitler and his men at its head, was a united movement that had spread throughout Germany, Austria, and the German-speaking regions of Czechoslovakia and Poland. It was still, however, in its early stages and not important enough to be more than one of several potential dangers to European development.

But it was British policy, together with the official policy of Germany, that was of paramount importance in the twenties, for those who wished to achieve a revision of the Versailles system. The first general criticism of that system had in fact come from Britain even before it had taken proper shape, in *Economic Consequences of the Peace* by the British economist Maynard Keynes, published in 1919, which provided the basis for the economic argument against the Versailles treaties. To this were added the views of various British politicians, who saw the new states of Central, Eastern, and South-Eastern

Europe as one of the absurdities of the post-war situation rather than a realistic basis for further development. That is why the German critique of Versailles was able to find sympathetic listeners in Britain.

The German Army became the subject of the first revision of the Versailles treaties. The initial postponement of the date set for its disarmament, decided upon at a conference in Spa in July 1920, already opened the door for the resurrection of the German Army, that dangerous nucleus of German militarism. But this was only the beginning, and was followed by further successes. The democratic German politician Erzberger was murdered, because he had had the courage to sign the Compiègne armistice as a prelude to the Versailles treaty. Another democrat, the Minister of Foreign Affairs Rathenau, who insisted that Germany should adhere to the terms of the treaty and who, moreover, signed a treaty with the Soviet Union, was also shot by Bavarian counter-revolutionaries.

Then in 1925 at Locarno, with the German Army commanded by General Seeckt virtually built up and ready for action, the whole problem of revising the Versailles system turned to a question of territories. By means of the Rhine guarantee pact, negotiated by Gustav Stresemann, an experienced diplomat of the old monarchist school, the German Republic guaranteed its Western frontiers – those with France and Belgium. The silence over her Eastern border – the entirely new border with Poland – meant that the guarantors of the Rhine pact, Britain and Italy, did not exclude the possibility of its later revision. And in the last year of Stresemann's life, towards the end of 1928 and the beginning of 1929, this problem was carefully prepared for international discussion.

A closer look at the diversified trends of European development in the twenties, at its various ramifications and aspects, will show that, despite all the heterogeneous and qualitative differences, they all led to a single goal: to changing the face of the new Europe which had been born out of the horrors of the Great War, the Europe created in 1918 by the peace of Versailles.

The position of Czechoslovakia, too, changed radically as a result of the complicated and contradictory situation prevailing in Europe at that time, the changes affecting both the international standing of the Republic and her inner political character.

## A Small Country's Security

The determined efforts to change the Versailles *status quo* closely concerned Czechoslovakia's very existence, though during the twenties there was as yet no immediate threat. With the sole exception of Hungarian policy, which was aimed directly at achieving the breaking up of the Czechoslovak Republic, all the other movements demanding revision were for the moment more of a potential than an actual danger. British policy, the weakening of France, the revival of German militarism, the birth of National Socialism, and Stresemann's German policy all affected and limited the scope for Czechoslovakia's independent action; but for the time being did not jeopardize her statehood. Nevertheless, these developments unavoidably caused considerable concern to those responsible for Czechoslovakia's foreign policy.

At first, in the early twenties, before the revisionist movements had been fully developed and crystallized, Czechoslovak foreign policy concentrated on the normalization of relations with other countries on the basis of the peace treaties. It was to secure adherence to the treaties that Czechoslovakia, in 1921, struggled against the attempt to restore the Habsburg monarchy in Hungary. Going against the wishes of Britain, with France sitting on the fence, she and Yugoslavia did not hesitate to mobilize their armed forces when this became necessary. The two members of the Little Entente, with Rumanian support, were defending the Versailles *status quo*, which such a restoration would have jeopardized. Once on the Hungarian throne, Charles Habsburg would have launched an open campaign for the integrity of Hungary, and this would have been a direct threat to her newly-independent neighbours. The Act stipulating the dethroning of the Habsburgs, adopted by the Hungarian Government under pressure from the Little Entente, was a great victory for the three countries which formed that new European bloc.

The removal of the danger of a Hungarian restoration immensely improved Czechoslovakia's position, in that Austria and Poland, as well as the members of the Little Entente, now sought co-operation with her. As 1921 ended and 1922 began, Czechoslovakia had not only considerably strengthened her international position, she had, *via facti*, become the leading state of the new Central, Eastern, and South-Eastern Europe. Also, in 1922 Britain made the first attempt to bring together all the countries of Europe – the victors and the vanquished, the capitalist states as well as Soviet Russia – outside the Versailles system. They met at a conference in Genoa, but the experiment proved a complete failure. No new basis for negotiation was set up, and the old one, the peace treaties, was undermined.

Czechoslovakia was well aware of the consequences. The peace treaties had ceased to be the foundation on which it was possible to build the existence of the new state in peace and safety. For this reason Czechoslovakia took immediate steps to sign a treaty with Soviet Russia, a treaty which had been in the making for some time. By doing so, she gave the Soviet Government *de facto* recognition, establishing official relations with the U.S.S.R. on the basis of the provisional treaty. Thus Czechoslovakia tried, as early as 1922, to outweigh the first symptoms of its vulnerability by adding Soviet Russia to France as a pillar to safeguard her existence.

Simultaneously, Czechoslovakia concentrated on fostering international relations through the League of Nations, which it had regarded from the very start as the best means for achieving progress and peace. She took an active part in all its work, and together with France and Greece helped to draw up the Geneva Protocol, with which the League was concerned throughout 1924. The Protocol supplemented the Covenant of the League of Nations and was intended to prevent the outbreak of another war by means of collective defence. It was to give life to the principles of collective security, more important than ever now that the peace treaties were being devalued. But this intention was not to be really fulfilled through the League of Nations, partly because the Protocol was also conceived to preserve the Versailles *status quo*, which was opposed at the decisive moment by the new British Conservative Government. The draft was rejected, and the Locarno conference met in October 1925 instead.

Locarno was to deal the first serious blow to Czechoslovakia's international position. With the pre-war system of power alliances revived, small countries like Czechoslovakia again lost their opportunity to be heard when decisions on important international issues were taken.

This was very clearly demonstrated in the relations between Czechoslovakia and Germany. Since the signing of the peace treaties the two countries had had good official relations, Czechoslovakia being a welcome, if small, partner for her larger neighbour. The identical policies of the Social Democratic parties helped to foster this understanding between them. Czechoslovakia was the first state with which Germany established official contacts after the war, and this led in June 1920 to the signing of a trade agreement with definite political implications. Wishing to come to terms with her powerful neighbour, Czechoslovakia relinquished the right to confiscate German property in Czechoslovakia, which had been one of the conditions imposed by the peace treaty, so that the trade agreement was negotiated on the basis of absolute equality. In these circumstances the agreement was instrumental in strengthening Czechoslovak-German relations.

Czechoslovakia maintained strict neutrality in all Franco-German conflicts, endeavouring at the same time to soften the strongly anti-German bias of French policy. The German Government asked Czechoslovakia on a number of occasions to mediate between Germany and France.

Locarno brought a fundamental change to this relationship. Although the two countries continued to maintain correct neighbourly relations, the new German policy, as the democratic principles of the Weimar Republic were being abandoned, became that of a major power towards an unimportant partner.

The German Foreign Minister, Stresemann, expressed this change in somewhat brutal but accurate terms when, talking about the Locarno Treaty of 1925, he said: 'Messrs Beneš and Skrzyński had to sit in the next room until we let them in. Such was the position of countries hitherto riding high because they had been the servants of others, who dropped them the minute they believed they could reach an understanding with Germany.'

Czechoslovakia realized the consequences of Locarno even before the treaty was actually concluded, and she did her utmost to prevent its being signed. Finding, however, that Britain was determined to go ahead with it and to come to terms with Germany as soon as possible, she tried at least to ameliorate its unfavourable effects where she herself was concerned. Czechoslovakia therefore endeavoured to strengthen her ties with the countries of Central, Eastern, and South-Eastern Europe, but even in this respect she was hampered at every step by Germany's growing influence. This influence proved most damaging to Czechoslovakia's relations with the other countries of that region. Austria ceased to co-operate with her, turning instead to Mussolini's Italy, and to Germany. Imperceptibly the rapprochement, or *Ausgleichung*, was initiated, beginning with the setting up of an identical apparatus of administration and ending with close collaboration in military matters. The way was being paved for a future union of Germany and Austria.

The resurgence of Germany revived a multiplicity of old ties between that country and the post-war succession states; ties which had never been completely severed despite the radical changes that had taken place in the region. The German minorities, which existed in all the countries concerned, actively pioneered the renewal of contacts, and this trend appeared all the more desirable to most of Germany's partners by virtue of the marked swing to the Right that was then taking place in the Weimar Republic.

All these circumstances combined to loosen the connections between the countries of the Little Entente, Czechoslovak efforts to maintain a united front having already run aground in the political conflicts leading up to the conclusion of the Locarno Treaty. One of the reasons for this was the narrow territorial limitation of the Little Entente's joint interests, which did not go beyond Central Europe. The three countries of the Little Entente had a common enemy in Horthy's Hungary and its revisionist policy, but this identity of interests did not apply to their relations with Germany. This became increasingly apparent in the latter half of the twenties.

Nor did Czechoslovak - Polish relations, improved and strengthened by the agreement signed by the two countries in April 1925, survive Locarno for any length of time.

Czechoslovak foreign policy scored a partial success in its attempts to alleviate the effects of Locarno by the signing of the Czechoslovak-German agreement on arbitration. Germany concluded a similar agreement with Poland. The agreements, obliging the contractual parties to solve all mutual disputes by negotiation through the League of Nations rather than by war, were based on the same principles as the treaties Czechoslovakia had concluded earlier with the members of the Little Entente; and with France and Austria, the principles which had led to the Geneva Protocol and formed the basis of international efforts for collective security.

The Czechoslovak-German agreement on arbitration was of particular importance for relations between the two countries, although it was not part of the Locarno treaties nor linked with any international guarantees. It was to be the only political agreement between them in the inter-war period, and Czechoslovakia invariably referred to it in the years that followed. The agreement did not, however, in any way confirm the *status quo*, and as distinct from the Rhine guarantee pact, it did not give guarantees on the eastern and southern German frontiers drawn up at Versailles. It was for this very reason that at the same time Czechoslovakia and also Poland signed a guarantee treaty with France. This treaty was meant to strengthen the alliance forged by the Czechoslovak-French treaty of 1924, and in it France undertook to give Czechoslovakia immediate aid and support if the latter became the victim of aggression.

France was thus the only big power to promise Czechoslovakia assistance in the event of attack. The treaty came at a time when Czechoslovakia's international standing was badly shaken by the effects of Locarno, and it undoubtedly strengthened Franco-Czechoslovak relations. On the other hand, the treaty was both a symptom and consequence, not only of the deterioration of Czechoslovakia's international position but also of the increasing isolation of France, of her gradual but quite unmistakable decline as a leading European power.

Conscious of her own weakened international position, Czechoslovakia now also strove to bring about closer ties with the Soviet Union. The negotiations aiming at a complete normalization of relations between the two countries, begun by the signing of the provisional agreement of 1922 and continued ever since, entered their final stages immediately after Locarno. But these hopes were never to be realized, partly because of strong opposition in right-wing quarters at home, and partly because the Soviet Government, which in 1922 signed the Rapallo Treaty with Germany, quickly lost interest in relations with Czechoslovakia.

Locarno had thus dealt the first blow to Czechoslovakia's international standing. It was clear to her leaders that the country had been pushed into a blind alley where relations with others were concerned. Speaking on the Locarno talks and on Czechoslovak policy in the negotiations in the Standing Committe of the National Assembly in October 1925, Dr Beneš revealed the first hint of pessimism when he said that the intention had been, 'to resolve the problem of security in Central Europe, in so far as this *can* be resolved under present circumstances'.

## Developments in Czechoslovakia

Czechoslovakia's changed international position naturally affected political developments at home. The trend of international politics was now in sharp contrast to the tendencies that had brought the Czechoslovak Republic into being. It was in contrast not only with the country's foreign policy but also with Masaryk's ideas on her internal political system. This was why, just at a time when the *bourgeois* democratic regime had succeeded in consolidating itself by defeating both the extreme Right and the extreme Left, forces were coming into play which would undo the good work. And although this deterioration was in the main due to circumstances beyond Czechoslovakia's control, some part in it was also played by developments inside Czechoslovakia herself, by the mechanism of the *bourgeois* democratic system.

Masaryk's broadly based democracy, which in the first few years after the war had enabled the country to concentrate on the defence of the new Republic, now helped to put in train a process of internal political fragmentation. The existence of Czechoslovakia had been safeguarded; there was no longer any immediate external threat to unite the nation in its own defence. The democratic principles of freedom and tolerance which had brought about that vital unity now gave the various political groups in the country the opportunity to crystallize their views and go their own way. The bonds of national solidarity, forged when the new state was being established, now became loosened, and the political lines in a complex and advanced capitalist society became drawn in such a way that the various Czechoslovak political groups became linked with similar movements in other European countries.

The Communist movement was organized in the Third Communist International, but there also existed an agrarian movement with its Green International. The Christian movement was linked internationally by the Catholic Church, with the monarchist movement also finding support in the Vatican. The Social Democratic movement was united in the Second International, while the Fascist movement at this time looked to Fascist Italy. The Fascists had no international organization comparable to the other movements, simply because this was a highly nationalist creed. Yet even they had their international contacts. And finally there were the German National Socialists, with organizations in Germany, Austria, Czechoslovakia, and Poland.

The strength of these movements varied considerably, and depended not only on the number of supporters each could muster but also on whether the particular movement had a power base, in other words whether it was a leading force in any country and, if so, in which country. It made a great difference whether the strength and influence were rooted in a major European power or in a small, insignificant state. There was also the question of organization; the better the organization of a movement, the more influence it was likely to have.

The first sign of this process inside Czechoslovakia had appeared in the earlier twenties, with the formation of a revolu-

tionary movement in the united Communist Party of Czechoslovakia. This lasted throughout 1921, when the individual
revolutionary movements of the various nationalities in the
country came together to form a single international organization, as part of the world revolutionary movement belonging to
the Communist International.

Naturally enough, all this did not come about without a great
deal of discussion within the revolutionary movement. At their
congress in Lubochňa, as early as January 1921, the Slovak
and Ruthenian left-wing representatives came out in full
support of the twenty-one points that were a condition of
acceptance into the Communist International. In this they had
the majority of organized workers behind them. In March, the
same step was taken by the German left wing in Czechoslovakia
led by Karel Kreibich, but they only managed to gain the
support of a minority of the German Social Democrats.

The Czech left wing, numerically the strongest, and under
Šmeral's leadership the most important revolutionary group in
the country, held its congress in May, also accepting the twenty-
one conditions of the Communist International. The Communist Party of Czechoslovakia then actually came into
existence at a joint congress held in Prague between 30 October
and 2 November 1921. The national divisions inside the revolutionary movements were thus removed and a united,
strong Communist Party was created which was to play an important role in the future of the Czechoslovak Republic.

The aims of the revolutionary Communist movement were
those set down in the programme of the Communist International: the revolutionary restructuring of society and the
establishment of a Soviet-type republic ruled by a dictatorship
of the proletariat.

This basic line of policy was modified in the course of the
twenties. When the Communist Party of Czechoslovakia was
born, Šmeral, basing his view on Lenin's analysis, refuted
suggestions that there existed favourable conditions for immediate revolutionary action by the proletariat. 'Everything
seems to indicate that we are in the middle of a lengthy process of decay rather than faced with imminent catastrophe',
Šmeral declared, saying that what the Party had to do in the

immediate future was to gather its energies for a confrontation at some later date.

Following a temporary setback caused by the December defeat, the revolutionary movement recovered quickly once the Communist Party of Czechoslovakia had been formed. One contributory factor was the economic crisis that reached its worst period in the winter of 1922–3. Almost a quarter of all the industrial workers in Czechoslovakia were unemployed, and the employers were putting on the pressure by lowering their wages. This critical economic situation called for more radical measures by the working class, and the number of strikes as well as their intensity increased. Even though these were mostly defensive strikes, as opposed to the revolutionary period immediately after the war, there was no doubt about the increasing militancy of the workers.

The policy laid down by the Communist International in the autumn of 1922, calling for governments composed of workers and peasants, sounded the signal for a new revolutionary offensive. It found supporters in Czechoslovakia, too, where an anti-Šmeral opposition was formed within the Communist Party, led by Josef Haken and demanding that the Party go over to the attack. In 1924, with the aid of the Communist International, this opposition assumed leadership of the Czechoslovak Party. This was the beginning of the bolshevization of the Party, which was meant to form the hard core of revolutionaries preparing to overthrow the existing regime. The process of bolshevization continued throughout a period of crises in the Party, and the Bolshevik policy finally won a complete victory at the Sixth Congress of the Comintern in 1928. The programme of the Comintern was then adopted by the new leadership of the Communist Party of Czechoslovakia taking over at the Fifth Party Congress in February 1929, with Klement Gottwald at its head, and immediate steps were taken to prepare a proletarian revolution.

The Social Democratic Party also underwent changes in the course of the twenties. Critically weakened by the formation of the Communist Party, it sought to compensate for this by acquiring new allies.

The groundwork of its co-operation with the German Social

Democrats had already been laid, and after a number of joint actions the two parties agreed, in April 1925, to merge their trade union organizations, and negotiations were opened for the fusion of the parties themselves. And although this did not actually take place until January 1928, the Czech and German Social Democrats in Czechoslovakia worked closely together throughout the twenties.

The Social Democrats also intensified their co-operation with the Czechoslovak National Socialist Party, of which Beneš had emerged as leader following a serious internal crisis. The two parties were the chief supporters of Masaryk's 'Castle Group', their aim being to preserve democracy in Czechoslovakia.

The agrarian movement, having won mass support in the political struggle for land reform, began to organize itself in 1921 and 1922. By championing the demands for the distribution of confiscated land, the Agrarian Party had won over the rural middle class in particular, for it was to these 'people who have the necessary means, the farm buildings and machinery, and who can at once take over the land formerly belonging to the great estates' that the land reform had brought the greatest benefits. The Agrarian Party was also backed by poorer country people, who had likewise benefited, however little, from the land reform. Leadership of the Agrarian Party fell into the hands of the agrarian middle class, which had reaped the greatest gain and which now formed a new and numerically large social group.

During this period the Agrarian Party, led by Antonín Švehla, gradually shook off Masaryk's influence and began to implement its own policies. In 1922 it joined together with the Slovak and Ruthenian agrarian movements to form the Republican Party of Agricultural Workers and Small Farmers, at the same time establishing contacts with the *Bund der Landwirte*, the German agrarian party in Czechoslovakia.

The agrarian movement did not have as its goal a democratic republic of the type envisaged by Masaryk, but rather a so-called agrarian democracy which saw 'the soil as the chief source of national life' and the foundation 'for the brotherhood and unity of all who live on it'. It was a programme of the rural middle class, the programme of a conservative *bourgeois* republic.

The Catholic movement was less successful in forming a united bloc, though the Czech People's Party did establish contacts with the German Christian Socialists, and these links were further strengthened by the creation, in June 1922, of a united organization of Czech and German industrialists. But on the other hand the formerly united Czech and Slovak Catholic movement was split in 1921 when Hlinka created the independent Slovak People's Party, with Slovak autonomy as its chief aim.

In any case the Catholic movement in Czechoslovakia was not a movement in any real sense of the word, rather it was a loose association linked by a common Christian programme. It did not have any concrete political programme, its main importance deriving from its contacts with the Vatican.

Inspired directly by Mussolini's *putsch* in Italy, the Fascist movement became increasingly active in Czechoslovakia at the end of 1922 and the beginning of 1923. Owing to its nationalist character the movement developed in several separate national groups, but these began to establish mutual contacts, as well as having close links with Fascist organizations abroad. The German Fascists were the best organized, their roots in the German national workers' movement which had, since the 1880s, had its greatest following in the German-speaking regions of Bohemia and Moravia. Following the formation of the Czechoslovak Republic, the German National Socialist Workers' Party (*Deutsche national-sozialistische Arbeiterpartei*) came into being, with similar German organizations in Austria, Poland and Germany.

The first ideological programme of the movement, *Der nationale Sozialismus*, was drafted in 1921 by Rudolf Jung, the leader of the German National Socialist Party in Czechoslovakia. In the same year Adolf Hitler and his group – Röhm, Göring, Goebbels, and Rosenberg – took over the leadership of the Bavarian National Socialist organization, ousting the former leaders. This gave the movement a new, dynamic impetus, backed by the practical measures of para-military bands of ex-soldiers, to which Hitler himself had belonged until 1920. Under his leadership the whole movement acquired a new vigour. Hitler rejected any agreement on a republican platform, refusing all attempts at parliamentary negotiations. Power was for him the only means, the only argument, and the only goal: the power wielded by the para-military S.A. and S.S. organizations, with mass support provided by the members of the Nazi Party. This power was to help destroy 'rotten democracy' and install the new German order throughout the world. Exceptionally close relations existed between the Nazi group in Czechoslovakia and the Bavarian movement, borne out among other things by the fact that Rudolf Jung was one of the few who were on Christian name terms with Adolf Hitler.

The German National Socialist Party had very little influence in Czechoslovakia in the early twenties. Such importance as it had lay rather in its international associations and in the fierce nationalist campaign by which it maintained, and indeed frequently provoked, friction between the Czech population and the German minority. Having as its aim the break-up of the Czechoslovak Republic and the unification of all European territories inhabited by Germans in an all-German Reich (*Alldeutschland*), it tried in every possible way to prevent a Czech-German rapprochement, which was obviously being achieved by the Czechoslovak Government. By 1923 the Party had reached a stage where it was preparing an open revolt in the German-speaking parts of Czechoslovakia, timed to coincide with Hitler's Munich *putsch*. When Hitler failed to bring it off, the National Socialist plans for a rising in Czechoslovakia were quickly shelved, and the Party devoted its energies to building up and organizing the movement. In doing so it established the first contacts with the emerging Fascist wing of Hlinka's People's Party in Slovakia.

After the Slovak branch had split off from the Czech People's Party a determined bid for its leadership was made by Vojtech Tuka, a professor at Bratislava University. The Party's official newspaper, *Slovák*, of which Tuka was the Chief Editor, actively propagated the ideas of Italian Fascism, painting a rosy picture of conditions in Italy, and waxing especially enthusiastic about Mussolini's measures against the workers. Tuka, who acted on behalf of the Hungarian Foreign Ministry, was in direct touch both with Horthy's Hungary and Fascist Italy. In 1923 he visited Hitler's headquarters in Munich, where he knew a *putsch* was being prepared. He used the Hungarian, Italian, and German model for the 'Home Guard' he founded as part of the People's Party. These were armed units of storm troopers which were intended to stage a Fascist takeover in Slovakia in 1923, after which Slovakia would be annexed by Hungary. The failure of the *putsch* in Munich, however, put paid to Tuka's schemes, which encountered uncompromising opposition from the other Slovak political parties.

Fascist organizations sprang up in the Czech lands too in this particular period, basing themselves on the extreme right wing in Karel Kramář's party. This right wing, which included many former legionaries, had been campaigning against Masaryk and his concept of a democratic republic on an extreme nationalist platform. In international affairs the Kramář group was in favour of the Russian monarchist anti-Soviet intervention. They seized on the signing of the provisional agreement between Czechoslovakia and the Soviet Union in 1922 as a launching-pad for an all-out attack on Masaryk and his supporters. This group, too, considered Mussolini's regime in Italy to signpost the way forward.

Towards the end of 1922 and the beginning of 1923 two Fascist groups – the National Movement and the Red-and-Whites – were formed under the aegis of Kramář's National Democratic Party, with the aim of establishing a Czechoslovak national state on the Italian Fascist model. The attempted assassination of the National Democratic Finance Minister, Alois Rašín, on 5 January 1923 gave them the pretext they needed to make their bid for power. Under the slogan of 'Forward the Red-and-Whites', Fascist avengers organized street demonstrations, calling for tough action against the Communist Party of Czechoslovakia and against all democratic parties and organizations which tolerated its activity.

The demonstrations were dealt with by the authorities before the Fascists could take matters any further, and in actual fact they lacked the forces necessary for a fully-fledged *putsch*. At the same time, and at Masaryk's personal request, the National Democratic leadership dissociated itself from the abortive revolt. The Czech socialist parties and the *bourgeois* centre –

the Social Democrats, the National Socialists (not to be confused with Nazi organizations of the same name) the Agrarian Party, and the People's Party – formed a political bloc which quickly drafted the Act for the Defence of the Republic. The Act became law at the beginning of March 1923. Intended to safeguard the *bourgeois* and republican character of Czechoslovakia, the law was aimed, on the one hand, against the Communists and other left-wing revolutionaries trying to overthrow the existing regime and set up a proletarian republic, and on the other, against all right-wing groups wishing to turn Czechoslovakia into a Fascist state. The new law, backed by the political parties which had co-operated in drafting it, helped Czechoslovakia maintain her democratic character until the next political conflict that took place in the middle of the twenties.

## A Step to the Right

It was not to be expected that so radical a change in the general trend of European politics and in the international standing of Czechoslovakia as that produced by the Locarno Treaty could be without its repercussions on the internal politics of a country lying in the very heart of Europe. The changed European situation led to the first frontal attack on the democratic character of the Republic, now increasingly at odds with developments in the neighbouring states, as well as to an attack on the Czechoslovak foreign policy, which the Treaty of Locarno had shunted into a siding.

The political crisis was to be solved by the parliamentary elections of November 1925. The election results were eagerly awaited, and they proved even more surprising than had been expected. Two parties emerged as victors – the Agrarian Party with 970,000 votes and the Communists with 934,000. The Social Democrats suffered a serious defeat, polling a mere 630,000 votes as against 1,500,000 in 1920. In Slovakia, Hlinka's People's Party made considerable gains, while in the German regions victory was shared by the German Agrarian and Social Democratic parties. Except in Slovakia, the Fascists did very badly. On the strength of these election results the following

year brought a fight for power between the parties, all of whom
wished to be in a position to implement their own domestic and
foreign policies.

The Agrarian-Catholic bloc was the strongest, consisting of
both Czech and German Agrarian and Christian parties, and
gaining, after a bitter struggle, the co-operation of Hlinka's
Slovak People's Party, which succeeded in suppressing its own
Fascist wing led by Tuka. This bloc wanted to turn Czechoslovakia into a conservative republic, similar to the regimes
that came to power in Germany, Austria, and France in the
mid-twenties. The Conservatives had also won the elections in
Britain. The bloc further demanded a change in Czechoslovakia's foreign policy, the aim being to weaken the alliances
of the Little Entente and to bring the country closer to Stresemann's Germany.

President Masaryk and his supporters, who had hitherto been
the decisive factor in Czechoslovak politics, were forced on to
the defensive. His position was undermined by the disappointing
election results of the Social Democratic and National Socialist
parties, which provided most of his following. The Castle
Group now tried to create a bloc for the defence of the
*bourgeois* democratic republic by forming a coalition of these
two parties and the Communists, but the Communists refused
to join.

The Communist Party, completing the first stage of its
process of bolshevization, renewed its fight against the Agrarian-
Catholic bloc on the one hand and the Castle Group on the
other. In the summer of 1926 it led the workers in staging
widespread demonstrations against high prices, the introduction of agrarian taxes, and the proposed rise in priests' salaries.
In the sphere of foreign policy the Communist Party demanded
the immediate *de jure* recognition of the Soviet Union, complete normalization of relations, and Czechoslovakia's backing
for Soviet policy.

The Fascists also took a hand in the struggle for power. The
Czech Fascist movement formed the National Fascist League,
led by Rudolf Gajda, who had been in command of the officers'
clique which in 1918 plunged the Czechoslovak legions in
Russia into the anti-Soviet war of intervention. The National

Fascist League made the following demands: the replacing of the republican system by a Fascist dictatorship; the suppression of the workers' movement and banning of the Communist Party; the introduction of national and racial discrimination; limited rights for the Germans, foreigners, and Jews; in foreign policy, it rejected negotiations through the League of Nations and all the treaties concluded in Locarno; it demanded a consistently anti-German policy and the breaking off of all relations with the Soviet Union, with whom Czechoslovakia was not to negotiate in any circumstances.

With this programme as its aim the National League planned a Fascist coup, which was to take place during the Eighth Sokol Festival. Gajda and Tuka had reached an agreement under which the Fascist wing of the Slovak People's Party was to go into action at the same time. Tuka maintained direct contacts with the German Nazi movement, whose leaders were watching the Fascist preparations in Czechoslovakia with great interest. The Press reports about these preparations, at first sparse, but as time went on increasingly more detailed, helped to create an atmosphere of tension and fears for the future in Czechoslovakia during 1926.

At this juncture President Masaryk and his supporters took decisive political action against the Fascist danger and in defence of the Republic. The Agrarian-Catholic bloc, both Czech and German, came out on their side, and the Fascists found themselves totally isolated. The Sokol Festival passed without incident, and the Republic was saved.

The Castle Group, which had led the fight against the Fascist menace, turned out to be too weak to control further developments. The weakened socialist parties, on which it depended for support, were forced to take a back seat, assuming the role of an opposition to the Agrarian-Catholic bloc which now took the initiative. The various parties which made up the bloc came to an agreement in connection with the adoption of a law on agrarian taxes, which was bitterly opposed by the rest of the parties, in particular the Communists, who tried to obstruct the bill by staging stormy scenes in Parliament. A new political coalition, which was later joined by Kramář's National Democrats, had come into being. It found its expression in a new

Cabinet, formed in October 1926. Czechoslovakia was changing into a conservative *bourgeois* republic.

That this was no coincidence is shown by the fact that a similar trend made itself felt even in the very cradle of *bourgeois* democracy, France, as well as in all the new Central European republics: Germany, Austria, and Poland. Conservative tendencies had also come to the fore in Britain and in a number of succession states that had retained the monarchy.

The new Czechoslovak Government was favourably received in all these countries. It had the blessings of German governmental circles, which had earlier tried to hasten its formation by demanding that representatives of the German minorities be included in the Czechoslovak Government. It also had the support of the Austrian Catholic regime led by the prelate Seipel. The Vatican could claim some credit in the matter, having given open support, during 1925, to Catholic groups in the Czech lands and in Slovakia, even resorting to complicity in a campaign against Masaryk and his Castle Group. And of course the new Government was viewed with favour by all the similar agrarian regimes of the succession states.

The new Government tried, unsuccessfully, to change Czechoslovakia's foreign policy, hitherto the undisputed domain of the Castle Group. But in this respect it came up against Masaryk's adamant refusal to approve any Cabinet in which Dr Beneš would not be Foreign Minister. Nevertheless, the conservative forces exerted a continuous pressure on Beneš's policy, which was in any case becoming increasingly ineffective as a result of European developments.

The new Government endeavoured to weaken the pro-French bias of Czechoslovak foreign policy, and it resolutely rejected all attempts to link this with closer relations with the Soviet Union, demanding that the worsening in Czechoslovakia's international position and her growing isolation be compensated for by intensifying relations with Stresemann's Germany. This was a Germany that, in contrast to the violent revisionist, militarist, and pan-German currents which existed and were gaining in strength underneath the surface, was working for a gradual transformation of Central, Eastern, and South-Eastern Europe by means of treaties with the individual countries of the region. Stresemann's foreign policy, backed by the People's Party, did not openly demand a new Eastern, and perhaps also Southern, frontier; it simply refused to guarantee the existing ones. It did not demand an *anschluss* of Austria; it merely started the preparatory process of *Ausgleichung*. It did not openly demand the return of former German territories in the East, but it organized a European minority movement, which demanded unification with the Fatherland. It did not demand the creation of a German-controlled economic system in Central and Eastern Europe, but it was buying up the successor states' bonds in America, and systematically restored the old economic links which favoured her agrarian partners.

In Czechoslovakia itself it was now possible for Czechs and Germans to co-operate in the Government, and closer co-operation was also established between the Czechs and Slovaks, since the new policy was more in harmony with Slovakia's agrarian character. Milan Hodža, an Agrarian politician, became the new Prime Minister.

The new coalition Government made changes in social legislation and, in carrying out the land reform, weakened its fundamental principles. Its home policy was aimed at diminishing the influence of the working class in general, and the persecuted Communist Party in particular.

However, this new concept of a conservative republic safeguarded by co-operation with Stresemann's Germany was doomed to failure, showing itself to be unstable and without perspective. The forces of European development brought it crashing down and buried it in the debris of the Weimar Republic. The German policy did not outlive its creator, who had made defeated Germany a world power once more. When Stresemann died in October 1929, Germany's economy collapsed amidst a world crisis, and her political downfall was assured by a fierce onslaught of reactionary forces. Germany was hurtling towards a crisis of gigantic dimensions. Would the coming deluge also swamp Germany's neighbour, the Republic of Czechoslovakia?

# CHAPTER IV

# *THE STRUGGLE FOR FREEDOM AND DEMOCRACY*

When the New York Stock Exchange collapsed on 24 October 1929, it brought down with it the main pillar of the world's capitalist economy. Economic catastrophe overwhelmed the world. Signs of danger had appeared before the First World War, and at the end of hostilities a major crisis had developed, but of short duration. Now, however, on the threshold of the thirties, the entire old-style capitalist system collapsed. The economic crisis went hand in hand with social and political crises, so that the generation which ten years previously had come out of the trenches firmly convinced it would never have to fight again, was suddenly faced by a new catastrophe, not unlike the horrors of war.

The old world which had given birth to capitalism had been rocked to its foundations and now the economic crisis brought yet another shock. Millions of people lost their jobs and means of subsistence. In their fight for the barest essentials of existence large masses came into conflict with a society unable to provide for them. The call for the overthrow of this society, for a world-wide proletarian revolution, now sounded with a new urgency.

Having escaped the direct effects of the crisis by virtue of its closed socialist economy, the Soviet Union became an attractive example, and the Communist International, which in 1928 had succeeded in getting all its national organizations to follow the same policy, called for the overthrow of capitalism and the establishment of a dictatorship of the proletariat. These revolutionary appeals found ready listeners among the miserable proletariat, the rural poor, the impoverished middle classes, the unemployed millions, and the young generation unable to find its place in a crisis-torn world. The Communist Parties, now completely Bolshevik in character, stood at the forefront of this radical movement. Huge demonstrations and strikes took place throughout Europe, leading to bloody confrontations between the organs of state authority and those who were seeking a revolutionary way out of the crisis. This sudden intensification of the socio-political tensions in the European capitalist countries resulted in an open class war.

The revolutionary struggle reached its highest pitch in Germany, where the large proletariat led by a strong Communist Party attempted to seize power. This gave encouragement to the proletariat of other countries, in particular those having a common frontier with Germany. The Communist International once again counted on a victory of the German proletarian revolution as the first act in a revolution that would sweep the whole of Europe and the world. But the international revolutionary solution proposed by the Comintern was not to remain the only attempt at resolving the crisis. Capitalist society produced several different movements which tried to find a way out.

The economic crisis had two contrasting aspects. It was a crisis affecting the whole world, but its effect was to break up the economic unity as individual countries, making desperate efforts to ward off the catastrophe, introduced import tariffs and restrictions in an attempt to safeguard their home market. At the same time they strove to gain as large a share as possible of foreign markets. These efforts naturally brought the various countries into conflict, economic competition turning gradually into a trade and tariff war, which caused a worsening of political relations between the countries concerned.

Compared with the earlier period, which had given rise to international political currents far transcending the frontiers of the individual capitalist countries, there was now a growing endeavour to create smaller, closely-knit communities, each preoccupied with saving itself from the crisis.

As a result of this new trend, the capitalist countries adopted one of two lines in their European policy. The first, though modified in various ways, was to all intents and purposes the old big power policy which had already found its application in Locarno. This policy was based on the assumption that the superior strength of the major powers was to play the decisive role in international relations. In the thirties this power policy found expression in the attempts of the big powers to shield themselves from the effects of the crisis at the cost of the small and the weak. In Europe they did so by trying to dominate above all the various succession states, many of which were on the brink of disaster owing to the crisis.

The first such attempt was made by Germany, which tried to achieve economic domination, having laid the foundations for such a step in the preceding years. In 1931 Germany negotiated a customs union with Austria, the supposition being that other countries, notably Hungary, Yugoslavia, and Rumania, would join at some later date. Feelers were also put out to Czechoslovakia. But the German plan had to be abandoned after a fierce diplomatic exchange, when France, Czechoslovakia, and to some extent Italy came out against it, and the German-Austrian customs union had to be revoked.

A similar attempt was made a year later by France, Tardieu's *aide mémoire* on the Danubian Federation proposing closer economic links between Czechoslovakia, Austria, Hungary, Rumania, and Yugoslavia. On the face of it the big powers would not have been concerned, but in fact the whole plan was conceived in such a way as to bring the federation under French influence. However, Tardieu's plan remained on paper, due to German and Italian opposition.

With Germany and France having failed to make good their individual plans for the domination of Central, Eastern, and South-Eastern Europe, this power policy found its culmination in the Four Power Pact, officially put forward by Italy in March 1933. According to the pact, it would be up to the four capitalist powers – Britain, France, Germany, and Italy – to decide the future fate of the region, and to take similar decisions on colonial problems. It was a new attempt to divide the world into spheres of influence.

The Italian proposal was intended to separate the big and the small. Co-operation between the big powers was based on both psychological and practical considerations, the psychology of power and superiority, and the practical endeavour to create a kind of world *élite*, determined to survive at all costs, even if this meant letting the less powerful die. But before it could be implemented, this policy was outstripped by a related, though at the same time distinct, movement.

On 30 January 1933 Adolf Hitler assumed power in Germany. He cut off Germany from the rest of Europe and, hoping to widen the gulf as much as possible and thus cushion the country against the effects of the world crisis, made use of extreme German nationalism. This found its first outlet in the struggle against the international Communist movement, which 'eroded the unity of the German people'. The path was lit by the flames of the Reichstag. A second outlet was provided by a fanatical anti-Semitism, with the Nuremberg Laws giving legal sanction to crimes against people of Jewish origin and their property; a third by the old pan-German aim of uniting all Germans in one state, which could only be accomplished by annexing those parts of other European countries inhabited by 'German compatriots'.

At the same time, by fighting against all the *bourgeois* political parties which had formed part of the previous republican system, Hitler's nationalist regime gave the appearance of waging a revolutionary struggle against capitalism, and thus gained the support of the workers, whom the crisis had hit very hard. The final aim of this 'National Socialist revolution' was the creation of a new German Empire – the *Grossdeutsches Reich* – which would dominate the world.

To achieve this final aim, Nazi Germany, just as the other capitalist powers before it, had undermined the fundamental principle of international politics to come out of the First World War, that of collective security. In its place, and also in the place of the Four Power Pact, Germany followed a policy of bi-lateral pacts. These, concluded with different countries for limited periods of time, served Germany as a flexible instrument, giving her freedom to manoeuvre. They had an obvious political aim. When concluded between two major powers, such pacts helped to make both more powerful; when concluded between unequal partners, they left the small country at the mercy of the big power.

Difficulties in implementing her final aim made it necessary for Germany to change her line of approach, and the Berlin-Rome axis was expanded into a triangle that added Tokyo to the alliance. And when even this was not enough to get him what he wanted, Hitler would temporarily resort to the four-power method, as in the case of Munich. The final aim, however, remained unchanged, and so Germany's struggle for world conquest became once again the dominant theme of international politics.

Thus the economic crisis led to the widening of the rift between the powers, the big power solidarity of the Four Power Pact being substituted in Nazi Germany by the expansive nationalism of a single power – by pan-Germanism. Its historical roots, its unity, and its monolithic character made Hitler's National Socialism much more dynamic, militant, and aggressive than the loose alliance of the Four Power Pact.

In their different ways both these European trends represented attempts to restore world unity by force. They both tried to liquidate the revolutionary movement, and they posed a grave threat to the smaller countries. But their common struggle for power that could temporarily bring them together carried with it at the same time the danger of mutual conflict. A closer look at their aims will show that these were twofold: against the small countries on the one hand, and against the Communist movement on the other.

The Four Power Pact had put in jeopardy the existence of the new states created in 1918 – Poland, Czechoslovakia, Rumania, and Yugoslavia – and it also affected Austria and Hungary. Hitler's takeover made this threat still greater, accompanying it with an attempt to transform the internal politics of those countries in accordance with the Fascist model of society.

It was Czechoslovakia, which had always acted as a seismograph where European developments were concerned, that took the initiative in trying to save the situation.

When the disarmament conference split up in 1932, it became quite clear that the League of Nations had failed, that it lacked the authority to solve international problems. This realization led to the setting up of the Four Power Pact. In October 1932, as Hitler prepared to make his bid for power, his representatives met Mussolini in Rome, their negotiations ending in an agreement on the division of spheres of interest between the two countries. Poland, Czechoslovakia, Hungary, and Rumania were to be Germany's domain, while Fascist Italy, whose support Hitler badly needed at the time, was to have a free hand in Austria and in South-Eastern Europe. The threat to the whole region had become acute.

Czechoslovak intelligence received detailed reports on these negotiations, on the strength of which Foreign Minister Beneš went direct from the abortive disarmament conference in Geneva to a special meeting of the Little Entente in Belgrade. In January 1933 Czechoslovakia submitted to her partners the draft of a pact for the organization of the alliance, which was signed on 16 March. In effect it was another attempt to form a Central and Eastern European federation along the lines suggested by Masaryk during and immediately after the war. Its chief aim was to combine three small states in a larger entity, to make one power out of three small countries. It was to be 'the first step towards integration, towards a synthesis, a new international community'.

The Little Entente, which represented 45,000,000 people, was headed by a Permanent Council, whose initial aim was the co-ordination of the foreign policies of the member states. This meant organizing a joint struggle against the external enemy. Economic integration was to follow, and at the beginning of 1934 an economic pact was concluded as a further step on this road.

The efforts to bring about political and economic integration did not remain confined to the Little Entente. Due to the skilful policy of the Rumanian Foreign Minister Titulescu, they spread further afield, to the Balkans and Asia Minor. The Balkan Pact, signed in 1934, linked Rumania, Yugoslavia, Greece, and Turkey on principles identical to those of the Little Entente. There was close co-operation between the two groups, especially on international affairs; the Little Entente and the Balkan Pact represented a broad and important alliance of smaller states in defence of their freedom and independence, based on the principles of collective security.

Unsuccessful efforts were made at this time, especially by

Czechoslovakia, to establish closer contacts with Austria and Poland. There was also an attempt to revive the League of Nations and make it work in accordance with the principles on which it had been founded, but which had been abandoned. The small countries of Central, Eastern, and South-Eastern Europe were not strong enough in themselves to effect this, but they found support in the policy of two European powers, in Barthou's French and Litvinov's Soviet policy.

The Four Power Pact, which was meant to decide the future of Central, Eastern, and South-Eastern Europe by means of a round-table conference, was very important from the point of view of France, which had a strong but now threatened interest in that region. The arrival of Hitler had increased this danger still further, with Germany, her old enemy, making no efforts to conceal her aggressive plans.

The Four Power Pact also affected the one European power which had hitherto played next to no part in European diplomacy, the Soviet Union. The Pact offered the possibility of concerted action against her, both in Europe and Asia.

Hitler's rise to power, his anti-Communism, and his *Drang nach Osten* closely concerned the Soviet Union as a state in general and as a socialist state in particular. And by means of the German-Polish treaty of January 1934 the influence of Nazi Germany reached the Soviet frontier. As a result there was a change in Soviet foreign policy. Relations with Germany, based on the 1922 Treaty of Rapallo, confirmed and widened in scope by another treaty signed in 1926 and extended in 1931, gradually deteriorated. Soviet diplomacy, conducted by Litvinov, started to establish contacts with France where democratic politicians such as Herriot, and in particular Barthou, were sympathetically inclined. In 1934 Litvinov and Barthou held talks on the setting up of a so-called Eastern Pact. This was intended to supplement the Locarno treaties of 1925 on the inviolability of Germany's Western frontier with a similar treaty on the Eastern borders.

At the same time the Soviet Union drew closer to the Little Entente and to Turkey. The protocol on naming the aggressor, signed in 1933, was the first step in this rapprochement, and was followed by further defensive measures.

France, the Soviet Union, the Little Entente, and the Balkan Pact countries, were making a concerted effort to resurrect the League of Nations which had become virtually defunct. After the failure of the disarmament conference in 1932, it was abandoned by the powers seeking to set up the four power bloc, and immediately afterwards Japan, Italy, and Hitlerite Germany walked out, intending thereby to cripple the League and gain complete freedom of action.

It was then that the League of Nations was given a new lease of life. In the autumn of 1934, supported by France, the Little Entente, and the Balkan Pact, the Soviet Union became a member of the League, and took her place among the major powers. Czechoslovakia played an exceptionally important role in bringing the Soviet Union into the League of Nations as Dr Beneš, the Chairman of the League's autumn session, had paved the way for her entry and introduced her to this international body.

The third trend in European politics had thus crystallized bringing together the imperilled small countries with the democratic forces in France and with the revolutionary Soviet Union. This rapprochement had been achieved within the revived League of Nations and on the basis of the principles of collective security, in defence of the *status quo* in Central, Eastern, and South-Eastern Europe. It was a policy of defence against the new division of the world by the big four, and in particular against the aggressive plans of Nazi Germany.

## Two Fronts in Europe

At the end of 1934 and throughout the following year, the struggle to determine the future of Europe came to be waged on two fronts, one led by Germany, and the other consisting of the alliances of small eastern European nations with Franco-Soviet co-operation. Both camps had their sympathizers, some successes, and their weak points.

The Nazi regime in Germany, which many people had thought would not last very long, consolidated its position. By destroying all the other parties in the country, one after the other, Hitler came to hold all the important offices and, after

Hindenburg's death in August 1934, became Germany's chief representative as Führer and Reich Chancellor. With the huge Nazi Party backing him up he instituted and fortified the Fascist dictatorship, his regime giving international political support to the Fascist groups and parties which existed, without exception, in every European capitalist state.

Nazi Germany soon chalked up its first international victories. It established contacts with Mussolini's Italy, but their co-operation at this time was not particularly close. Italy was trying to protect her own sphere of interest in Central Europe by closer ties with Austria and Hungary, with whom she signed the Rome Protocols in March 1934. The German-Polish pact of January 1934 was very important to Hitler as it ended the isolation in which Germany had found herself when she left the League of Nations. This agreement was a blow not only to France, but also to the incipient new bloc of the Little Entente and the Balkan Pact. And the annexation of the Saar in the autumn of 1934 was another German triumph, especially important for her internal policy.

In March 1935 Hitler officially renounced the Versailles undertakings concerning disarmament, which had of course never actually come into force, and announced the formation of a new German Army. In June 1935 Hitler followed this with an even greater achievement when Germany and Britain signed a naval treaty. Even though the treaty was very limited in scope, dealing with the purely technical aspect of relations between the two countries, and despite British reservations regarding Hitler's Nazi regime, its political significance was not to be denied. It was the first official British sign of acceptance of Nazi Germany, and this in itself was extremely valuable to Hitler. Added to this were the diplomatic contacts maintained with Berlin, in the conviction that not only was it possible to come to some sort of understanding even with a power like Nazi Germany, but that this was the best, quickest, and simplest way of solving international problems.

German policy had the further advantage of being single-minded. The dictatorship enabled quick and flexible manoeuvering as well as authoritative decisions. The policy of the Nazi Party had its own dynamics, and each new success won more and more supporters among the masses, whom it did not give a moment's breathing-space. It was full of vitality, driving what used to be a defeated Germany forward in pursuit of the great national goal of world domination.

But Germany still had a long way to go. She had very little influence abroad, and at home the regime had not succeeded in liquidating the opposition despite the burning of books, police raids, and concentration camps. The leaders of democratic and revolutionary German parties and organizations found political asylum in Czechoslovakia, France, the Soviet Union, Britain, America, and elsewhere, devoting their energies to an anti-Nazi campaign in exile. The brutal methods used by the Nazis outraged public opinion and caused people abroad to look upon Germany with horror and disgust.

The other front formed in the years 1934-5 covered a much larger territory, its potential strength incomparably greater than that of Germany. It had considerable successes to its credit. It was based on the Franco-Soviet treaty of May 1935, which rounded off the rapprochement between the two powers, one of whom was Germany's neighbour to the west and the other a near neighbour to the east. Both sides undertook to give the other effective military aid in case of an attack by an aggressor. Czechoslovakia had been exceptionally active in promoting this treaty, supported in her endeavour by Rumania. And it was Czechoslovakia who suggested that the treaty should be emulated by others.

On 16 May 1935 Czechoslovakia and the Soviet Union signed a treaty of alliance, linked by special clauses with the Franco-Soviet agreement. It sought to make the Paris-Moscow treaty the supporting pillar of a wider system of alliances to be joined by others, in particular by the countries of the Little Entente and the Balkan Pact. Titulescu's policy in Rumania was designed to take the necessary preparatory measures for such an eventuality. This aim was expressed during the signing of the Czechoslovak-Soviet alliance treaty by the following words: 'It was concluded with a view to the creation in Eastern Europe of a regional security system, the foundations for which were laid by the Franco-Soviet treaty of 2 May 1935.'

The bloc consisting of France, the Soviet Union, and the

small nations of Central, Eastern, and South-Eastern Europe, and of Asia Minor, gradually became a defensive ring encircling Nazi Germany. It was a very powerful bloc covering a vast expanse of territory, and it received strong international support, in particular from all the democratic forces of the world, which regarded the Nazi dictatorship with repugnance. Their own activity was in turn helped by the bloc's existence. Numerous bodies, such as the various anti-Fascist intellectual organizations and the international organizations helping the victims of Fascism and championing the cause of German political exiles throughout Europe, all allied themselves with the bloc.

In the summer of 1935 the bloc succeeded in gaining the support of the international Communist movement. The Seventh Congress of the Communist International adopted the policy of the popular front, which was to channel the immense strength of the proletariat away from the revolutionary struggle and concentrate instead on the creation of a broad defensive front against the brutal menace of Fascism.

The real strength of the Paris-Moscow-Prague coalition lay not merely in its sheer size, measured in terms of territory, or its improving organization, but more in the ideas upon which it had been built: the defence of Europe from Fascism and war, the defence of the freedom and independence of the small countries, and the defence of people, nations, and races condemned by the Nazis to extermination. These humanitarian ideas now brought the democratic and revolutionary forces together, making them allies in a common caue.

Yet the bloc did have its Achilles' heel, and in spite of all efforts it never managed to achieve a tightly-knit organization. All that was achieved in this direction was the alliance between France, the Soviet Union, and Czechoslovakia. The bloc was too complex and diverse a mosaic of states, interests, and political aims which had in the past been opposed to one another. There was not sufficient time to create the necessary understanding and dispel distrust. In each of the countries there were, moreover, forces working against the bloc, and to overcome this much effort, patience, and resolve was needed. To succeed, the bloc needed unity, but unity was directly dependent on the internal political development of the countries concerned. It was this labyrinth of internal political developments that posed the biggest problem.

In Western Europe, Britain was now governed by the Conservatives, who took over in June 1935 after a period of coalition government. And just as in 1924 Baldwin's premiership meant the end of the Geneva Protocol as Britain set out on the road to Locarno, now his Government's first foreign policy move was the signing of a naval treaty with Germany.

In France, the assassination of Foreign Minister Barthou in Marseilles in October 1934 and the fall of the government that followed cleared the way for changes in French foreign policy, now in the hands of Pierre Laval. Despite having signed the alliance treaty with the Soviet Union, France now became more cautious in her dealings with the Communist power. But she drew closer to Italy and Great Britain, and opened negotiations with Germany. At the same time the popular front was being formed in France, trying to find new ways of strengthening French democratic traditions in its struggle against Fascism. Spain, which had just become a republic, was making heavy weather of the process of consolidation.

The whole of Northern, Central, and Southern Europe was politically under the influence of German Nazism and Italian Fascism. Austria had Dollfuss' Austro-Fascist dictatorship, whose basic principles were continued by his successor, Schuschnigg, after the Chancellor's murder in 1934. Gömbös's dictatorship assumed power in Hungary. Czechoslovakia was the sole exception in retaining its democratic form of government.

Eastern and South-Eastern Europe was in a political turmoil. In Poland, Beck's foreign policy, with its pro-Nazi bias, helped to bolster Piłsudski's authoritarian controlled democracy. Developments in the Balkan states took their own specific turn. Their collaboration in the Little Entente and the Balkan Pact had been dictated by fear of aggression and the desire to safeguard their newly-acquired independence. The policy behind the new bloc geared to Paris and Moscow ran directly counter to their internal trends, with most of them replacing monarchy with a monarcho-military dictatorship.

Strong Fascist groups and parties gave new significance to their old links with Germany, which had been renewed during the twenties.

The assassination of King Alexander in Marseilles had, on the one hand, weakened the Yugoslav dictatorship, but on the other it led to greater autonomy of the individual countries, notably Croatia, and thus to a weakening of the Yugoslav State. Germany's economic and political influence grew rapidly, Hitler sending Göring as his personal representative to King Alexander's funeral. All told, Yugoslavia was clearly becoming the weak link of the Little Entente.

In Rumania there was a powerful Fascist movement, centred on the Iron Guard. Titulescu's foreign policy, forging close ties with Czechoslovakia, France, and the Soviet Union, was one of the chief barriers holding back the Fascist onslaught.

Bulgaria went from one crisis to another, while the newly restored Greek monarchy strove to maintain strict neutrality in the coming conflict.

The Soviet Union, stretching from Eastern Europe deep into Asia, was not altogether united despite its monolithic character. There evidently existed differences of opinion between various groups of diplomats, politicians, and military men. It is impossible to say what were the aims of these groups, but the Moscow trials which took place in the late thirties bear out the hypothesis that such differences did exist. All this, however, in no way affected actual Soviet policy, whose greatest asset lay in its outward unity, which greatly increased Soviet influence in international affairs at that time.

The labyrinthine politics of the various European countries cut across the two sharply defined fronts of 1935, bringing with them the possibility of change.

## Poverty and Hunger

With this outline of the extremely complex European political situation in the mid thirties, a closer look must be taken at the important part the developments in Czechoslovakia had played in it. Czechoslovakia's strenuous efforts to maintain a European outlook in her foreign policy were inevitably reflected in the country's internal developments. The fall of the right-wing coalition government at the end of 1929 coincided with the beginning of the thirties' economic crisis. This crisis hit Czechoslovakia very hard. It first showed itself in agriculture. Produce prices fell sharply, bringing the income of small farmers and peasants down below subsistence level. Numbering almost 60 per cent of the entire population, they were unable to purchase even the most basic industrial equipment. This helped to exacerbate the existing crisis in industry. The farmers also had no money to invest in their properties and were forced to borrow. As the situation dragged on, they found they could not repay these loans and went bankrupt. The farms became inactive and fell into disrepair, and agriculture as a whole suffered a decline.

In industry the crisis progressed more slowly than in other capitalist states, its effects only becoming really pronounced in the latter half of 1930, reaching its zenith in 1933, when industrial output in Czechoslovakia fell to 60 per cent of the 1929 figure. A financial crisis followed. And the whole process culminated catastrophically in a universal stagnation of international trade, which made matters in industry still worse.

The result of the industrial crisis was a massive increase in unemployment. First of all production was merely cut back, the factories working only a few days a week, but as the crisis continued an increasing number of plants had to shut down completely, as they were unable to sell their products. Thousands of workers were made redundant. The unemployment figures were highest in the winter of 1932-3, when official statistics gave the number of people out of work as 920,000. Unofficial estimates put it as high as 1,300,000. Counting one unemployed worker as the wage earner for a family of three, this meant that at the peak of the crisis there were between three and four million people – a quarter of the entire population – without any means of subsistence. The brunt of the crisis was therefore borne by the two numerically strongest classes, the farmers and the industrial workers.

Of course the crisis affected all sections of the population, leading to the collapse of independent businesses and the impoverishment of the middle classes. It hit public employees, white-collar workers, and the intelligentsia as well as capitalist enterpreneurs. A discernible social hierarchy existed among the victims, the weakest members of each class or group being the worst affected: agricultural workers and crofters, unqualified and young workers, women, small traders and craftsmen, the lowest paid office workers, young intellectuals, and the smaller industrialists. A similar hierarchy applied in respect of territory. The worst effects of the crisis were felt by the economically more backward areas such as Ruthenia, Slovakia, and South Bohemia.

The appalling crisis, its absurdity, which was to be seen in the huge stocks of unsaleable goods on the one hand and the starving masses on the other, and the hopelessness and misery it engendered, produced a great wave of discontent in Czechoslovakia as in all the other countries. As the crisis dragged on, this dissatisfaction mounted, to culminate eventually in a determination to destroy the system that had caused it; and as everywhere else, the worst hit social classes – the agricultural workers and the industrial proletariat – became increasingly more radical in their outlook.

The unemployed, the hungry, and the poor had their spokesman in the Czechoslovak Communist Party. Like all the other branches of the Communist International, it too was trying to bring about a revolutionary solution, pointing out that the crisis of capitalist economy was one of capitalist society as a whole. The new Party leadership, headed by Klement Gottwald, was committed to the preparation of a proletarian revolution, as proposed by the Sixth Congress of the Comintern in 1928. As soon as it had assumed control, it gave first priority to the revolutionary struggle.

This Bolshevik line culminated in the resolution passed by the Sixth Party Congress in May 1931, at a time when the crisis had reached terrifying proportions, and social conditions in the country had become intolerable. The resolution, defining the Party's political line, emphasized the basic revolutionary tenet that the genuine liberation of the Czechoslovak working people can only be achieved by the destruction of Czechoslovak imperialism, the revocation of imperialistic treaties, the cancellation of the war debt, the defeat of our own *bourgeoisie*, and the establishment of fraternal relations with the people of other nations within a framework of soviet republics. The Communist Party went on to suggest how the crisis should be solved by means of a programme of soviet power in Czechoslovakia, underlining that the struggle for the daily needs of the working masses is a fundamental condition of the struggle for a proletarian dictatorship.

With this revolutionary programme the Communist Party led the working class into the attack on capitalist society and for a world revolution. The Communist Party took a very active part in most of the industrial strife of the period, which had intensified greatly as a result of the crisis following the temporary calm during the prosperous twenties.

Demonstrations by the unemployed were one of the new forms of class struggle at the time of the crisis. Organized by the Communist Party, they gradually grew into a powerful movement all over the country, and were usually at their strongest during the winter when the number of unemployed was at its highest. The hopeless situation in which these people found themselves gave their demonstrations a truly revolutionary character. The movement had its first success in the demonstrations of March 1930. By the end of the following winter, it had become a mass movement, a total of 200,000 people taking part in a demonstration held on 25 February 1931, which was proclaimed the day of struggle against unemployment. By this time the movement had become organized, with local action committees of unemployed preparing demonstrations, laying their demands before the authorities, and organizing hunger marches.

In the course of 1931 the workers took action against dismissals and wage reductions. The two biggest strikes were those of metal workers at Karlova Huť, which lasted two months, and of agricultural workers in South Slovakia. These were followed by the greatest struggle of the period – the month-long miners' strike in the North Bohemian coalfields in the spring of 1932, personally organized by members of the new Communist Party leadership. The strikers had the support of the whole region, with the small traders, farmers, and intellectuals solidly behind them. Their example led to strikes by miners at Kladno, in the Ostrava region, at Sokolov, and at

Handlová in Slovakia. In May 1932 Slovak agricultural workers staged a hunger strike with the slogan 'Unity – Strike – Victory' as their motto, first coined by the miners at Most. Building workers, too, went on strike, particularly in central Slovakia, where the movement reached its peak when the men working on the new Červená Skala–Margecany railway line downed tools in June 1932.

Revolutionary action by the workers led to the adoption of more severe measures against them by the state authorities. The Slovak Agrarian politician, Dr Juraj Slávik, who was Minister of the Interior from the end of 1929 to the end of 1932, was the prime mover, and a number of serious incidents between the police and the hungry demonstrators and strikers occurred during his term of office. Shots were fired at a procession of children at Radotín near Prague in April 1930. On 5 February 1931, four workers were killed and four others seriously wounded when *gendarmes* opened fire on demonstrators at Duchcov, while in May there was more shooting in South Slovakia during an agricultural workers' strike organized by the Communists and the trade unions.

Three people were killed at Košúty in Slovakia on 25 May 1931, and one worker died at Chust in Ruthenia on 20 July 1931 during similar incidents. In November there were more deaths at Frývaldov, where the workers had declared a general strike in the whole district and staged a demonstration in protest against the employers. The funeral of the victims turned into a massive political demonstration by the workers of Frývaldov. In June 1932 police fired at Slovak workers at Holič, Telgárt, and Pohorelá, and the following month at Sutory near Rimavská Sobota, where small farmers clashed with a bailiff who had carried out 140 evictions in the course of three days. There was a similar incident between the police and farmers at Nižní Apš in Ruthenia in September 1932, and two Slovak workers were shot and wounded at Polomka in November.

These shootings heightened political tension in the country, each event becoming a political issue and arousing sympathy for the workers. Protest demonstrations and strikes were held, money was sent to the victims and their families, and this created a broad front of solidarity within the working class and brought other groups over on to their side. Czech and Slovak intellectuals came out very strongly in support of the workers and against the brutal methods of the police.

A broad political front came into being which demanded that the police be prevented from firing on the workers. Asking for the removal of Minister Slávik, it also urged the Government to take immediate steps to combat the crisis and its social consequences. Apart from the Communist Party with its revolutionary programme, there was now also a reformist bloc of the two socialist parties, the National Socialists and the Social Democrats, the former taking the initiative by adopting a new programme in April 1931, which envisaged a number of far-reaching reforms while retaining the *bourgeois* democratic system. In the economic field it demanded nationalization and control of industry, as well as the planning of trade policy.

With this programme there came to the fore in Czechoslovakia a politico-economic movement for reform that wanted to change capitalist society and give the State considerable powers in the economy. Although it had not yet fully crystallized, the movement represented a new direction of capitalist policy on an international scale, combining the ideas of both Czechoslovak and foreign economists, the teaching of John Maynard Keynes, as well as the experience of the Soviet Five Year Plans, reinforced by the realization that the economics of the liberal capitalist era were a thing of the past. Apart from the international revolutionary solution to the crisis which the Communists tried to put into practice, and these attempts at a reform of capitalism, the crisis also strengthened efforts to find a solution on a nationalist basis.

The social consequences of the crisis were more severe in Slovakia and Ruthenia than in the Czech lands. This was due to the economic imbalance inherited from the days of the Austro-Hungarian Empire and from earlier times. Owing to lack of capital and the technical obsolescence of many of its branches, Slovak industry could not keep step with the more advanced industrial establishments in the Czech lands in the fiercely competitive struggle in the years of the depression. It had even less chance of competing on an international level.

The most heavily hit was the Slovak timber and woodwork industry which was geared mainly to export trade. The situation became particularly critical after the Czechoslovak-Hungarian trade agreement was rescinded in 1930. By 1933 only half the Slovak timber mills were working, and even their capacity was reduced to 30 per cent.

The crisis also dealt a heavy blow to the ore-mining industry, the output of iron ore falling in 1933 to only 20 per cent of that achieved four years previously. Coal mines and ironworks also suffered badly, and output fell considerably in every other branch of Slovak industry.

Slovakia was already experiencing great difficulties in finding sufficient work in her undeveloped industry for all the people who came looking for jobs from the relatively overpopulated rural areas where farming also lacked modern equipment and up-to-date methods. This had resulted in thousands of Slovaks leaving the country each year, some to take up seasonal work in neighbouring Austria or Hungary, many others emigrating for good, chiefly to America.

The crisis brought a sharp rise in unemployment. Inadequate administrative facilities existing at the time make it impossible to give any reliable figure: official sources gave the number of unemployed in Slovakia at the worst period of the depression as 88,000, contemporary estimates put it as high as 250,000. Unemployed workers could not find jobs either at home or abroad, as all the capitalist states drastically reduced their quotas or stopped immigration altogether in those years. Slovak agriculture was incapable of feeding the population, and so there were whole areas, both in Slovakia and Ruthenia, where people were literally starving.

Faced with this terrible and incomprehensible suffering, the ordinary Slovaks and Ruthenians became radical in their outlook, turning in many cases to the Communist movement. But Hlinka's People's Party, the strongest single political organization in Slovakia, channelled this radical feeling into an increasingly nationalist mould, which in its simplicity was easier for the ordinary man to understand. There were still many Czechs in the country's administration and in various cultural institutions who had come to work in Slovakia immediately after the Republic was founded in 1918. In the meantime a new generation of Slovak intellectuals had grown up, and these young, educated people were prevented by the crisis, as were the Czechs in their part of the country, from finding jobs in the civil service, in schools administration, and in the universities. The Slovak man in the street looked upon the Czechs as his overlords and for that reason alone as being responsible for his present misery.

Hlinka's People's Party made political capital out of such sentiments. By fighting against Communism, it helped to prevent the Slovak proletariat from joining forces with the numerically stronger and far better organized Czech working class. By fighting against 'fiendish progress-mongers' it helped to combat the anti-clerical forces. Hlinka's main political aim was Slovak autonomy. Following the imprisonment of the chief author of this political programme, Vojtech Tuka, on charges of sedition, younger People's Party representatives took up the campaign. One faction, led by Ďurčanský, adopted what was to all intents and purposes Tuka's policy, co-operating with Fascist circles in Hungary, Austria, and Germany. Another, led by Sidor, fostered links with Poland instead. Both these Slovak groups were supported and misused by these countries as one of the means of weakening their Czechoslovak neighbour.

There was also a sharp upsurge of nationalism among the German minority in Czechoslovakia. The crisis had struck harder and more swiftly in the German-speaking regions than in the Czech areas, partly because the light industries in the German regions were more vulnerable, and partly because they had close economic links with Germany, so that the economic chaos in that country could not but have its repercussions across the border.

Meanwhile, the German National Socialist Party in Czechoslovakia reacted to the advent of the crisis by intensifying its nationalist campaign, pointing to the existence of the Czechoslovak Republic as the chief cause of the predicament in which the German workers now found themselves.

It has already been shown that the German National Socialist Party was not an independent organization, being linked with the Nazi movement in Austria and, above all, in

Germany. In 1931 Hitler and Jung came to an agreement on their joint action in carrying out a Nazi coup throughout Central Europe.

Early in 1932, the leadership of the Nazi Party in Germany sent the following instructions to German Nazis in Czechoslovakia: 'Prepare for the moment when the Führer gives the order to take up arms in the cause of unity . . . That day is not far distant, and the unification must be carried out with your help and the help of Austria.' And at the same time German S.S. and S.A. detachments were helping to arm and train a similar, para-military organization of the Nazi Party on Czechoslovak soil – *Volkssport*, or V.S. for short.

Czech Fascists, too, attempted to solve the crisis by closing their ranks on a nationalist platform. Their campaign was directed against the Communists and their policy of international revolution, against all democratically inclined groups for their national and political tolerance, and against the Germans. In the early thirties there were further violent anti-German demonstrations in Prague, organized under the leadership of Kramář and Gajda, during which an attempt was made to storm certain German buildings such as the *Deutsches Haus*, the German Theatre, and the editorial offices of German-language newspapers. They were, however, cordoned off by the police, and the demonstrators had to content themselves with looting German cafés and Jewish shops.

## The Czechoslovak New Deal

What was the official Czechoslovak policy at the time of the crisis, when the Government had to contend with the revolutionary activity of the Communists, attempts at evolutionary reform, as well as with various nationalist movements?

After the first coalition government fell in 1929, a so-called government of the broad coalition was formed under the Agrarian Party politician Udržal. As its title indicates, this was a more broadly based coalition than the Agrarian-Catholic bloc that had made up the previous government. The latter had been seriously weakened, partly by the waning influence of the German parties and the Czech National Democratic Party, and partly by the withdrawal of Hlinka's People's Party, which went over to the democratic bloc, now without the right-wing groups, led by Masaryk's followers. This bloc had, on the contrary, gained in strength, and its younger members, headed by Dr Edvard Beneš, began to assert themselves. There was thus once again a government representing all the nationalities in the country, but this time its political composition was different, signifying a distinct move to the Left and helping to reinforce Czechoslovak democracy. The main task of Udržal's Government, from its formation in December 1929 to its fall in October 1932, was to fight the crisis and its international, social, and political consequences.

The catastrophic downfall of the Weimar Republic in early 1933 put an end to the policy of the previous Czechoslovak coalition, which had tried to safeguard the country's existence in the international, political, as well as economic sphere by establishing close relations with Germany. This close relationship proved a liability when Germany collapsed, threatening to drag Czechoslovakia into the abyss. The only way out lay in severing contacts and freeing Czechoslovakia from all dependence on Germany. That is what Udržal's new Government set out to do.

In foreign policy this meant forging stronger ties with France and renewing contacts with the Soviet Union. It also meant bringing the Little Entente back to life, although a first step towards this goal had been taken at the Štrba conference in 1930. The quick switch was facilitated by the failure of the Agrarian-Catholic bloc to make Czechoslovakia's foreign policy its own instrument, so that it had never become as strongly pro-German as the bloc would have liked to make it.

On the home front the endeavour to loosen Czechoslovakia's ties with Germany was directed first and foremost at cutting contacts between the extreme right-wing German nationalists in Germany and in Czechoslovakia. The chief blow was aimed at the Nazi movement. In March 1931 the Government launched what was to be a systematic attack, the Czechoslovak authorities banning public appearances by Nazi speakers from Germany and the wearing of brown uniforms and swastika insignias. Public meetings and celebrations organized by the

D.N.S.A.P. were likewise prohibited, and every effort was made to sever the existing links between the Nazi movement in Czechoslovakia and Hitler's in Germany.

The climax of the anti-Nazi campaign mounted by the Czechoslovak authorities came with the trial of the paramilitary Nazi organization Volkssport in Brno in the summer of 1932. This was the Czechoslovak Government's reply to the preparations made by that organization and the D.N.S.A.P. as a whole for a Fascist *putsch*, the trial providing proof of its direct links with the German S.S. and S.A. It served as a warning of the dangerous plots being hatched by Nazi Germany, not only to the Czechoslovak public but to the whole world.

In the economic quarter an attempt was made to intensify trade relations with those countries and regions with which Czechoslovakia was drawing closer politically, though this presented considerable difficulties owing to the nature of capitalist economy.

The crisis and its terrible social effects made it incumbent on the new Udržal Government to try and solve the most burning social problems. It sought to alleviate the crisis by supporting the capitalist economy. This made it impossible to prevent the capitalists from putting the blame for the crisis chiefly on the working classes. With right-wing parties in the coalition, the Government was unable to put through any really effective social programme. All it did, under pressure from below and especially from the workers' movement, was to initiate various relief operations.

In order at least partly to compensate for the measures taken by the Government in favour of the capitalists, the socialist parties insisted on steps being taken to improve the lot of the unemployed. Unemployment benefits were increased in the case of workers who were members of trade unions, while those who were not received food coupons to the value of between ten and twenty crowns per week. Potatoes, bread, milk, and other foodstuffs were also distributed to ensure that the unemployed, and in particular their children, received at least basic sustenance. But as the crisis deepened and the ranks of the unemployed kept swelling, these relief measures could not substantially alter the plight of the workers and their families, providing no solution to the social problems caused by the crisis.

At the same time the Government's anti-Communist measures led to new political conflicts, police brutality in dealing with strikers, and in particular their use of firearms against demonstrating workers, giving rise to a broad opposition front.

It was the Government's inability to solve, in any effective way, the economic and social problems brought on by the crisis that led to its fall at the end of October 1932.

The new Government had much the same party composition as the previous one, differing only in personalities. Juraj Slávik was dropped as Minister of the Interior, and another Agrarian, Malypetr, replaced Udržal as Prime Minister. As soon as it took office, it became apparent that a markedly different political course would be steered than under the previous administration, and that considerable changes would be made in the economic and socio-political structure of the country. This at a time when, by putting forward a proposal for the setting up of an Organizational Pact of the Little Entente, Czechoslovakia gave new impetus to the defence of the Versailles *status quo* in Central, Eastern, and South-Eastern Europe. There was an easily discernible connection between Czechoslovakia's domestic and foreign policy, the common denominator being the Foreign Minister Beneš, who had become a leading member of the Castle Group supporting President Masaryk.

The Malypetr administration based its policy on the new programme of the Social Democratic Party, which Masaryk had personally helped to draft and which was adopted in 1928, and the new National Socialist programme of 1931, which was the brainchild of Eduard Beneš. The socialist bloc now had a commanding position in the Government, and it thus determined the internal policy of the country, Malypetr's Government using the authority of the State to control and influence the capitalist economy in an effort to overcome the crisis. In a declaration the Government stated that 'It is not possible to keep using the old methods and forms of enterprise, we can no longer rely simply on the once effective and instructive "*laissez-faire, laissez-passer*". Unless we wish to see complete anarchy in production and marketing, private enterprise must adapt itself to controls in both these fields'. And in June 1933 the Government adopted a bill which gave it powers to regulate 'certain economic matters and ensure that a balance is maintained in the economy as a whole'. On the strength of this law, the Malypetr administration issued 240 decrees dealing with the organization and control of the economy.

The Government's actions were of a similar nature and followed the same aims as the grandiose New Deal with which President Roosevelt was at that time trying to rescue the American economy and put an end to the crisis.

All these measures, immediately put into effect by the Malypetr Government, were vehemently opposed by groups favouring unrestricted free enterprise. Politically this found expression in the withdrawal, in January 1934, of the National Democrats from the Government. Their departure made it possible for the administration to go ahead faster and more directly with its programme of economic reform.

The trend which sought to give wider powers to the State in economic affairs was also reflected in politics, the new Government making determined efforts to strengthen the authority and military readiness of the State against both the internal and external enemy. To this end a law curtailing the freedom of the Press was passed in the summer of 1933. Another law gave the Government special powers with a view to safeguarding the country's integrity, its republican form of government, its constitution, and public order. The Law for the Defence of the Republic was extended by the addition of new clauses, a new law was promulgated on the prosecution of State employees guilty of subversive activity, and in October yet another law, passed after long and heated debates, enabled the Government to suspend and ban political parties.

All these new laws were a reaction to the Hitlerite *putsch* in neighbouring Germany. The assumption of power by the Nazis, pledged to implement the political programme contained in Hitler's *Mein Kampf*, imperilled Czechoslovakia not only on the international level, but also from within. The successful coup gave encouragement especially to the German Nazi organizations in Czechoslovakia, but the fact that the Fascist model of society had triumphed in the largest Central European country also invigorated Fascist movements of every nationality.

The importance of this internal danger can be deduced from the prompt action taken by Hitler, who immediately after his takeover on 8 February 1933 summoned the Czechoslovak diplomatic representative in Berlin, ⸢exerting pressure on him in trying to exact assurances of the unhindered and legal development of the German nationalist movement in Czechoslovakia.

But the Malypetr Government went ahead with its drive against the Nazi movement. Four D.N.S.A.P. leaders – Jung, Krebs, Schubert, and Kasper – were put on trial, as were members of other anti-State organizations, which term applied to all National Socialist bodies in Hitler's Germany: the N.S.D.A.P., the Hitler Jugend, the S.A., and the S.S. The law empowering the Government to dissolve political parties, passed in October 1933, was invoked on 4 November to ban the German National Socialist Party in Czechoslovakia, which was simply a branch of Hitler's own party on Czech territory.

The move effectively paralysed the Nazi movement in Czechoslovakia. The banning of the D.N.S.A.P. deprived the Nazis of their organizational and political base in the country and prevented them from using the Party in the preparations for a *putsch* stage-managed from Berlin. The two top leaders of the Nazi movement, Jung and Krebs, fled the country and took refuge in Germany.

The Czechoslovak Government made similar use of the new legislation in its fight against the indigenous Czech and Slovak Fascist movements, which reared their heads in 1933, encouraged by developments in Germany.

The first blow was struck by the Czech Fascists when they made an abortive attempt to seize the Army barracks in Brno as a prelude for their coup. When this failed, Hlinka's People's Party in Slovakia staged a political demonstration at the State and Church festivities in Nitra in the summer of 1933. These were held to commemorate the 1,000th anniversary of the founding of the first Christian church at Nitra by Prince Pribina. During the celebrations, attended by members of the Government, the Church hierarchy, and the diplomatic corps,

Hlinka addressed the crowd with a declaration that ended with the following words: 'They've told us we'll get autonomy if we want it. Well, we want it!' His audience, many thousands strong, chanted in unison: 'We want autonomy, we want autonomy!', and went on to sing folk songs in order to prevent the official programme from being carried out. The whole occasion was turned into a political manifestation, the People's Party giving it a decidedly chauvinistic, anti-Czech character.

At the same time, Hlinka's People's Party, the Slovak National Party, and the Czech Fascist groups – the National Fascist Union, the National Fascist League, and the right wing of the National Democrats – held a conference, which adopted a manifesto demanding that Czechoslovakia cease to be a democratic republic and change its foreign policy. In this way a bloc of Czech and Slovak Fascist groups was formed under the leadership of the People's Party, seeking to subvert the Republic. Consequently the new political legislation passed by the Malypetr Government was invoked once more, this time against the Czech-Slovak Fascist front. And on the basis of the same political laws the Malypetr administration proceeded to attack the Communist Party of Czechoslovakia.

As soon as the Nazi dictatorship was installed in Germany, the Communist Party took up the fight against German Nazism and its henchmen in Czechoslovakia, conducting an anti-Nazi campaign in the Press, through its members of Parliament, and by means of strike action that culminated in actual skirmishes with German Nazis in the border regions and with Czech Fascists in the interior. The large and successful protest demonstrations that took place in Czechoslovakia in the spring of 1933, following the Reichstag fire, and in the autumn of that year during the Leipzig trial were chiefly the work of the Czech and Slovak Communists.

Along with the majority of European public opinion, the Communist Party did not believe that the Nazi regime in Germany would last very long, basing this view on the resolution passed at the Thirteenth Plenary Session of the Communist International's Executive, which considered the Nazi dictatorship to be only temporary and which predicted a revolution in the near future. The Communist International and all its branches in the various European countries were busily preparing such a socialist uprising. The Communist Party of Czechoslovakia had organized an underground network for this purpose, stretching from factory and local Party organizations to the illegal Central Committee. 'Soviets the only salvation' was the slogan under which the Party waged this struggle.

It was from this revolutionary viewpoint that the Communist Party assessed the actions of the Malypetr Government. While fighting against the Agrarian-Catholic bloc which formed part of the Government, the Party directed its chief political campaign against the socialist bloc, and in particular against the Castle Group, which represented the main influence behind the Malypetr administration. The Communist International held that the socialist parties were only the other side of the coin whose obverse was the Fascist movement, and so, making this equation between the socialist and the Fascist parties, the Communists regarded the Malypetr Government as a Fascist one. Its new measures for the economic and political bolstering of the State – which undoubtedly modified the principles of *bourgeois* democracy – the Communists considered part of a process that brought Czechoslovakia increasingly closer to Fascism.

Thus the Communist Party came to the conclusion that the political regime in Czechoslovakia was identical with Hitler's in Germany, and this was emphasized by one of its leaders, Václav Kopecký, who said 'the difference is purely a formal one, but in fact it's the same Fascism, the same reaction, the same danger, the same dictatorship'. This deduction led the Communist Party of Czechoslovakia to oppose forces which, though by other means and on a different class and political platform, were nevertheless fighting the same enemy as the Party itself.

This Communist policy culminated in a fierce personal campaign against President Masaryk at the time of the presidential elections in May 1934. Coining the motto 'Masaryk – No!, Lenin – Yes!', the Communist Party asserted that Masaryk 'is the patron of war preparations and is to be placed at the head of an openly Fascist dictatorship'. During the actual election ceremony in the Vladislav Hall of Prague Castle, Communist deputies and senators created stormy incidents as they tried to obstruct the proceedings.

This brought the conflict between the Communist Party of Czechoslovakia and the Malypetr Government to a head. Warrants were issued for the arrest of four leading Communist members of Parliament – Gottwald, Krosnář, Štětka, and Kopecký – who were to be put on trial. They avoided a prosecution by 'going underground' and then leaving the country for the Soviet Union. The Communist Party now found itself in a semi-illegal position, with its activities severely curtailed.

This, however, was to be only a temporary setback. The attempted Nazi *putsch* in Austria in July 1934, when Hitler planned to march into Vienna, sounded a stern warning to Czechoslovakia, even though this time the Nazi dictator did not succeed. As a result of these events, anti-Fascist forces in Czechoslovakia sought to unite and take joint action in defence of the Republic.

## Two Fronts in Czechoslovakia

The dividing line between the two fronts dominating the political scene in Europe at the end of 1934 and beginning of 1935 did not represent the sum total of the complex political situation of that period. Specific conditions existed in the individual countries that were the combined results of their past history and the actual political constellation prevailing at the time.

In Czechoslovakia, it was the socialist bloc, with the Castle Group at its head, that came to stand at the helm. But there was also another strong political group that stood in opposition to it, so that the situation in Czechoslovakia was identical to that in Europe as a whole, with two opposing fronts facing one another.

The product of a complex process of crystallization and segregation, a right-wing Fascist bloc came into being in direct dependence on international developments.

After the National Democrats left the Government they formed the National Unity Party with Karel Kramář as its leader. Thus, in the autumn of 1934, Czech Fascism received a new and very important political and organizational base. In Slovakia, meanwhile, Hlinka's People's Party extended its influence by building a bloc whose aim was to achieve political autonomy for the country. Both these centres saw the Fascist dictatorship of Mussolini's Italy as their ideal, and both sought to change Czechoslovakia's foreign policy in her favour. At the same time, the Czech and Slovak Fascist movement gained a new, if for the time being only potential, ally in the members of the extreme right wing of the Agrarian Party. It was their common interest in effecting a change in Czechoslovak foreign policy that brought them together, the Agrarian right wingers being strongly opposed to co-operation with the Soviet Union and wishing to establish contacts with the signatories of the Rome Protocols – with Austria, Hungary and, through them, with Italy herself.

The Slovak People's Party on the one hand and the Agrarian right wing on the other simultaneously acted as a bridge that offered links with the German Nazi movement of Konrad Henlein.

Following the dissolution of the Nazi Party as a result of the ban of October 1933, the German Nazi front in Czechoslovakia was resuscitated in another guise with the creation of a new movement led by Henlein and called the *Sudetendeutsche Heimatfront*. The movement took over the former membership of the banned Nazi Party, as well as its entire organizational structure. This time, however, it was headed by a group of German intellectuals belonging to a small, exclusive secret organization called the *Kameradschaftsbund*. Taking its ideas from the tenets of the Austrian sociologist Othmar Spann, the group was closer to the Italian model of a corporate Fascist state than to the Nazi dictatorship as practised in Germany. The leader of this new movement, Konrad Henlein, represented a central position between the Nazi rank-and-file and the intellectuals.

The diversity of views held by its members enabled Henlein's movement to establish contacts in a number of different quarters. Via its Nazi majority it was linked with Hitler's Germany, which provided much-needed financial support. The *Kameradschaftsbund* group maintained contacts with the German Agrarian and Christian-Socialist Party, with which it began to

build a united German conservative bloc, linked both by means
of personal contacts and by its political platform with Austria,
Hungary, and Italy, most especially with the first and its
Austro-Fascist regime. And here again it had common interests
with the Slovak People's Party, Kramář's National Unity Party,
and the right wing of the Agrarian Party.

The Fascist front that had come into being in Czechoslovakia
by the end of 1934 was thus linked by a common affinity for
Mussolini's Italy, while the Nazi rank-and-file of Henlein's
movement had close contacts with Hitlerite Germany. This became particularly important in the first half of 1935 as the movement prepared for the decisive struggle in the Parliamentary
elections that were to take place in May 1935, when the number
of votes gained by the Henlein organization would determine
its future political strength.

The anti-Fascist groups did not remain idle at this time,
drawing together in their constant struggle against their opponents, so that they gradually formed a united front of democratic and revolutionary forces determined to halt the Fascist
tide.

This bloc contained the nucleus of the Malypetr administration: the socialist bloc which relied on the close co-operation
between the Czechoslovak National Socialist Party and the
Czech, Slovak, and German Social Democrats. Then there was
Monsignore Šrámek's Catholic People's Party, collaborating
with the German Christian-Socialist Party. Another, somewhat unreliable, partner in this bloc was the Agrarian Party.

The Communist Party of Czechoslovakia, whose policy had
taken on some new features in the latter half of 1934, became
yet another member of the anti-Fascist alliance. With the
changed international situation, and with the Soviet Union now
a member of the League of Nations, the Communist Party
concentrated its efforts on the struggle against Fascism.

Following a report by Jan Šverma, the Tenth Plenary
Session of the Communist Party's Central Committee in
November 1934 adopted a new policy, expressed in the following
slogan: 'Against co-operation with the *bourgeoisie* – for a fighting
Socialist coalition.' This meant co-operation with the Czech
and German Social Democrats, the National Socialists, and

with the organizations of peasants and small farmers. Thus the Communist Party of Czechoslovakia entered upon a Popular Front policy. The growing Czechoslovak-Soviet co-operation in international politics helped to bind this alliance together.

In this way the foundations were laid for a broad anti-Fascist movement in Czechoslovakia, due to which this country became an important centre of European anti-Fascism and provided asylum for thousands of victims of Hitlerite Nazism and Austrian Austro-Fascism.

The Parliamentary elections of May 1935 were to give the two fronts in Czechoslovakia the opportunity to measure their respective strengths. But before that, an important development took place inside the Henlein movement. At the beginning of 1935 the Nazis from the former D.N.S.A.P. party managed to take over leading positions in the movement. As they had close personal contacts with Nazi Germany, this assured Henlein of increased political and financial support from that quarter, enabling him to conduct an ambitious election campaign. He aimed to break up the German democratic parties, thereby depriving the Czechoslovak anti-Fascist front of a valuable ally. After that he hoped to come to an official agreement with the Czechoslovak right wing and Fascist bloc, which would pave the way for far-reaching changes in both Czechoslovakia's internal politics and her European foreign policy.

The Socialist bloc within the Malypetr Government demanded that Henlein's party be prevented from conducting, with German financial backing, unbridled Nazi progapanda intended to subvert the Republic. At the beginning of April 1935 the Social Democrats laid before the Government a proposal for the banning of the Henlein movement, asking that it be disbanded on the basis of the Law for the Defence of the Republic.

A fierce political battle followed this proposal, the Agrarian Party coming out against it. President Masaryk was asked to decide the issue and, faithful to his democratic principles, the 85-year-old President ruled that it was incumbent on Czechoslovakia as a democratic state to allow all opinion to be expressed. Henlein's movement, now called the *Sudetendeutsche Partei* (S.d.P.), took advantage of this to launch a violent attack on that very democracy.

D.D.—7

In the elections of May 1935 the Czech and Slovak democratic bloc held its own, retaining its leading position in the Republic. The revolutionary forces in the German movement also suffered only insignificant losses. The German democratic bloc, however, was completely disrupted, with the German Agrarian, Christian-Socialist, and Social Democratic parties splitting down the middle. Czech Fascism made very slight gains, but the Slovak Fascist bloc scored a marked success. Henlein's party polled 1,250,000 votes, thus becoming the spokesman for 66 per cent of the German minority in Czechoslovakia and the strongest single political party in the country.

## The Triumph of Democracy

In the sultry atmosphere that prevailed in Europe in the autumn of 1935 there were growing signs that a major conflict was approaching in which the two opposing fronts would clash head on.

In October, Italian troops invaded Abyssinia. This was the first instance since the war in which one member state of the League of Nations attacked another. The Abyssinian crisis became a test case, not only for European anti-Fascist forces but for the League itself. Democratic and revolutionary world public opinion took a firm stand against Mussolini's aggression, in defence of the helpless Abyssinian people. But as the bombs fell, sympathy alone was not enough. And so the League of Nations became an arena for the struggle to gain more concrete help for the victim of Fascist aggression.

It was no coincidence that it was the Czechoslovak representative, Beneš, who presided over the plenary session called to discuss the Abyssinian affair. The Emperor Hailé Selassie, pleading in Geneva for assistance, was the personification of all small countries in danger of foreign aggression. The realization that it could just as easily be a Czechoslovak representative demanding aid against an invader gave an added incentive to Beneš's policy. The Czechoslovak chairman tried to get the League to declare Italy as the aggressor and to adopt effective economic and political sanctions against her. A resolution on sanctions was, in fact, passed on 9 October 1935. Their implementation, however, was hampered by the opposition put up by France, by British indecision, and by the general disinclination of the big powers to take sides against Italy on behalf of backward little Abyssinia.

At the same time, Nazi Germany was sounding the alarm against the threat posed by Communism to European civilization.

At the Nazi Congress in Nuremberg, held in September as a 'freedom congress', Germany was pledged to conduct an implacable struggle against the Soviet Union and against 'Bolshevism as the invention of an alien race'; against 'Bolshevism, which is the arch enemy of all nations'. Hitlerite Germany, the champion of 'the universal spiritual, cultural, and economic traditions of Europe' also declared its steadfast intention to fight against all those who opened the doors to Europe for this 'enemy of all mankind' – those who had 'dared' to sign alliance treaties with the Soviet Union: France and Czechoslovakia.

German verbal attacks on France maintained a certain diplomatic restraint with the intention of leaving the way open for a possible agreement. They were conducted primarily along legalistic lines, claiming that by signing the treaty with the Soviet Union, France had violated the Locarno Agreements. On the other hand, Goebbels's campaign against Czechoslovakia was quite unrestrained and aimed to discredit that small country in the eyes of the world. Czechoslovakia, which had had the audacity to try and erect a defensive barrier against Germany, was described as an instrument of Moscow, a pillar of Soviet foreign policy, a Red Army stronghold in the very heart of Europe. This Nazi scaremongering campaign bore fruit – in Britain and France, as well as in a number of countries in Central, Eastern, and South-Eastern Europe. And in Czechoslovakia itself, it gave rise to uncertainty, nervousness, fear.

At the end of October 1935 the Agrarian Party in which the right wing, represented by its new chairman Rudolf Beran, had gained the ascendancy, tried to bring about a change in governmental policies by recalling Malypetr, and replacing him with Milan Hodža as the new Prime Minister.

Hodža was not, however, a right-winger, belonging to the centre of his Party. But he had often in the past criticized

Czechoslovak foreign policy for its pro-Soviet and anti-Italian line, the latter becoming more apparent than ever at the time of the Abyssinian invasion. On the home front he had opposed the co-operation of the Socialist parties with the Communists and had tried to come to terms with Henlein, hoping in this way to woo the Sudeten Germans away from Hitler. The anti-Fascist front took a firm stand against all such attempts, their clash with the forces of reaction coming to a head in the Presidential elections of December 1935.

On 14 November Masaryk informed the Premier Hodža of his intention to abdicate, recommending Beneš as his successor.

The Agrarian Party, taken by surprise and quite unprepared for this development, found itself on the defensive. It tried to gain time, fully aware of the importance the new incumbent of the highest office in the state would have in determining Czechoslovakia's future policies. But on 14 December President Masaryk abdicated officially, again giving Beneš as his choice for the next President of the Republic. An attempt by the Agrarian Party to form an alliance between the right wing parties and the Fascists, aimed at preventing Beneš's election, failed when the bloc disintegrated before it had been properly constituted.

Beneš's candidature had the backing of the Czech People's Party, the National Socialists, the Czech, Slovak, and German Social Democrats, and the Communists. When even the Slovak People's Party decided to vote for Beneš, and when the opposition within the Agrarian Party grew stronger, the right-wing Agrarians withdrew from the bloc they had themselves brought into existence, their candidate, Professor Němec, stepping down shortly before the election.

Beneš's election was greatly helped by the votes cast by the Communists, who had originally intended to put up their own candidate, Klement Gottwald. But they were persuaded by the very real danger represented by the Fascist front to support Beneš instead, despite the fact that they disagreed with many of his policies, and on 18 December, Beneš was elected President by an absolute majority of 340 votes. His election constituted a great victory of the democratic, anti-Fascist forces in Czechoslovakia and helped to strengthen the anti-Fascist front in Europe as a whole.

One of the first steps taken by the administration immediately after the election was to take action against Henlein's S.d.P., which represented the greatest internal threat to the Republic. Having defeated the most reactionary forces in the country and neutralized the Slovak Fascist centre, the Government now was free to deal more radically with the Henlein movement.

Despite its convincing victory in the Parliamentary elections, the S.d.P. lacked inner unity and cohesion. It was made up of a large number of groups holding different political views and struggling with one another for power within the Party. Full of internal conflict, the Party badly needed a period of calm in which to consolidate its ranks if it was to exert real political influence. This it was not to have. The Government now banned all its public activities, including the Party Congress that was to have been held in April 1936, the 'Sudeten German Cultural Festival', and political speeches by Nazi leaders. The Nazi Press was censored, and the Government passed a number of bills severely curtailing the political and propaganda activity of the S.d.P., which was in danger of being banned altogether.

All these measures proved highly effective, preventing the Party from achieving the unity it so badly needed and sowing discontent within its ranks, which culminated in the first half of 1936 in a full-scale crisis. 'Courts of honour' were set up in the Party to expel individual members and whole groups. Party meetings became the scene of bloody battles between opposing factions as the struggle of the old Nazis against the *Kameradschaftsbund* group grew in intensity, the former finally turning against the Party Chairman, Konrad Henlein. The S.d.P. was becoming increasingly isolated and losing its political influence. It disintegrated and as it did so became incapable of action. Berlin had failed once more in its attempts to build up a reliable Nazi bastion inside Czechoslovakia.

The victory of the democratic bloc in the December Presidential election also helped to ensure the continuity of Czechoslovakia's foreign policy, which remained anchored to the Little Entente, France, and the Soviet Union, and, on a broader level, to the European democratic and anti-Fascist front. This front had been considerably strengthened by these developments in Czechoslovakia. More successes were to follow in other countries.

In December 1935 a new Constitution was adopted in the
Soviet Union. In France, the Socialist groups joined together
in the Socialist-Republican Union, which, together with the
Radical Socialists and the French Communist Party formed the
Popular Front that was to exert a growing influence on French
policy, both at home and abroad. And in February 1936 the
Popular Front triumphed in Spain. Each of these victories by
the anti-Fascist front brought new hope to Europe and the
world.

# CHAPTER V

# *THE DOOMED DEMOCRACY*

~~~~~~~~~~~~~~~~~~~~~~~~~~~~~~~~~~~~~~~~~~~~~~~~~~~~

### Hitler's Attack Begins

By the beginning of 1936 Hitler realized that to wait was a disadvantage. If he delayed, he would only be giving his anti-Fascist opponents time to organize and gather strength. He therefore decided to go over to the offensive, to break the barrier that was beginning to encircle Germany. He had to break up the French-Czechoslovak-Soviet bloc, reinforced by democratic and revolutionary forces throughout Europe, and he turned his attention to the link he considered to be the weakest, France.

On 7 March 1936 the troops of Nazi Germany marched into the Rhineland, occupying the demilitarized zone whose inviolability had been guaranteed at Locarno. Faced with German aggression, the question was, would France fight and defend herself? Would she do so in the knowledge that she was risking another war as the inevitable result of such an action? The Soviet government advised its French ally to stand firm.

'The Soviet Government does not consider this German disavowal of the Locarno treaties to be an isolated act. In its opinion, the unlawful occupation of the Rhineland is merely a link in a chain of events, all of which are inspired by a spirit of aggression. The Soviet Government is convinced that if the countries concerned resign themselves to this latest instance of German perfidy, the results will be catastrophic, as the aggressor will be rewarded and given encouragement for the dishonouring of further international obligations. The Soviet Government believes that there is yet time to

save Europe from the threat of a war of aggression, provided
a firm stand is taken; on another occasion it will be too late
to stop Hitler.'

The Soviet Government considered the re-militarization of
the Rhineland to be a *casus foederis* calling for the implementation of the Franco-Soviet treaty of alliance. Czechoslovakia
adopted a similar viewpoint, the Czech government informing
the French Ambassador in Prague that 'we shall follow suit if
France decides to take steps against Hitler'. Czechoslovakia
considered herself bound by her alliance treaty with France of
1925, and was ready to go to her assistance. The Little Entente
and the Balkan Pact were also willing to help France, and even
Polish military leaders indicated that they would assist their
old ally. Britain and Italy, on the other hand, categorically
refused to defend the Locarno Treaty, which they had signed
in 1925, by force of arms, and urged France to come to terms
with Germany.

France dragged her feet. The spectre of renewed German
aggression loomed large, and France had faced it twice before
within living memory. Her ancient foe had grown strong once
more. And France feared the possible consequences of her
resistance; she feared war. And more than the war itself, she
feared entering it at the side of her new ally, the Soviet Union,
and of the small countries of Central and Eastern Europe, without the support of her old partner, Britain. Nor did she relish
having Italy as an adversary. The situation was further complicated by the growth of the Popular Front within France herself.

In the end, France rejected the idea of resistance to Hitler,
signing the so-called White Paper in London on 18 March
1936. By her signature on this document, which affirmed her
co-operation with Britain, France gave her seal of approval
to Hitler's annexation of the Rhineland. By refusing the help of
the anti-German bloc, she decisively weakened it. The Franco-
Soviet Treaty of Alliance having been negated, the alliance
itself, which had been the mainstay of the bloc, lay in ruins.

France turned away from her allies in Central, Eastern, and
South-Eastern Europe, as well as from the League of Nations.

She went outside the League to sign her treaty with Britain, who seemed to offer greater guarantees of defence against Hitler than the anti-Fascist bloc. By doing so, France adopted the British policy of appeasement, and by coming to terms with Hitler endeavoured to divert German aggression from herself, offering as ransom the states of Central, Eastern and South-Eastern Europe.

Thus, at the time when Europe was first faced with the dilemma of choosing either defence or retreat, France, who carried the main burden of responsibility, opted for the latter. And though this helped to avert a world war, which in March 1936 had again become a real danger, it also seriously affected the balance of power between the two political fronts in Europe, weakening and threatening with disintegration the anti-Fascist and anti-German front.

The Rhineland crisis was to have catastrophic results. France had publicly admitted her weakness, the Soviet Union lost interest in co-operation with the capitalist countries of Europe, and Hitler followed up his triumph by further steps aimed at world conquest. Aided and abetted by Mussolini's Italy, Nazi Germany launched an all-out attack, which was accompanied by political pressure from international Fascism, on all European democratic and revolutionary forces.

In May 1936 the victorious troops of Fascist Italy entered Addis Ababa, the capital of defeated Ethiopia. July saw the outbreak of the Spanish Civil War, with Germany and Italy lending their support to the Spanish Fascist front. Hitler's intention was to threaten the French southern frontier in the Pyrenees and to pave the way for his future expansion into Africa and Asia, where he hoped to gain colonies. By his anti-Comintern pact he wanted to bring about the containment of the Soviet Union between the pincers of the German-Japanese front.

All these events and preparations were of immediate importance to the highly exposed region of Central, Eastern, and South-Eastern Europe, where the break-up of the Franco-Soviet alliance had quite tangible consequences. The French Popular Front Government, set up in May 1936, did try to breathe new life into the alliance treaty with the Soviet Union, but without avail. Too much mistrust had built up between the two countries for these efforts to be successful. After March 1936, the Soviet Union had ceased to give credence to French protestations of their willingness to stand up to Hitler. It was indeed with increasing scepticism that the Soviet Union viewed the Franco-British policy of appeasement and the efforts made by France to achieve some sort of rapprochement with Germany and Italy. The French '*Non*' of March 1936 had dealt a heavy blow to Litvinov's foreign policy, which was aimed at co-operation with Western Europe. And the Moscow trials helped to create still more distrust of the Soviet Union in France. In August 1936 leading Soviet politicians, headed by Zinoviev and Kamenev, were put on trial in Moscow, accused of collaboration with the exiled Trotsky and, through him, with Nazi Germany. In May 1937 the army leader Tukhachevsky was sentenced to death and executed for alleged collaboration with the Germans.

Despite attempts made by both sides in early 1937, no marked change appeared in the atmosphere that now existed between France and the Soviet Union. Their alliance treaty was a dead letter, with no genuine co-operation to give it substance. The Little Entente and the Balkan Pact had lost their chief pillar of support, and a new power vacuum appeared in Central, Eastern, and South-Eastern Europe. Hitler's success in the Rhineland opened the door to this formerly German-dominated region.

In July 1936 Hitler strengthened his position in Austria by means of a special treaty, and he began to exert pressure on the Little Entente. When the anti-Fascist bloc in Rumania collapsed, its major champion, Titulescu, lost office. The country was drawn into co-operation with Hitlerite Germany thanks to the influence of the Germanophiles surrounding King Carol, the Fascist Iron Guard, and the political advances made by Germany herself. While not completely severing her ties with Czechoslovakia and France, Rumania set out on the road of co-operation with Poland and Germany.

Yugoslav policy took a faster and more radical turn. In the autumn of 1936, Yugoslavia entered into negotiations with Mussolini's Italy, which led to the signing of an alliance treaty the following year. A similar treaty was later signed with Germany, Yugoslavia passing into the German-Italian camp and joining the Berlin-Rome Axis.

Czechoslovakia's international position had become critical. The Rhineland crisis had disrupted all of the country's foreign political ties. Though the Popular Front Government of Léon Blum in France tried to maintain Franco-Czechoslovak contacts, it did not have sufficient strength to establish new ones. The Little Entente was falling apart, and everything that Czechoslovakia did in her desperate attempts to save it proved in vain. The British Government was urging Czechoslovakia more openly and insistently to come to terms with Hitler, explaining that while British public opinion was sympathetic towards Czechoslovakia, 'it would be wrong to imagine that in case of war Britain could give Czechoslovakia any concrete assistance'. Anthony Eden, speaking at a meeting of the League of Nations, referred to 'the impracticability of maintaining the *status quo*' in Central, Eastern and South-Eastern Europe. Britain demanded a thorough revision of the League and of the principles on which the organization had been based. The French, too, urged Czechoslovakia to show restraint and good will so that neighbourly relations with Germany could be initiated.

In these circumstances, the Soviet Union and the Czechoslovak-Soviet Treaty assumed an exceptional importance for Czechoslovakia. The two countries had an identity of interests, the Soviet Union being directly concerned in the situation developing in Central Europe, whose countries were its neighbours. It felt threatened by German expansion in the area. That was why Soviet People's Commissar Litvinov defended the *status quo* in the League of Nations. In this, the Soviet Union found itself completely isolated, with its only support coming from the small Czechoslovakia. As a result, the Soviet Union showed understandable caution, and the collapse of the Franco-Soviet alliance was reflected in a weakening of Soviet-Czechoslovak co-operation.

At the same time, the Moscow trials had a profound effect on the political situation inside Czechoslovakia, sharply exacerbating the atmosphere of political insecurity and disorientation.

Right-wing groups launched successful attacks on the country's alliance with the Soviet Union. Nevertheless Czechoslovakia continued to have good relations with Soviet Russia and even to extend them further, though owing to the changed circumstances they were now conducted on levels other than official diplomatic ones.

The disruption of the European anti-Fascist front, in which Czechoslovakia had played so prominent a role, meant a decisive defeat for Beneš's foreign policy. But more than that, all the principles on which the State had been founded in 1918 were being destroyed.

All that remained was the country's internal democratic system. The anti-Fascist front of democratic and revolutionary forces, which had helped to strengthen Czechoslovakia's democratic, republican character just before the Rhineland crisis, was also active in defence of the country's independence in the face of growing German aggression. However, her staunchly democratic character left Czechoslovakia completely isolated in the Central, Eastern, and South-Eastern Europe that emerged after the Rhineland crisis, this having become exclusively the domain of Nazi and Fascist forces. The noose around Czechoslovakia was being drawn ever tighter.

It was at this period of international isolation that a frontal attack was launched from various sides on Czechoslovakia's inner structure. For this, the European Fascist and right-wing forces needed to have an operational base inside the Republic, but the Fascist forces in the country had been defeated and considerably weakened. There was no united Fascist front, and the individual organizations lacked the strength to create one. In 1936 a fresh attempt was made to reconstitute the Fascist front in Czechoslovakia from without. Its largest and numerically strongest component – Henlein's S.d.P. – was revived.

In the summer of 1936 this party had been in the doldrums, engaged in a debilitating internecine struggle. It was at this time that Henlein received help from three international centres which, each for a different reason, were interested in maintaining the unity of the S.d.P. These centres were Vienna, Berlin, and London. In Vienna, Othmar Spann spoke up in support of the *Kameradschaftsbund*, but his intervention was without success and did not solve the crisis within the Party. Of cardinal importance for the further development of the S.d.P. was the support its leader, Konrad Henlein, received from London.

The British Government based its view on the assumption that Henlein was a 'moderate' who had links with the Nazi leadership in Germany without himself being a Nazi. It therefore argued that it was necessary to support Henlein in order to prevent his replacement by 'other minority leaders, who are far more radical and show greater sympathies for National Socialism in Germany'. That was why the British Government through its spokesman, the Under-Secretary for Foreign Affairs, Vansittart, assured Henlein during his visit to London in 1936 that it would give him every support. The British would endeavour to achieve an agreement between the S.d.P. and the Czechoslovak Government, and they were 'in principle ready to advise and assist the Sudeten Germans also on an international platform'.

From that moment the British Government intensified its pressure on the Czechs with a view to lifting the restrictions on the S.d.P. and arriving at some sort of settlement with it. The Foreign Secretary, Anthony Eden, personally intervened a number of times, at international conferences, in debates, as well as by exerting pressure on the Czechoslovak Minister in London, Jan Masaryk, T. G. Masaryk's son.

In this way the British Government helped to prop up the S.d.P. at a time of its profound inner crisis, while rendering the Czechoslovak authorities helpless and making it impossible for them to continue their struggle against the party with anything like their former determination. Henlein's prestige gained immensely as a result of this British support, both internationally and at home.

The British were not, of course, motivated by any desire to create a Fascist front. Quite the contrary – by lending their support to Henlein, who proclaimed openly that he was no Nazi, they hoped to make his party a bulwark against Nazism. This was a typical manifestation of the policy of appeasement, which tried to halt the growth of Fascism by means of negotiation with its more moderate representatives. But in helping them, the British Government was in fact – as was to appear later – helping the Nazis. The British attitude to Henlein was also influenced by distrust of Czechoslovakia in general and the strong dislike with which British Conservative circles regarded her regime in particular. The British authorities viewed the actions taken by the Czechoslovak Government to combat Fascism with disfavour, considering them too radical and left-wing. Czechoslovakia's anti-German foreign policy was likewise not popular with British conservatives, who considered the anti-Fascist bias of the Czech Government to be due to its close co-operation with the Soviet Union. All this awoke suspicions of 'Bolshevism' and led Britain, in 1936, to lend its support to Konrad Henlein. But in doing so, Britain struck a blow against Czechoslovak democracy. The first step had been taken for the political reinforcement and revival of Henlein's movement. Then came yet another intervention, which was to have a decisive effect on solving the crisis within the S.d.P., this time from Berlin.

Nazi Germany had tried before to influence events and to help the Nazi wing of the party achieve a dominant position, sending a specialist to Prague for the purpose. Immediately after Henlein's success in London, K. H. Frank, the leading representative of the Nazi group in the S.d.P., was invited to Berlin. His visit, in July 1936, resulted in an offer being made to Henlein by the Nazi leaders, asking him to withdraw his support from the *Kameradschaftsbund*, in return for which the Nazi wing of the S.d.P. would cease to attack him and Berlin would recognize him as the head of the party. As an expression of their new-found confidence in him, the German Nazi Government invited Henlein to attend the Olympic Games to be held in Berlin the following month.

The crisis inside the S.d.P. was solved on the lines suggested by Berlin. With British support, Henlein's party became an offshoot of Hitler's Nazi Party in Czechoslovakia, as the banned D.N.S.A.P. had been. At the beginning of August, Henlein, as the official guest of the German Government, had talks with the highest representatives of Nazi Germany, with the Reichsminister for Foreign Affairs Neurath, Hitler's deputy Hess, Goebbels, and others. His triumphant visit to Berlin was concluded by an audience with the 'Führer and Reichs Chancellor', Adolf Hitler.

Returning from Berlin full of self-confidence, Henlein steered the Sudeten German Party on its new course, launching a large propaganda campaign to make public his party's programme, this being something he had until now intentionally avoided. His demands included territorial autonomy for the Sudeten Germans, the recognition of the German minority as the second nation in the Republic, the right for the Germans to proclaim their allegiance 'to the hundred-million-strong German people and to consider themselves a part of it', and the holding of new elections, which were to bring about a radical change in Czechoslovakia's internal policies.

Hitler himself now tried to persuade the Czechoslovak Government to accede to Henlein's demands and, in particular, to give him a seat in the Cabinet. At the end of 1936, Hitler's envoys Trautmansdorff and Haushofer paid a secret visit to Prague in order to discuss this 'Sudeten German question' directly with President Beneš.

Thus in the latter half of 1936, with the aid of London and Berlin, the German Nazi front in Czechoslovakia was successfully reconstituted, the British and the Nazi German governments at the same time exerting strong pressure on the Czechs to come to terms with it.

Hitler's anti-Czechoslovak campaign culminated during the Nazi Party Congress held in Nuremberg in September. The democratic regime in Prague was abused as 'Bolshevik' and Czechoslovakia decried for her close contacts with the Soviet Union. Alfred Rosenberg spoke of 170 airfields in Russia and thirty-six airports in Czechoslovakia which were to serve as Soviet bases for an attack on Europe. Goebbels also referred to the Czechoslovak airports, from which Red bombers would take off on their missions to destroy European capitals. He told his listeners in exactly how many minutes individual German cities and other Central European centres could be wiped out by Soviet aircraft operating from Czechoslovakia. All these speeches, which were based on lies and fabrications, created mass hysteria in Germany and helped to influence public opinion throughout the world.

Czechoslovakia's democratic regime, which was daily becoming a greater anomaly in the political conditions of contemporary Europe, was discredited by the Nazis and was viewed with growing distrust by the other European nations. The French Ambassador to Berlin assured the Czechoslovak representative that France would not abandon her allies in any negotiations, but he warned that Czechoslovakia was overdoing things as far as Russia was concerned, and that by constantly emphasizing her alliance with Russia, which was to him incomprehensible, they were playing into Hitler's hands, making it possible for the Germans to claim that it was a military alliance and not merely a pact of mutual aid. As a result, it was not only Britain but also France who urged Czechoslovakia not to provoke her German neighbour but rather to try to reach a settlement.

At the same time Hitler offered to conclude a bilateral pact with Czechoslovakia. His envoys Trautmansdorff and Haushofer, who in November and December had tried to provide Henlein's S.d.P. with freedom of action in Czechoslovak internal affairs, laid the draft of this pact before Beneš as the second part of their mission to Prague. It was basically the same approach as Hitler had used in Austria, binding that country completely to Germany with the pact of July 1936.

Beneš rejected both proposals: the first – support for the Sudeten German Party – categorically, the second in a diplomatic fashion. He was ready to sign a treaty with Germany, but only within a wide European framework, in other words on the principles of collective security. Instead of the bilateral pact suggested by Hitler, he put forward his own draft, based on the Czechoslovak-German arbitration treaty signed in Locarno in 1925. For Hitler, who had successfully broken the Versailles Treaty, as well as the Locarno pacts, this was unacceptable. The negotiations were broken off by the German side, but Hitler used this as yet another proof that Czechoslovakia did not wish to come to an agreement despite all the good will shown by Germany.

The intensified international pressure, which also made itself felt internally through the agency of the reconstituted German Nazi front, could not but leave its mark on political developments within the country.

a   22 September 1938, Prague. The acceptance by the Right-wing Czechoslovak Government of the Franco-British note led to massive
demonstrations. On that day the government
resigned. *Karel Hájek, Prague*

13b   The new Czech National Government
immediately mobilized. The reservists responded enthusiastically. *Karel Hájek, Prague*

13c   The Czechs were not without friends in the West. London, September 1938

14a  Chamberlain's arrival in Munich,
29 September 1938.
*Fotoarchív VHU, Prague*

14b  Chamberlain, Hitler and interpreter Schmidt in Munich

15a  Hitler enters Czechoslovakia,
1 October 1938

15b  Czech refugees from the territory ceded to Hitler.
*Karel Hájek, Prague*

16a   Czech defences turned into rubble without fight. *Jan Lukas, New York*

16b   German army enters Prague, 15 March 1939. Hitler himself broke the shameful pact.
*Fotoarchiv SPB, Prague*

The pressure exerted by Berlin, London, and finally Paris was also concentrated on the group which made up the chief political force behind the defence of the Republic and the core of the Czechoslovak anti-Fascist front – the Castle Group based on the Socialist bloc. Henlein's political campaign was likewise aimed against them. The foreign policy of the bloc was increasingly coming into conflict with the trend of development in Europe as a whole, losing international support as a result. This led to its growing isolation at home as well, and the political front that had come into being before the Rhineland crisis began to fall apart.

The first to break away were those right-wing *bourgeois* groups which had only joined the front as a result of their waning fortunes rather than out of any real conviction. The Agrarian right wing led by Beran and supported by Hlinka's People's Party in Slovakia demanded a change in Czechoslovakia's foreign policy, in particular the country's relations with the Soviet Union. They wanted Czechoslovakia to adapt herself to the changed situation and adopt policies conforming with those pursued by her neighbours, and urged closer ties with Poland, whose policy of direct negotiations with Germany they wanted Czechoslovakia to emulate.

In the autumn of 1936 this group launched an open attack on Czechoslovak foreign policy. Its attempt to change that policy was, however, unsuccessful. In a heated parliamentary debate, the old political bloc managed to win the day, in particular preventing an anti-Soviet bias from being introduced. In his closing speech Foreign Minister Krofta declared: 'A great many slanders, absurdities, and downright lies have been uttered about our relationship with the Soviet Union. That relationship has found its expression in a simple defensive treaty concerning mutual aid against aggression. That is all there is to it.'

The Agrarian right then tried to establish direct links with Berlin, but Nazi Germany laid down the same conditions as before, demanding the implementation of Henlein's political programme. To meet these demands would in fact have meant destroying the Republic. The Agrarian right wing knew this well enough, but on the other hand, inspired by the British appeasement policy they still hoped that by coming to terms with Henlein they might achieve some kind of agreement with Germany. For this reason they advocated agreement with Henlein.

The Communist Party of Czechoslovakia split off from the bloc led by the Castle Group, intensifying its own revolutionary policy independent of the various political combinations.

As early as February 1936, after Klement Gottwald's return from Moscow, the Central Committee met in a session at which the Party's work was subjected to criticism. It was stated that the Party had gone too far in pursuing 'reconciliation with this regime and with the *bourgeois* state', succumbing to 'the tendency of obliterating the distinction between the Communist policy of class struggle and the Social Democratic policy of class peace'. The Party had suffered from 'a diminution of revolutionary vigilance and a grave, opportunistic distortion of the line adopted at the Seventh World Congress of the Communist International'. On the strength of this criticism, the Seventh Congress of the Communist Party of Czechoslovakia, held in April 1936, issued new directives for the Party's policy. 'The Communist Party's position as regards the threat posed to Czechoslovakia by Hitlerite Fascism is the position of the defence of the country against Hitler, the defence of Czechoslovakia against Fascism', it was stated at the Congress. This defence, though, was to be achieved by the Communist Party by means of an independent class policy of the Czechoslovak working class. The popular anti-Fascist front was to be one in which the Communist Party played a leading role. This meant an end to the Party's participation in the anti-Nazi front led by the *bourgeoisie*, that is, by the Castle Group.

The new policy, outlined at the Seventh Congress, brought the Communist Party a number of successes during 1936 and 1937. But it did not succeed in achieving its ultimate aim, which was to create a popular anti-Fascist front under its own leadership.

Another splinter group to leave the Castle bloc in 1936 was that centred around Milan Hodža. The following year this group attained a leading position in the country, its foreign policy being based on Hodža's Central European concept. It tried to prevent Hitler from dominating the region by close collaboration with Schuschnigg's Austria and Darányi's Hungary. It was given additional importance by having the support of British governmental circles. Hodža's group expressed the view of the Slovak Agrarian Party and of certain Czech Agrarians, but it was out of step with the right-wing Party leadership under Beran. On the other hand it enjoyed the support of Kramář's National Unity Party and, above all, of the remnants of the German republican parties, and this considerably enhanced its influence, both at home and abroad.

Following their defeat in the parliamentary elections of 1935, the leadership of the German Agrarian, Christian-Socialist, and Social Democratic parties was taken over by groups which tried to save their parties from Henlein's movement by promulgating a new activist programme in April 1936. They supported the Czechoslovak State but demanded a weakening of its *bourgeois* democratic character and changes in its foreign policy on the lines of Milan Hodža's Central European plan.

In co-operation with these parties Hodža, at the beginning of 1937, tried to reach a new Czech-German settlement which was to be based on a draft bill of 18 February 1937, the so-called nationalities statute. The draft never became law, the main obstacle being that the Sudeten German problem was not a purely internal one where Czechoslovakia was concerned, but was part and parcel of German policy towards that country. With strong support from Berlin, Henlein launched a fierce campaign against such a settlement, demanding that Hodža's Government conduct any negotiations on the subject with his party, the only one that was, according to him, entitled to speak on behalf of the Sudeten Germans. This standpoint was backed not only by Berlin but also by British policy. And the right-wing circles in the Agrarian Party advised Hodža to do the same.

In September 1937 both Hodža and other Agrarian spokesmen tried to establish contacts with Henlein's S.d.P. in a realistic attempt to set up a right-wing government with Sudeten German participation. But by that time Henlein had received other orders.

By the autumn of 1937 Hitler had judged the international situation, as well as the situation in Czechoslovakia itself, to be

sufficiently ripe for his direct assault. The groundwork was laid
by Goebbels's systematic propaganda, and this was followed by
diplomatic activity. The regular September Nazi Congress in
Nuremberg was, for the first time, officially attended by the
diplomatic representatives of other countries, in particular the
British and French. In their discussions with Hitler it was
stressed that all those concerned were anxious to achieve
mutual agreement. British and French diplomats urged Czechoslovakia to come to terms with Germany, the German Embassy
in Prague exerting continual pressure on the Czechoslovak
Government to this effect.

On 17 October 1937 the S.d.P. held a regional conference at
Teplice, which was to serve as a signal for an all-out attack.
Henlein started it off by making a fiercely aggressive speech in
which he demanded fundamental changes in Czechoslovakia's
internal and foreign policies.

A group of Nazi deputies led by K. H. Frank made use of
their parliamentary immunity and organized an anti-govern-
mental demonstration on the main square of Teplice during
which they clashed with Czechoslovak police. At a meeting of
the leading S.d.P. representatives on the night of 17 October,
Henlein announced that the hour of their 'liberation' had struck
for the Sudeten Germans, saying that Germany would come to
their assistance with the benevolent neutrality of Britain and
France.

It was on the strength of this supposition – that the break-up
of Czechoslovakia was imminent – that Henlein drafted his open
letter to the President of the Republic, Eduard Beneš. Before
the letter had been delivered to its recipient the radio in Nazi
Germany had broadcast its text. Goebbels's anti-Czechoslovak
propaganda had attained fantastic proportions, creating the
impression that 'Germany was about to launch a punitive ex-
pedition against the Republic', to quote the Czechoslovak
Foreign Minister Kamil Krofta.

But that was to be the end of this particular German campaign. Czechoslovakia did not wait for the fatal blow to be
struck, the authorities taking all the necessary measures to prevent further disturbances. The Government warned the world of
the danger facing it by openly revealing Germany's plans, thus

successfully making the Nazi provocation an international issue and informing the world about Hitler's intentions before he was able to realize them. All this turned the situation to Hitler's disadvantage, preventing him from bringing off the prepared coup and forcing him to withdraw.

The events of October 1937 proved that the anti-Nazi bloc in Czechoslovakia, which had shown signs of disintegration after the Rhineland crisis, still existed. They proved that although isolated and considerably weakened, Czechoslovakia was still capable of defending herself against the Fascist enemy inside as well as against Hitler's onslaught from outside.

## The Mark of Cain

The end of 1937 and the early months of 1938 had brought Germany a number of indisputable successes and victories, the most important of these being the liquidation, following Hitler's Rhineland triumph, of the organized anti-German and anti-Fascist front of European democratic and revolutionary forces. Yet at the same time Germany's plans of world conquest suffered a series of major setbacks.

Hitler failed to achieve his purpose in Spain, where he had hoped in a matter of a few short weeks to clear the way for his advance into Africa and Asia. He came up against the determined resistance of the Spanish people, and against the resistance of the Spanish popular anti-Fascist front, which received international aid from the world's democratic and revolutionary forces. With the help of international brigades, the Republicans halted German expansion, changing a *blitzkrieg* into a lengthy war.

His failure in Spain was one of the reasons why Hitler did not launch his attack in the East, which he had obviously been preparing. At the end of 1936 the German anti-Soviet campaign had reached such proportions that the possibility of a German-Soviet conflict became a very real one. Yet Hitler did not take the expected step. There were many reasons for this, and while we cannot at this time tell exactly what they were, it is certain that Hitler had called off his anti-Soviet campaign. This represented a defeat and forced him to modify his policy, with the result that he concentrated on Russia's neighbours in Central, Eastern, and South-Eastern Europe. But here again, though he scored some undoubted successes, Hitler did not have it all his own way. Another painful defeat came in October 1937, when Germany had to abandon its drive against Czechoslovakia.

Nevertheless, Central, Eastern, and South-Eastern Europe was the most exposed region, where German aggression was most likely to succeed. That was why, in 1938, Hitler renewed his efforts in this direction, British policy giving him a free hand in the hope that a world crisis would thereby be averted. In his talks with the Führer at Berchtesgaden in November 1937, Lord Halifax emphasized that Germany's demands in Central Europe 'concern changes in the European order which will have to be made sooner or later', and that 'Britain is anxious that these changes should take place by peaceful evolution without resort to methods that could cause further upheavals, undesirable from the Führer's point of view as well as from that of other nations'.

Hitler's speech in the Reichstag on 20 February 1938 was a signal for the solution of the Central European question.

'We can see what painful economic and political consequences were caused by the map of Europe juggled about by the lunacy of Versailles: in two of our neighbouring countries alone there are over ten million Germans, who were prevented, against their will, from becoming part of the Reich. . . . It is unthinkable for a self-respecting world power to stand by and see members of its nation continually humiliated on account of their sympathies and their oneness with their motherland, its destiny and its world view'.

As a first step towards the solution of the acute Central European crisis Germany 'solved the Austrian problem'. In a matter of hours on 11 March 1938 Nazi troops occupied Austria and incorporated it in the Reich. It was obvious that it was now Czechoslovakia's turn.

Preparations for its destruction were started immediately after the _Anschluss_. They took place on a number of levels. On the diplomatic side, Hitler reiterated his assertion that he wanted nothing but peace, giving Czechoslovakia explicit assurances that he had no aggressive intentions towards her. At the same time he stopped accusing Czechoslovakia of being a Soviet tool and concentrated all his propaganda on the Sudeten German issue which he claimed was the sole reason for his interest in Czechoslovakia. He continued to emphasize that the just solution of that issue – the self-determination of the Sudeten Germans as demanded by Henlein – was a necessary condition of good neighbourly relations between Czechoslovakia and Germany.

Speaking at a Reichstag meeting on 18 March, Hitler gave Prague the following warning: ' . . . let no one think that it is a mere figure of speech when I say that Germany will on no account go on indefinitely witnessing the suppression of its brethren.'

The German general staff, which had made its plans for a military attack on Czechoslovakia (these were known under the code name *Fall Grün*) now revised them in view of the changed situation after the Austrian *Anschluss*. The German invasion was to take the form of a pincer movement in the region of Moravia.

Hitler laid the main stress on internal developments in Czechoslovakia itself, on the policy of Henlein's S.d.P., which was to camouflage the invasion by making it appear that it was no more than the solution of an internal political crisis. Hitler took personal charge of Sudeten German affairs, giving Henlein and K. H. Frank his own instructions at private meetings with the Sudeten German leaders. At a conference in Berlin on 28 March, he instructed Henlein to 'make demands on behalf of the S.d.P. which would be unacceptable to the Czechoslovak Government'. Henlein promised to 'ask for so much that we can never be satisfied'.

At a congress held in Karlovy Vary on 24 April, Henlein put forward these unacceptable demands in the form of his new Party programme.

1. Complete equality and equal rights for the German national group.

2. Its recognition as a legal entity.

3. The determination and recognition of a German national territory.

4. The setting up of a German administration in all sectors of public life concerning the interests and affairs of the German national group.

5. The establishment of legal safeguards for those Germans who live outside the German territory.

6. The righting of the injustice perpetrated against the Sudeten Germans since 1918 and reparations for the damage caused by that injustice.

7. The recognition and practical implementation of the principle that only German public employees should work in the German territory.

8. Complete freedom of choice in matters of allegiance to the German nation and German world view.

The Karlovy Vary programme thus significantly widened the S.d.P.'s demands of late 1936. Yet Henlein declared the eight points of that programme to be the minimum they were willing to accept, going on to mention a number of other vaguely defined demands, the intention clearly being to leave the door open for their modification in either direction at some later stage, according to the circumstances.

The Karlovy Vary programme provided Nazi Germany with its new weapon in its struggle against Czechoslovakia, the slogan now being the self-determination of the Sudeten German minority. Significant changes had taken place in the German political camp in Czechoslovakia, which made this new move possible.

The *Anschluss* of Austria had brought about the collapse of Hodža's Central European policy, as the liquidation of Austria deprived him of his chief prop. At the same time it meant the collapse of the German neo-activist front in Czechoslovakia. At the end of March the entire German Agrarian and Christian-Socialist parties went over to Henlein, with only the German Social Democrats and Communists continuing to co-operate with the Czechoslovak Government. But even the Social Democrats were weakened by Hitler's propaganda and by internal strife, with the young generation led by W. Jaksch standing in opposition to the old leadership of L. Czech under the slogan of 'popular socialism'.

Henlein's S.d.P. now had 83 per cent of the German seats in the National Assembly, thus becoming the only true representative of the Sudeten Germans. This made the S.d.P. even less interested in any settlement with the Czechoslovak Government. The Party's only aim now, as well as the sole task given it by Hitler, was to clear the way for a Nazi occupation of Czechoslovakia. The Sudeten Germans, and Hitler himself, were to be aided in achieving their purpose by the political leaders of Western Europe.

In spite of the isolation in which she found herself after the Rhineland crisis, Czechoslovakia was still part of an international system of treaties. Unlike Austria, which had no such treaties with anyone but Germany, Czechoslovakia, despite all that had gone before, had an alliance with France, the Soviet Union, and the countries of the Little Entente. It also had a treaty of arbitration with Germany. These treaties had never been annulled, and even though their usefulness had become limited since the Rhineland affair, they still bound the beleaguered Czechoslovakia to the rest of Europe.

At the time of the *Anschluss*, when it became clear that the defence of Czechoslovakia against German aggression was entering a crucial stage, the Czechoslovak Government tried to revive the old alliances, asking her allies, France and the Soviet Union, whether they still felt bound by their undertakings. On 17 March both these countries gave an unambiguously affirmative reply. The Soviet Government declared the *Anschluss* to be the beginning of German aggression not only against the small states but also against the big powers.

'The Soviet Government,' declared People's Commissar Litvinov, 'is fully aware of its own share of responsibility ensuing from the stand taken by the League of Nations, the Briand-Kellogg Pact, and its treaties of mutual assistance with France and Czechoslovakia.'

The Soviet Government accordingly assured the Czechoslovak Government immediately after the annexation of Austria that it considered the Soviet-Franco-Czechoslovak

treaty to be valid and binding and was ready to give Czechoslovakia active assistance in the event of German aggression.

A similar proclamation was made on the same day by the
French Premier Léon Blum. It was no accident that this
announcement was made by a government newly formed after
the *Anschluss*, which tried to restore the anti-Fascist Front
Populaire. Blum gave Czechoslovakia assurances that France
would honour her commitments and, in case of either direct or
indirect German attack, would provide 'immediate, effective,
and full assistance'.

Even the British Prime Minister Chamberlain emphasized at
the end of March, on the request of the Czechoslovak Minister
in London, Jan Masaryk, that, although Czechoslovakia was in
an 'area in which her [Britain's] vital interests are not at stake,
where it is a question of war or peace, legal obligations are not
the sole consideration'.

Thus the German aggression in Austria had helped to a
certain extent in reviving Czechoslovakia's international
alliances. As a result, for the first time since the Rhineland
crisis, there appeared a certain, if fairly slight, chance of the
creation of an all-European anti-German front.

In the circumstances, Hitler's plans for attacking Czechoslovakia ran into difficulties, giving added strength to his
adversary. Beneš's old foreign policy could now again be put
into practice. The Czechoslovak system of alliances was given
a new lease of life and an over-riding commitment to the defence
of the Republic restored political unity within the country.
All this brought back into European and world politics a
spectre that had been laid to rest in the Rhineland, that of a
general war.

The leaders of world reaction now flocked together under the
banner of peace. They did not demand that Germany cease her
aggression, which was the chief cause of international tension,
wishing on the contrary to silence those who were calling for
energetic action against Hitler. The campaign of the 'peacemakers' turned into a fierce attack on the Soviet Union, bringing down Blum's Government in France, which was to be the
last government of the anti-Fascist popular front, and concentrating its strongest onslaught against the country which

was the source of all the tension – Czechoslovakia. The campaign was backed up by German, Italian, Polish, and Hungarian propaganda at their most strident. In his official report from Paris, Czechoslovak envoy Osuský stated that 'There has never before been such a devilish and cynical campaign as this in Paris'.

This frenzied campaign, conducted against the victim of German aggression with the proclaimed intention of safeguarding peace, bore fruit in the Anglo-French intervention in Prague of 7 May.

The champions of appeasement struck a damaging blow at the Czechoslovak endeavour to renew the system of alliances, posing a condition which considerably limited Czechoslovakia's freedom of action in defending herself against Nazi Germany. That condition was the categorical Anglo-French demand that the Czechoslovak Government should without delay come to a full agreement with Henlein's S.d.P. by accepting his Karlovy Vary programme.

Czechoslovakia was trapped, for to accept meant disintegration of the Republic and her domination by Germany; a refusal would nullify the system of alliances, as a German attack could then be interpreted as having been provoked by Czechoslovak intransigence and her unwillingness to come to terms with the Germans. Neither the Czechoslovak-French nor the Czechoslovak-Soviet treaty were applicable in such a case, and Czechoslovakia would lose the right to lodge a complaint with the League of Nations. The step taken by the British and French representatives had only a single aim: to leave the way clear for Hitler and thus rid the world of the tension created around Czechoslovakia.

Pressure was applied on all Czechoslovak diplomats in the West. Osuský reported from Paris: 'Bonnet urges that Prague should go to the limit where concessions are concerned, and do so as quickly as possible.' Jan Masaryk wrote from London: 'Britain will advise us to make concessions which I fear will be very far-reaching, more so than we imagine.' Heidrich cabled from Geneva: 'I have gained the impression that although London realizes it would be dangerous to give autonomy to the Sudeten Germans, they will nevertheless demand ever greater

concessions from us in the hope that it will be possible to appease
Henlein even though they do not know how.' At the same time
the British Ambassador in Berlin, Neville Henderson, officially
informed the German Government of the action taken by
Britain and France.

Germany, thinking the road was clear, started making new
preparations for an attack on Czechoslovakia. Having gratefully
received the news of the British and French intervention in
Prague, Ribbentrop emphasized that, 'while Germany has no
intention of solving the Sudeten German problem by force, it
would have no alternative but to send in troops should the blood
of Sudeten Germans be spilled in Czechoslovakia'. And at the
same time Goebbels's propaganda machine was paving the way
for the German invasion by means of a fierce anti-Czechoslovak campaign, directed against 'the intolerable oppression of
the Sudeten Germans'.

Throughout Germany celebrations were held on the fortieth
birthday of Konrad Henlein, 'the champion of Sudeten German
unity and freedom'. The German Press asked the Sudeten
Germans 'to still more firmly pull down their helmets and set
out on their victorious march to freedom'. At a number of
meetings and demonstrations officials of the N.S.D.A.P. pro-
phesied that by the autumn, at the latest, the Czechoslovak-
German frontier would cease to exist. Leaflets printed in Czech
were distributed in Czechoslovakia, describing the Republic's
hopeless position. Rumours were rife in the Sudeten areas about
the imminent German invasion.

But Czechoslovakia had no intention of surrendering, despite
certain critical developments at home. Immediately after the
*Anschluss* and the strengthening of Henlein's party, a Slovak
People's Party congress in Bratislava recommended co-operation with the German and Hungarian minorities with a view to
achieving autonomy for Slovakia. Nothing came of Hodža's
intensive efforts to bring the People's Party into the government.
On the credit side, however, all the Czech and Slovak political
parties and groups, with the exception of the People's Party and
a section of the Agrarian right wing, joined together to form a
united front for the defence of the country. A broad Czecho-
Slovak coalition was thus formed to avert the threat to the

Republic's existence, such as had been the case shortly after its birth in 1918. The Communist Party of Czechoslovakia, though not forming part of the coalition, was a powerful factor in the defence of Czechoslovakia undertaken by it. The only minority group to support the coalition government, which was again led by the Castle Group headed by President Beneš, were the German Social Democrats, who became a kind of loyal opposition.

In the international sphere it was only the Soviet Union which provided Czechoslovakia with any support. While Britain and France were forcing Czechoslovakia to give way to Hitler, the Soviet Union made approaches to France and Czechoslovakia, urging that their general staffs hold immediate joint conferences. But Bonnet, 'after due consideration', warned Czechoslovakia not to take precipitate action, saying that 'we must exercise great care where the Soviets are concerned'. The Soviet Union invited Czechoslovak and Rumanian representatives to Moscow for talks on a tripartite agreement which would give Soviet aircraft the right to fly over Rumanian territory.

On 14 May 1938 the Czechoslovak Government rejected the Anglo-French intervention in a special memorandum, emphasizing its responsibility for the defence of the integrity and inner strength of the Czechoslovak Republic. The Government refused to negotiate with Henlein on the basis of the Karlovy Vary programme, pointing out that on 26 April it had already set out its own proposals for the solution of the Sudeten German problem within the framework of the Czechoslovak constitution.

It was on this basis that the Czechoslovak Government actually opened unofficial, informative talks with Henlein's S.d.P. At the same time it did in part accede to Henlein's demands by announcing that on 22 and 29 May and on 12 June local elections were to be held. But the S.d.P. broke off the negotiations on 19 May, and Henlein left the country to pay a visit to Germany.

Czechoslovak military intelligence learned that S.S. and S.A. units in Germany had been put on stand-by for the dates of the local elections, and that ever since 7 May German troops in Saxony had been moved to positions close to the Czechoslovak frontier. It was obvious that a military attack was imminent, and the secrecy with which the preparations had been made indicated that the aggression was to be carried out as in the case of Austria – an overnight *fait accompli* before anyone could do anything to prevent it.

It was Czechoslovakia's aim to foil such a *fait accompli* at all costs. Consequently, Czechoslovakia informed her allies – France, Britain, and the Soviet Union – about the German troop movements in the vicinity of her borders. Henderson, the British Ambassador in Berlin, at once lodged a protest with the German Government, asking for further information. At the same time the Czechs made a similar demand. The whole business had now become an international affair, which tied Hitler's hands. Germany reacted with angry outbursts of invective and threats against Czechoslovakia, testifying to the heavy blow the latter had inflicted on her.

On 20 May Ribbentrop summoned the Czechoslovak Minister in Berlin Mastný to give him the following message for the Czechoslovak Government:

> '1. that he was increasingly disturbed by the continued oppression of the Sudeten Germans, by the banning of their meetings and cases of ill-treatment, about which he had only today received fresh information; he would therefore remind us of Hitler's well-known statement that Germany will not tolerate the persecution of Germans outside her borders, pointing out that there were seventy-five million of them, ready to take action at any time;
>
> 2. that he could not tolerate any longer the false information given out by our Government in Prague about troop movements, and he stressed that the spreading of such information could result in a situation where armed forces would in fact be concentrated against Czechoslovakia.'

Czechoslovakia, however, further intensified her defensive efforts, carrying out a partial mobilization on 21 May 1938 with a view to 'safeguarding law and order at the present time, as well as preventing any repetition of the incidents which have taken place in some parts of the Republic'.

The democratic and revolutionary forces of the world welcomed Czechoslovakia's stand against Nazi Germany, and telegrams of congratulations poured into Prague. Anti-Fascists of various nationalities volunteered to help Czechoslovakia if fighting broke out, just as they had done in Spain. The Soviet Government sent an important message, as reported by Ambassador Fierlinger from Moscow: 'I have had a talk with Litvinov, who congratulated us on the energetic measures we have taken and on the policy adopted by our Government. He continues to follow developments with great interest.'

The partial mobilization carried out by Czechoslovakia created an extremely tense situation. There were now only two alternatives. Either Germany would go ahead with its plans for an invasion or it would back down. But the invasion could no longer be a secretly mounted surprise attack, the *fait accompli* Hitler wanted. It would have to be an open act of aggression for which Czechoslovakia was well prepared and which would bring with it the additional risk of triggering off the military aid provided for by the alliance treaties. This, of course, had been the main reason behind the mobilization, as Czechoslovakia hoped to bring the allies in on her side. World war would now have been the inevitable result of a German attack. Hitler backed down.

It was most humiliating for a power such as Germany to have to retreat yet again, before so small a country as Czechoslovakia. Hitler's humiliation expressed itself in the most vociferous anti-Czechoslovak propaganda campaign to date. Ominously for Czechoslovakia, this propaganda found receptive ears in Britain.

The Czech intransigence, which had created an international problem, was frowned upon by official British circles. The British Government had for a long time considered Central Europe to be the natural domain of Hitler's Germany, and its entire policy was framed in such a way as to allow the changes which it considered unavoidable in that area to be carried out in a peaceful fashion. A swift action such as the annexation of Austria did nothing to disturb the peace. But Czechoslovakia was not playing the game. Instead of keeping quiet, she had alerted all of Europe, and the Czech mobilization put Britain herself in a delicate position, for if armed conflict were to break out and the alliance treaties come into force, Britain would become directly involved. Britain was thus being pressurized by Czechoslovakia into joining the anti-German front, and not only at the side of France and Czechoslovakia but also that of the Soviet Union. From the British point of view it was unthinkable that a major power should find herself in such a position due to the action of an insignificant Central European state.

Thus it was that, by the joint efforts of Hitler and the British Government, the 'real culprit' of the May crisis was found. That culprit was Czechoslovakia. In vain did the Soviet representative Litvinov try to keep Britain, as well as France, from reaching an understanding with Germany, repeatedly telling Bonnet and Halifax that the Soviet Union was willing to take part in any collective action on behalf of Czechoslovakia. In vain did Jan Masaryk warn from London: 'It is extremely important that we should not make any tactical error giving the Germans, and also the British, the opportunity of putting the blame on us.'

On 21 May a series of Anglo-German talks was begun, with Germany protesting her peaceloving intentions. The British Foreign Secretary, Halifax, in a personal letter to Ribbentrop emphasized that a world conflict would profit those 'who wish to see our European civilization destroyed', by which he meant the Soviet Union.

Germany sidetracked the whole issue to make it exclusively a Sudeten German problem, reiterating that it had always been and still remained ready to solve that problem by peaceful means. The Czechoslovak Government, the Germans alleged, did not favour such a solution and was deliberately prolonging the negotiations in order to gain time, wishing to stir up an international conflict which would relieve it of its obligation to improve the lot of the 'terrorized' German inhabitants in Czechoslovakia. The British and French governments agreed with these assertions. After all, Czechoslovakia had rejected their own efforts to help resolve the Sudeten crisis. Moreover, Czechoslovakia had failed to accede to the Anglo-French demand for an immediate calling off of the partial mobilization.

Germany continued to claim that all the reports about German troop movements in the direction of the Czechoslovak frontier were totally unfounded. Their sole aim, the Germans said, had been to justify the Czech mobilization intended to provoke a world war. To prove their point, the Germans invited the British and French military attachés to visit the border areas in question. The result was that the attachés reported they had not seen any exceptional concentration of armed forces near the Czechoslovak frontier.

Czechoslovakia was thus accused before the whole world as the disseminator of false information in the hope of stirring up conflict. The country which had so indomitably defended its independence was branded with the mark of Cain as a war-monger.

## A Troublesome Ally

In May 1938 Czechoslovakia had warded off a German attack and gained a great victory. But the way the crisis was handled on the international level left Czechoslovakia in a critical position. From now on Czechoslovakia did not have only Germany to contend with, but was forced to fight also against the conservative ruling circles in Britain and France, which were determined not to have any repetition of the May events and to break the resistance of the Republic in order to save world peace.

Hitler drew back in May, but Goebbels's hate-filled anti-Czechoslovak and anti-Soviet propaganda, coupled with German Fascist provocations inside Czechoslovakia, sufficed to maintain tension, while Hitler intensified his preparations for another assault on Czechoslovakia at some later date. In his directives of 30 May, giving detailed plans for an invasion of Czechoslovakia, Hitler wrote: 'It is my irrevocable decision to destroy Czechoslovakia by military means in the near future.'

However, after his recent defeats he proceeded more cautiously. In a supplement to the *Fall Grün* directives of 18 June, he wrote: 'I shall only decide on action if I am absolutely convinced, as in the case of the occupation of the demilitarized zone and our entry into Austria, that France will not intervene and that, as a result, Britain will likewise do nothing.'

Hitler played a waiting game. He waited for the result of the Anglo-French moves, which were paving the way for his new assault.

The summer months of 1938 brought renewed and very determined pressure on Czechoslovakia from both her Western allies, aiming to destroy the system of alliances. If the Czechoslovak-French treaty could be made inoperative, Britain would no longer have any obligation towards Czechoslovakia. Secondly, the British and French effort was directed at paralysing the Czechoslovak-Soviet alliance. The third aim was the liquidation of the German-Czechoslovak arbitration treaty of 1925, under whose terms the two countries were pledged to resolve their mutual disagreements by means of negotiation. Britain played the leading political role in these efforts.

British policy was conducted along two parallel lines. On the one hand, while making it appear that it was a purely internal Czechoslovak matter, Britain tried to force the Czechs to accept Henlein's Karlovy Vary programme. Although she knew full well that its acceptance would mean the break-up of the Republic, Britain, with French support made the further existence of the Czechoslovak-French alliance treaty directly dependent on Czechoslovakia's acquiescence.

On the other hand Britain tried to solve the Sudeten German problem by means of a plebiscite. The example of the Saar and Austria showed that this would have been tantamount to ceding the Sudeten areas to Germany. In the middle of June two British representatives, Lord Noel-Buxton and an M.P., Riley, submitted a map to the French, showing the areas which were to be handed over to Germany.

Britain continued pursuing this policy, endeavouring to achieve the so-called neutralization of Czechoslovakia. On 17 June Halifax explained the exact meaning of this term to the British Ambassador in Paris, asking him to discuss with Bonnet the whole question of revising Czechoslovakia's foreign policy, in particular her treaties with France, the Soviet Union, and Germany.

The aim behind both these threads of British policy was to deprive Czechoslovakia of all her international treaties, instead of which she was to receive vaguely defined 'new guarantees'.

In other words Czechoslovakia was to be forced into the sort of isolation that Austria had been in before her. Without her system of alliances Czechoslovakia would no longer be in any position to endanger her former allies, because they would then be under no obligation to aid Czechoslovakia if she became the victim of aggression. The Czechoslovak-German conflict would be effectively localized, and the destruction of Czechoslovakia would have no international repercussions. The danger of war would have been averted and peace assured.

While combining both lines of policy, at this stage, in the summer of 1938, Britain concentrated primarily on the former – Czech acceptance of the Karlovy Vary programme. This had the advantage that Britain could play the role of an *éminence grise*, an adviser and friend, with Czechoslovakia in the limelight as the chief protagonist.

British pressure, backed up by France, made itself felt immediately after the end of the May crisis. The British Government sent a special observer, William Strang, head of the Foreign Office Central European Desk, to Berlin and Prague. He returned home from the Czechoslovak capital and reported to the British and French governments that he had received the impression that Czechoslovakia still failed to realize the necessity of quite extreme concessions to the Sudeten Germans. At the same time Britain urged France to be firm with Czechoslovakia, specifically to warn her clearly and unequivocally that if no agreement were reached with Henlein, France would be forced to rescind her alliance treaty with Czechoslovakia.

Official Anglo-French pressure was exerted on Czechoslovakia early in June. On the third of that month, the British Government sent a note to Prague in which it resolutely demanded that the Czechoslovak Government accept Henlein's programme. A French note followed on 7 June, emphasizing that if Henlein's requirements were not met, France would have to revise her attitude towards Czechoslovakia.

Czechoslovakia could now look only to the Soviet Union for support. Soviet diplomacy consistently kept aloof from the negotiations, owing to the clearly anti-Soviet tendencies not only of Germany but of France and Britain. In a statement made through Commissar Litvinov on 23 June, the Soviet Government stressed that:

'the Soviet-Czechoslovak pact is the most important factor relieving the tension around Czechoslovakia ... The Soviet policy of peace makes it incumbent on us to express the wish that the conflicts which have arisen between Czechoslovakia and her neighbours should be resolved by peaceful means, but we refrain from giving any unsolicited advice to the Czecho-slovak Government because we believe in its peaceful inten-tions and are convinced ... that it will of its own accord be able to determine what concessions it can make in conformity with the prestige, sovereignty and independence of the country. We believe that Czechoslovakia is merely defending herself, which means that whatever happens, the conse-quences will be borne by the aggressor.'

At the same time Czechoslovak-Soviet talks went on in Moscow, dealing with a variety of subjects. On 30 June an agreement on technical co-operation in industry was signed between the two countries, and a special agreement was nego-tiated with the Škoda Works. Talks on air transport between Czechoslovakia and the Soviet Union ended on 19 July with the signing of a protocol. Political discussions also took place, as witnessed by a three-hour meeting between two Czech repre-sentatives and Stalin and Molotov on 30 June 1938. That meant that at the time of continued Anglo-French pressure on Czecho-slovakia's system of alliances, Czechoslovak-Soviet co-operation, and thus the Czechoslovak-Soviet alliance treaty, remained unimpaired.

Anglo-French pressure led to the resumption of Czechoslovak talks with the S.d.P., broken off by Henlein on the eve of the May crisis. The Czechoslovak delegation was led by the Prime Minister Milan Hodža. But it was not long before the talks reached a stalemate.

Henlein's followers were full of justified confidence, safe in the knowledge that they had Berlin, London, and Paris behind them. Their demands were categorical and presented in the form of an ultimatum. The Czechoslovak representatives, their hands tied by London and Paris, were on the defensive.

They had no alternative but to accept the Sudeten German demands, which would mean the end of Czechoslovakia as a state. It would appear that the Czechoslovaks themselves were not united in their approach, the hopelessness of the situation no doubt making for depression and disunity. It seems that Hodža was ready to make greater concessions than President Beneš.

The Nazis took advantage of the stalemate to launch a fierce anti-Czechoslovak campaign in London, putting all the blame for the stalled negotiations on the Czechoslovak side, namely on President Beneš. They asserted that Beneš's tactics were to postpone the solution of the Sudeten German problem so as to avoid having to grant justified German demands for self-determination.

The British Government was showing increasing irritation at the way the negotiations were going, and particularly at Czechoslovakia's failure to comply with Britain's request and give way to Henlein. On 27 June Jan Masaryk reported from London: 'Halifax wants you to know that the British Government is disappointed at the lack of progress in the talks. They repeat that it is necessary to act quickly and make far-reaching concessions.' Two days later, Masaryk cabled:

'. . . In Parliament today, Chamberlain clearly accused President Beneš and the Government of deliberately holding up the negotiations, asking Halifax again to press in Paris for joint action in bringing pressure to bear on us. As I learn from those close to him, it is not out of the question that in his absurd endeavour to reach an agreement with Germany, Chamberlain will be ruthless towards us and try to discredit us in the eyes of British and French public opinion. . . .'

The blame for the lack of progress in the negotiations was thus placed squarely on Czechoslovakia. German propaganda, as well as British policy, now concentrated more and more obviously on one single man – President Beneš. This led to his increasing political isolation. Its effects were felt even inside Czechoslovakia, where it was intended to weaken Beneš's position and lead to his replacement by other, more conciliatory politicians.

The campaign was soon to bear fruit, in particular where the Slovak People's Party was concerned. At its June congress in Bratislava, the Party took an oath on the Pittsburgh declaration and on Slovak autonomy, at the same time publicly burning the text of the Czechoslovak-Soviet treaty, of which Beneš was the chief architect.

The anti-Beneš campaign of course also found willing ears in right-wing Hungarian, Polish, and Ukrainian parties, as well as within the ranks of the Czech Catholic clergy. Most important of all was its effect on the strongest political party in the country, the Agrarian Party. Beneš's domestic and foreign policies had been mostly unacceptable to the Agrarians throughout the life-time of the Republic, and they were therefore even less inclined to support them now that they had led Czechoslovakia up a blind alley. The extreme right-wing circles of the Agrarian Party around Beran and Preiss fully identified themselves with the official German, British, and French view that Beneš was the chief culprit who had resisted a 'peaceful' settlement of the Sudeten German problem. In the critical days of June 1938 Preiss wrote to Beran that 'only he [Beneš] is the obstacle' and asked, 'since he is the obstacle, can he guarantee the right course of action?'

These extreme right-wingers in the Agrarian Party exerted pressure on Hodža, and through him on Beneš, to make them adopt a conciliatory attitude. Hodža himself, following the failure of his Central European policy which collapsed with the *Anschluss*, saw a new opportunity to regain his influence. He was willing to accede to the wishes of Britain and France, whose representatives began to turn to him rather than the President.

It was in these circumstances, early in July, that the Sudeten German representatives broke off the stagnating negotiations with the Czechoslovak Government. The Goebbels propaganda machine immediately unleashed a campaign accusing Czecho-slovakia of unwillingness to come to an agreement and of trying, once again, to solve the Sudeten German question by provoking a war. As an example the Nazis pointed to the Sokol gymnastic festival, held in the last week of June, which had given expres-sion to Czechoslovakia's determination to defend her indepen-dence. The Germans also published a fabricated report that

Soviet military units had begun to march to the Western frontier of the Soviet Union, in an effort to aid Czechoslovakia.

The Czechoslovak Government attempted to resume the interrupted negotiations. It also tried to counter the Nazi propaganda campaign by offering to make public the proceedings of the talks with the Sudeten Germans, hoping thus to show Henlein's methods to the Czechoslovak, and especially the world, public. It therefore wanted to get the negotiations transferred to a parliamentary platform, setting the date of 25 July 1938 for the debate in the National Assembly. This suggestion was, however, rejected not only by the S.d.P. representatives, but also by the British Government, which refused to 'complicate' the issue in this way. In an effort to prevent a fresh European crisis developing out of the Czechoslovak problem, Chamberlain's Government decided to adopt a harsh course of action.

On 20 July the British Ambassador in Prague, Newton, laid before President Beneš a proposal according to which a special British representative, Lord Runciman, was to be sent to Czechoslovakia with the task of investigating the situation and mediating between the Czechoslovak Government and Henlein's party with a view to achieving an agreement between them. Beneš at first resisted this proposal, referring to Czechoslovakia's foreign political obligations and the political situation at home, pointing out that in so grave a matter Czechoslovakia was duty bound to consult her French partner.

With regard to the internal political situation, Beneš objected that a foreign mediator was incompatible with the sovereignty of an independent state. A crisis would develop which would lead to the resignation of the Government and his own abdication. Moreover, he was not in a position to accept the proposal, which exceeded the powers of the President of the Republic. The only possibility was to lay the proposal before Parliament, and Beneš asked for it to be submitted to the Speaker of the National Assembly and to the Minister of Foreign Affairs.

Newton's reply showed that the British proposal had been carefully prepared long in advance without Beneš having been notified. He informed the President that the French Government had been acquainted with the British proposal and was in agreement with it. Lord Runciman, too, had already expressed his readiness to take on the mission. Newton even indicated that the German Government had also been informed and found the proposal acceptable.

As for the political situation in Czechoslovakia, Newton, speaking for the British Government, categorically rejected any public discussion of the proposal, and in a written memorandum it was expressly stated that 'in the present circumstances Parliament should not be called into session'.

Most crucial of all, however, was Newton's reaction to Beneš's objections based on his fear of a possible crisis and the resignation of his government. Newton told him that Prime Minister Hodža had been informed about the proposal and was ready to go along with it.

The British Ambassador had received the first intimation of Britain's intention to send a mediator to Prague as early as 18 June, when he was asked to sound out the Czechoslovak Government in this respect. It is highly probable that he informed Hodža about it on that occasion, although explicit instructions to this effect from Halifax did not arrive until 15 July. When told that Hodža had been informed and had given his approval, Beneš found himself in a trap with no more arguments at his disposal. In his report to Foreign Secretary Halifax, Newton mentioned that Beneš 'appeared very surprised and shaken, only regaining his composure with some difficulty towards the end of our talk, which lasted two hours'. Finally Beneš asked Newton that their discussion should for the time being be treated as a preliminary one. This Newton categorically refused, having received a strict injuction from Halifax: '. . . to press Beneš to accept the proposal'. Should he nevertheless persist in his opposition, he was to be told that, 'His Majesty's Government could not refrain from publishing its proposals and the replies to them'.

This seemingly simple sentence concealed far-reaching consequences for Czechoslovakia. The political aim behind the threat to publish the exchange was officially to document Czechoslovakia's unwillingness to come to terms, not only with Henlein but also with the British Government. This would have carried with it mortal danger for the Republic, for if this unwillingness could be proved for the benefit of world opinion, German aggression would be seen in quite a different light. It would no longer be naked, unprovoked aggression against an innocent victim, for the victim would have brought it upon himself by his own intransigence. Czechoslovakia's alliances did not provide for such an eventuality, the treaty with the Soviet Union as well as the one with France being applicable only in case of unprovoked aggression. It was also only if attacked through no fault of her own that Czechoslovakia could turn to the League of Nations with a request for help. The threat was thus made with a view to discrediting Czechoslovakia once again in the eyes of the world, should she prove adamant, and the consequences would have been catastrophic. In these circumstances Newton could well report to Halifax that Beneš 'found himself under great pressure'. It was tantamount to a dagger held at his throat. Within an hour of their interview, during which time Newton again consulted Hodža, who 'pacified' Beneš, the Czechoslovak President had accepted the British ultimatum.

On 23 July Beneš handed a note to the British Ambassador, requesting that a mediator be sent to Prague. This was the way the Foreign Office wanted it to be done in order to conceal the pressure it had brought to bear on Beneš with its ultimatum. Lord Runciman arrived in Prague on 3 August. His arrival changed the nature of the negotiations between the Czechoslovak Government and the S.d.P., which were now conducted under British supervision and, to all intents and purposes, chairmanship.

The aim of the mission was determined quite clearly by all that had gone before. It was to persuade the Czechoslovak Government to accept Henlein's demands. That was borne out by the way the mission went about its work. Runciman and his colleagues established contacts with those circles in the Republic from whom they expected understanding and support in the furtherance of that aim. On the German side these contacts, both extensive and intensive, were with the S.d.P., above all with Henlein, whom the British considered (as opposed to K. H. Frank, Kundt, and others) to be a man of their own kind and a suitable partner in the negotiations. Among Czech politicians they concentrated on those who had already shown a desire to come to terms with the Sudeten Germans, the High Church hierarchy and particularly the right wing of the Agrarian Party, which meant men like Preiss, Beran, and, in particular, Hodža. Only formal contacts were maintained with President Beneš. A fresh series of negotiations between the Czechoslovak Government and the S.d.P. now began, under the patronage of the Runciman mission.

Hitler was quite openly and ostentatiously preparing to launch his military aggression. At the end of August massive manoeuvres took place in Germany, with a grandiose review of the navy, tanks, armoured cars, motorized infantry divisions, and aircraft. Using these manoeuvres as a pretext, Hitler called one and a half million men to arms.

In a number of different ways Hitler took charge of the German side of the negotiations with the Czechoslovak Government. He made his presence felt through the permanent Reich German adviser to the S.d.P., Kier, and by means of personal instructions and talks with Henlein, whom he adjured to make the negotiations as difficult as possible and to keep raising new demands without actually breaking off the talks. And all the time the special S.S. centre led by Obergruppenführer Lorens made ready to provoke a conflict in case the Czechoslovak Government did in the end accede to Henlein's demands.

Hitler had drafted a detailed political and legal motivation to excuse his move against Czechoslovakia. The German action was to be justified by reference to the 'intolerable oppression' of the Sudeten German minority and the reluctance of the Czechoslovak Government to come to an agreement on the issue. This was meant to prove that Hitler's action against Czechoslovakia was not aggression, so as to shift the chief political onus on to the victim. In Hitler's presentation it was Czechoslovakia, and particularly her President, who had provoked her mighty neighbour by her consistently anti-German attitude and her recalcitrance. Thus it was Czechoslovakia, and not Germany, who was to blame for the crisis which threatened to turn Europe into a battlefield. But Hitler went even further, warning France that should she decide nevertheless to come to Czechoslovakia's assistance, her action would necessarily be characterized as aggression against Germany. Similar threats were addressed to the Soviet Union. Anyone who helped Czechoslovakia would be dubbed an aggressor against Germany, who was merely intent on defending her own rights and those of her compatriots in the Sudeten regions. Tragically Hitler's arguments were not dismissed as absurd, but were accepted as objective and legally justifiable. They were, indeed, little more than a slightly exaggerated repetition of the official British, and for that matter French, view of Czechoslovakia's attitude.

At the same time Germany set about isolating Czechoslovakia from the rest of the world in a material sense as well. In collaboration with Poland and Hungary, the Germans arranged for all telegraph and telephone links from Czechoslovakia to be hampered and tapped. This seriously handicapped the Czechoslovak Government, which did not have adequate means of communication even with its own diplomatic missions abroad as a result, nor was it able to counter effectively Goebbels's furious propaganda, which to a large extent determined world public opinion on the Czechoslovak issue. And over all this loomed the spectre of the forthcoming Nazi rally at Nuremberg, which was to be opened on 6 September and at which Hitler was expected to make an official statement on his further course of action.

The negotiations between the Czechoslovak Government and the Sudeten German representatives had meanwhile reached their final stage under the aegis of the Runciman mission. The negotiations were highly complicated, various personal interests, ambitions, and political aims coming into play on every side. The Czechoslovak negotiators sought ways and means to calm the situation and save the Republic, while the Nazi representatives came forward with ever new demands, flooding the conference table with masses of documents in an effort to confuse and mislead the British participants.

As the negotiations went into their decisive phase in the middle of August 1938, President Beneš took over the leadership of the Czech delegation. He at once applied pressure to the S.d.P. representatives, demanding that they lay their cards on the table. He put forward a draft of Czech concessions, but at the same time wanted the Sudeten Germans publicly to express their readiness to co-operate and to undertake to respect the truce and stop their campaign of vilification in the press while the negotiations were in progress. The S.d.P. representatives were in a quandary. They could not accept Beneš's proposal, but to reject it would have meant to sacrifice the advantage of being able to put the blame for lack of progress on the Czechoslovak side. On the following day, 18 August, Henlein was to meet Runciman at Červený Hrádek to discuss the Beneš proposals. A private plane was hurriedly provided, and at one o'clock in the morning the Sudeten German leaders were in Berlin to receive further instructions from Ribbentrop. These stated that the demands contained in the Karlovy Vary programme were only the beginning, the minimum that the Sudeten Germans would accept. Hitler was in any case determined to solve the Czechoslovak problem by force of arms: 'He wants to lead the First Panzer Division into Czechoslovakia.'

In the morning, when Henlein met Lord Runciman at Červený Hrádek, their discussion was held on the basis of the new German line, the Karlovy Vary programme being proclaimed by Henlein as only a provisional compromise. The Nazi leader pointed out that Runciman had come to Czechoslovakia in order to settle the existing problem within the framework of the Czechoslovak State, but that such a solution was no longer possible. Henlein suggested that the Sudeten German territory be ceded to Germany on the strength of a plebiscite. Runciman then put a question to Henlein which foreshadowed the future course of British diplomacy on this subject, asking whether Henlein thought that an international conference might find the way to a solution. Henlein did not reply directly, but in further talks stressed with increasing emphasis that it was now not merely a Sudeten German problem but rather a question of the relations between Germany and Czechoslovakia as a whole. The British representatives wanted to know whether, if in the forthcoming week the Czechs showed no signs of wishing to come to an agreement, Henlein would be willing to find out from Hitler the possibility of having, before the rally, talks between the British representatives and the Führer, which would not be confined solely to the Czechoslovak question but would also deal with a pact on air transport, colonies, and a treaty on armaments. Henlein agreed.

New possible solutions of the Sudeten German problem had been proposed at the talks – a plebiscite and an international conference – both of them designed to leave the Czechoslovak Government out of the proceedings. A new element had now entered the picture, with the British showing their willingness to arrive at a broader Anglo-German agreement through Henlein's mediation, and at the expense of the Czechs.

Czechoslovakia knew all about these plans and, in an effort to circumvent them, the Czechoslovak Government presented, on 29 August, yet another proposal, the so-called third plan,  for a settlement with the S.d.P. This offered sizeable concessions, although still leaving a little in reserve by not fulfilling the Karlovy Vary demands in their entirety. They again represented an attempt to reach an agreement within the framework of the Czechoslovak State. But K. H. Frank, acting on instructions from the Führer and Reich Chancellor, ordered the Sudeten German delegation to insist on the eight points without the slightest compromise, and to interpret them extensively. On 2 September the S.d.P. rejected the third plan, putting forward new, 'extensive', demands.

Runciman's mission, too, turned the third plan down as inadequate and academic, warning the Czechs that it would draft its own proposals. At the same time Henlein, directly empowered to do so by the British Government, journeyed to Berchtesgaden to confer with Hitler on the subject of Czechoslovakia as well as the broader question of an Anglo-German treaty. In this tense situation, shortly before the Nazi rally was due to open in Nuremberg, President Beneš presented, on 5 September, the Runciman mission and the Henleinists with his so-called fourth plan. This not only acceded to the eight points of the Karlovy Vary programme but even included certain passages taken straight from Henlein's proposal of 2 September.

The fourth plan had an importance that far surpassed the Czechoslovak problem. It was, above all, an attempt to sabotage any possible Anglo-German treaty, a treaty that would have had catastrophic consequences for the whole world. Its chief aim was to preserve, at the cost of far-reaching concessions, the existing Czechoslovak system of alliances, and in particular the validity of the Czechoslovak-French treaty. When informing the French Government of the principles behind the fourth plan, the Czechs were careful to point out that it fulfilled the condition laid down by the French as indispensable for the further existence of the alliance treaty between the two countries. A similar statement was sent to the British Government. In this case, the Czechs were able to quote the opinion of the Runciman mission, which had acknowledged the fourth plan to provide full acceptance of Henlein's demands and to be a realistic basis for an agreement between the Czechoslovak Government and the S.d.P.

In this way Czechoslovakia sought also to stifle all attempts to name the Republic as the cause of international tension and the culprit in the Sudeten German issue, and to put the blame on her in case of an armed conflict. Any German attack would be totally unprovoked. This would have made it possible for her to appeal to the League of Nations and to invoke the Czechoslovak-Soviet treaty as well as the one with France. But there was still more at stake than that. It was an attempt to keep alive the anti-Hitler front which Britain was showing increasing signs of abandoning. Czechoslovakia was trying, at the desperate price of her own dismemberment, to keep British, and in the final analysis also French, policy from embarking on a course that was suicidal from their own point of view, a course that was to bring catastrophe for the further development of Europe and the world.

On 10 September, President Beneš broadcast a speech that was an appeal to world public opinion. He emphasized that with its fourth plan Czechoslovakia had made a great sacrifice for the sake of agreement with her neighbours, and in particular with Germany. She had made the supreme sacrifice for the sake of world peace. The fourth plan changed the situation entirely. Czechoslovakia had saved her system of alliances and removed the mark of Cain that had branded her a warmonger. Fresh international support was her reward.

Economic, political, and military contacts with the Soviet Union had continued throughout the whole crisis period, but now there were indications that a new policy towards Czechoslovakia might also be adopted by the West. In France, which had wavered and been reduced to the role of a second-rate power, there was growing opposition to the policies of Daladier and Bonnet. And in Britain, too, opposition to Chamberlain gained in strength, his opponents rallying around Churchill and Eden in the Conservative Party, and around the Labour Party and the trade unions. They demanded an end to the policy of appeasement. Even in Germany there was growing opposition among the generals against Hitler's brinkmanship, which combined verbal threats with concrete preparations for war, and in August their representative, Kleist, made contact with Churchill's group in London.

Czechoslovakia was well informed about all these events, being in touch with them primarily through its envoy in London, Jan Masaryk. The emergence and growing strength of the opposition in Britain and France gave new hope to Czechoslovakia, while Czechoslovakia's resolute stand against Hitler helped to strengthen the opposition groups in London and Paris. Whatever the price Czechoslovakia was forced to pay, the fourth plan preserved her system of alliances and by paralysing the Anglo-German rapprochement brought Czechoslovakia yet another victory over Hitler.

## The Crisis

The fourth plan proved an unexpected obstacle for the Nazis. They had suffered yet another defeat, which increased Hitler's fury. He decided to strike.

His first reaction to the plan, however, was absolute silence. In his opening address at the Nuremberg rally on 6 September he did not refer to Czechoslovakia once. It was only while the rally was in progress, during his meetings with Henlein and Frank, that a decision was taken on their further course of action. They agreed to provoke a rebellion inside Czechoslovakia and to break up the Republic by force by declaring the Sudeten territories part of the German Reich.

On 12 September Hitler mounted the rostrum at Nuremberg to make his final speech. He declared he would not tolerate any intimidation of the Sudeten Germans, 'whose suffering is beyond description'. He spoke of the 'deceitful Prague regime which in May ordered a mobilization and falsely accused the German Government of aggressive intentions, which it itself harbours towards the Sudeten Germans. Germany as a world power will not tolerate such provocation. . . . Nor does Germany intend to stand idly by while the Sudeten Germans are oppressed and who must be granted the right of self-dermination. . . . The Germans in Czechoslovakia are neither defenceless nor alone. I would ask that this is recognized.'

The apparatus of the S.d.P. went into action. Its representatives refused to discuss the fourth plan, Frank telling the Runciman mission quite openly that 'the situation has developed so rapidly since Hitler's speech at Nuremberg that only an *anschluss* is now possible'. Members of the party created incidents in sixty different Czechoslovak localities, hoping to provoke a rebellion which would grow into a *putsch* throughout the German areas. German propaganda called the situation in Czechoslovakia untenable. Not only was the Czechoslovak Government incapable of coming to terms with the German minority, it was no longer even able to keep law and order on its own territory. This propaganda campaign was meant as a preparation for the entry into Czechoslovakia of German military units 'in the interests of the preservation of law and order'.

But the Czechoslovak Government did not give the S.d.P. time to carry out its intentions. It took a firm stand, stating that the fourth plan had fulfilled all the S.d.P. demands, so that once they resorted to *putsch* tactics the Government was no longer bound by any obligations, either to them or to the West. In response to the efforts of the Runciman mission to save the day by suggesting further talks, the Government declared itself willing to take part, but at the same time it did everything in its power to localize the incidents and to prevent a full-scale rebellion from breaking out, taking harsh measures against the insurrectionists. Martial law was declared in most of the border areas, and the army, *gendarmerie*, and civilian volunteers restored order throughout the territory in a matter of days, so that the disturbances never got out of hand. In this way the S.d.P. and its leaders were quickly and effectively isolated.

On 13 September Frank cabled his ultimatum to the Prague Government, demanding the immediate withdrawal of the police, *gendarmes*, army, and civilian volunteers and the lifting of the martial law. The Government rejected his demands, and on the contrary issued warrants for the arrest of Henlein, Frank, and other Sudeten leaders. On 15 September they fled across the border to Germany. The Nazi *putsch* had failed, and the Czechoslovak Government immediately used its victory to disrupt the S.d.P. Having forced its leaders into exile, it now banned the party as a whole, effectively paralysing what had been a dangerous fifth column. The Führer had suffered yet another defeat, and once again, though she had appeared to be hopelessly trapped, Czechoslovakia had managed to preserve her internal democracy and her independence.

The Czechoslovak Ambassador Fierlinger cabled from Moscow:

'I have asked Potemkin once more to state the Soviet position. Potemkin accordingly outlined the whole situation, repeating that they were 100 per cent determined to help in every way. . . . In the military sphere they want joint action by all three [Russia, Czechoslovakia, and France] in order to stave off the campaign by certain British circles to the effect that the Soviets are urging us to be intractable and are pushing Europe into war.'

Yet on the very day that Henlein was making his escape and at a time when the Soviet Union was once again assuring Czechoslovakia of its willingness to help, a new assault against the Republic was being prepared in Berlin and London, an assault that was even more invidious and dangerous than the ones that had gone before.

From the point of view of Chamberlain's policy, the Czechoslovak fourth plan of 5 September was a complication which only postponed the final solution of the Central European problem, a complication that stood in the way of an Anglo-German agreement. Jan Masaryk reported that in a private conversation Chamberlain stated that though he was convinced that Czechoslovakia was in the right and he would help her if this were in the British interest, the situation was, unfortunately, different. 'Today there is no right and no truth. We are playing a colossal power game, with Czechoslovakia merely a pretext on both sides. . . .'

With her fourth plan Czechoslovakia had yet again manoeuvred the British appeasement policy into the anti-German front where it did not wish to be. And Chamberlain knew very well that she had done so quite intentionally, just as he was well aware of Czechoslovak links with those who stood in opposition to his policy at home in Britain. Czechoslovakia's action was therefore not only an unheard of interference in the sovereignty of British power but also a personal affront.

Chamberlain's appeasement policy was running aground in other respects as well. Official British circles were in vain trying to obtain closer contacts with Hitler and to start negotiations with him. Hitler either failed to reply to memoranda and personal letters or he would briskly reject the proposals made from the British side. And when the Nazis launched their attempt at a *putsch* in Czechoslovakia, Runciman's mission came to an end, thus closing yet another avenue of approach to Hitler.

Aware of the growing opposition to his policies, Chamberlain now decided to negotiate direct with Hitler. On the night of 13 September he offered to meet him in Germany, and on the 15th he flew to Berchtesgaden.

The talks envisaged by Chamberlain to last several days ended with the first meeting. Hitler flatly refused to discuss any broader Anglo-German agreement before the Czechoslovak issue had been settled once and for all. Hitler began by emphasizing his 'well-known desire for peace', but he pointed out that Germany now recognized only one problem, which was Czechoslovakia. The Czechoslovak question must definitely be settled 'one way or another', as he, Hitler, was no longer prepared to tolerate 'a small, inferior country treating a great, thousand-year-old empire as if it were of no importance'.

Chamberlain, disappointed in his hopes for an Anglo-German settlement, told the Führer that he himself was ready to solve the Sudeten German problem by annexing the territories in question to the Reich, but that he had to consult his

Government before anything could be done. That brought the Berchtesgaden talks to an end. The venue moved to London, Paris, and Prague.

The Czechs knew that their defensive struggle against German aggression, which had lasted many years, was now in its final and decisive stage. On 17 September President Beneš gave the French Ambassador an oral message for the Paris Government.

'A decisive phase has been reached in the struggle between ourselves and Berlin. It is not a question of our minority. Rather it is an age-old struggle for German hegemony in Central Europe. A fatal blow is to be struck against us, but this blow will affect all Central Europe, the entire French policy and thus France herself. We can stop Hitler only if we remain firm. I beg the French Government to take all this into account. We have kept our faith with France, and we shall remain faithful in the most difficult of circumstances. In making this emphatic appeal to the French Government we trust that, true to the spirit of our treaty of alliance, it will remain on our side whatever happens. If we remain firm, the rest of Europe will in the end go with us against Nazi Germany.'

The German Nachrichtenbüro (press agency) kept pouring out a stream of reports about the anti-German terror in Czechoslovakia. German newspapers came out with scare headlines such as 'Terrible Atrocities of Czech Bandits', 'Murderers Without Masks', 'Incredible Crimes of Czech Beasts', 'German Blood Accuses'; throughout special Sudeten German Freikorps units, in collaboration with the German S.S. and S.A., created disturbances all along the 2,000 kilometre Czechoslovak-German frontier, any of which could easily lead to a full-scale German invasion.

On 18 and 19 September dramatic Anglo-French talks were held in London. Their conclusion was that the chief responsibility for the critical situation and for the new German demands for the annexation of the Sudetenland lay with Czechoslovakia and, above all, her President. Chamberlain stressed that it had been primarily Beneš who had delayed the acceptance of Sudeten German demands, that he had always lagged behind events rather than anticipated them. This led to the following conclusions: A Czechoslovak-German agreement was no longer possible. There were now only two possible solutions – either to give Germany what she wanted or to risk war. Armed conflict, however, could not benefit Czechoslovakia in any way, for although her allies – France, the Soviet Union, and Britain – might become involved, they would be quite unable to provide effective protection. And not even when the war had ended would statesmen 'be able to maintain the boundaries of Czechoslovakia'.

Britain and France thus considered acceptance of Hitler's terms and the ceding by Czechoslovakia of her frontier regions to Germany to be the only possible solution. The remainder of Czechoslovakia would then be neutralized.

The problem now was how to persuade the Czechoslovak Government to accept such a solution. It was obvious that this would be no easy task. The Czechoslovak policy of resistance to Hitler had just scored a great victory by preventing a Nazi *putsch* and liquidating the German fifth column in the country. Czechoslovakia had triumphed over Hitler once more, and it was no small triumph.

On 19 September 1938 the British and French governments laid their London resolution before the Czechs. Completely disregarding the fourth plan submitted by Czechoslovakia, they said:

'. . . We are both convinced that, after recent events, the point has now been reached where the further maintenance within the boundaries of the Czechoslovak State of the districts mainly inhabited by Sudeten Germans cannot in fact continue any longer without imperilling the interests of Czechoslovakia herself and of European peace. In the light of these considerations both Governments have been compelled to the conclusion that the maintenance of peace and the safety of Czechoslovakia's vital interests cannot effectively be assured unless these areas are now transferred to the Reich. . . .'

A number of other provisions served to underline the fact that this was a thinly-veiled ultimatum. In order to scotch any independent action on Czechoslovakia's part, the two governments 'recommended' that the Czechoslovak Government should on no account resort to mobilization. Hitler, they said, had assured Chamberlain that while negotiations were in progress Germany would not go over to armed conflict.

The Czechs were given one day to make up their minds about the future of their Republic, the two governments doing everything in their power to ensure that the answer from Prague should be in the affirmative. They had agreed that 'the strongest pressure would have to be brought to bear on Dr Beneš to see that the Czechoslovak Government accepted the solution put forward by the British and French governments. Should, however, Dr Beneš reply in the negative, he would be accepting the idea of a war.' Though couched in diplomatic language, the note held the threat that if Czechoslovakia said 'No', she could once again be accused of trying to foment war.

The Czechs knew very well what this meant, and everyone made sure that they did, Bonnet telling Osuský ' . . . if the proposition is not accepted, Britain will withhold her support from France in case of a German attack on Czechoslovakia'. Without British support French aid would be so ineffective as to be practically non-existent.

On 20 September the French Ambassador, in co-operation with his British colleague, brought new pressure to bear on the Czechoslovak Government, in order to 'warn against the danger of haggling and creating a pretext for the unleashing of war'.

Thus on 19 and 20 September the Czechoslovak Government was faced with a terrible dilemma. If they said 'Yes', they would be giving their approval to the annihilation of the Republic and the liquidation of her system of alliances. By saying 'No' they would be registering a protest, but again the alliance system would be destroyed and the way left open for German aggression, which once more would mean the annihilation of Czechoslovakia as a state. They were being pressed to say 'Yes' by both Britain and France through diplomatic channels and by Nazi Germany with her strident propaganda and ceaseless incidents along the frontier, with which Czechoslovakia could not deal properly because her hands were tied by the 'recommendation' not to mobilize. An affirmative answer was also demanded by certain circles in Czechoslovakia itself. On 20 September the Slovak People's Party, on the direct instigation of some of the leaders of the banned S.d.P., issued a communiqué demanding the immediate and definitive settlement of the Slovak problem on the basis of the Pittsburgh Treaty. The Government was faced with a serious internal crisis, and various individuals now tried to avoid shouldering their share of responsibility, as witnessed by Hodža's attempted resignation.

But there were also forces encouraging Czechoslovakia to stand firm and say 'No'. On 19 September Beneš asked the Soviet Government for its view on the critical situation. Next day he received a reply. To his first question, whether the Soviet Government would honour its obligations as Czechoslovakia's ally if France stood by her, the Soviet Government replied 'Yes, at once and effectively'. The second question concerned the Soviet Union's attitude should France refuse to aid Czechoslovakia, who would then decide to resist Germany and appeal to the League of Nations. Would the Soviet Union be ready to fulfil her obligations in accordance with the League's articles 16 and 17? The Soviet Government replied 'Yes, in every respect'.

In France and Britain, too, opposition to the appeasement policy gained ground. It was seen that this policy would unnecessarily hand over to Hitler a country that formed an important anti-German base in Central Europe, despite the fact that Czechoslovakia herself wanted to resist with all the means at her disposal. Churchill now went to Paris to talk to the French opposition leaders, and Osuský phoned to Prague: 'All is not lost yet.'

The opposition in Paris and London had contacts with the Prague Government. Their advice to President Beneš was that he should reject the ultimatum. These moves helped to revive the Little Entente, and there were rumours that Titulescu, who had championed and helped to build the anti-Fascist front of the middle thirties, would be recalled to take charge of Rumanian foreign policy.

The situation prevailing in Czechoslovakia itself also spoke in favour of resistance to Hitler. The speedy liquidation of the S.d.P. attempt at a *putsch* had immensely strengthened the hand of those who wanted to defend the Republic at all costs. The knowledge that Czechoslovakia had a good, well-trained and well-equipped army lent added force to the anti-German resistance.

Shortly after 7 p.m. on 20 September the Czechoslovak Foreign Minister Kamil Krofta handed to the French and British Ambassadors his Government's reply to the ultimatum. The Czechoslovak Government said 'No'. The reply stated that the Czechoslovak Government wished to thank the British and French governments for their endeavour to solve the international problems concerning Czechoslovakia, but

'conscious of its responsibility for the interests of Czechoslovakia, the interests of friends and allies as well as for the interests of general peace, the Czechoslovak Government expresses the unshaken conviction that proposals which are contained in that communication are not calculated to attain the object at which French and British governments are aiming in the crucial efforts they are making in favour of peace.

'These proposals were drawn up without previous consultation with representatives of Czechoslovakia and an attitude hostile to her has been taken up without giving her a hearing although the Czechoslovak Government had already drawn attention to the fact that it could not accept responsibility for a decision taken without its participation. It is therefore regretted that it should not have been possible to draw up these proposals in a manner acceptable to Czechoslovakia. . . . In the Government's opinion acceptance of a proposal of this kind would be equivalent to acquiescence to complete mutilation of the State in every respect; from an economic point of view and that of transport, Czechoslovakia would be completely paralysed and from a strategic point of view she would find herself in an extremely difficult situation; and she would sooner or later fall under the absolute influence of Germany . . .'

The Government's reply stated further that relations between Czechoslovakia and Germany had been settled by a special arbitration treaty of 16 October 1925, which the present German Government had recently acknowledged to be still in force. The Czechoslovak Government wished to point out that this treaty was applicable in the present situation and its terms should now be enforced. In conclusion, Czechoslovakia turned to the British and French governments with a new and final appeal and begged them to reconsider their point of view. For 'at this decisive time it is not only the fate of Czechoslovakia which is in the balance but also that of other countries and particularly that of France'.

This rejection by Prague of the Anglo-French ultimatum which had been so laboriously prepared and had involved so much pressure being brought to bear on the Czechoslovak Government, caused much anger in Paris and London. Chamberlain was due to leave on the following day for another round of talks with Hitler, and he knew that Czechoslovakia's acceptance of the Berchtesgaden proposal was an essential precondition for any Anglo-German negotiations. By rejecting the proposal Czechoslovakia gravely endangered his whole policy, her stubborn resistance making her a troublesome burden to her former allies. Chamberlain was therefore determined to break Czechoslovakia's resistance at all costs. He had his personal motives as well, for he was not unaware of the growing contacts between the Czechs and those in England who stood in opposition to his policy.

It had been stated earlier in London that it could not be left to Beneš to decide on the issue of war and peace. And if Britain and France had been resolved to bring every conceivable pressure to bear on Czechoslovakia then, they were willing to go to any extreme now that only one night remained before Chamberlain was due to set off. With this in mind the two governments turned to those Czechoslovak politicians who had in the past showed themselves more willing to make concessions than President Beneš – to the Agrarian leaders and especially to Hodža. Hodža himself described the Czechoslovak Government's reply to the British and French initiative with the disloyal statement that it was a 'concession to the pig-headed elements'. Once again the Agrarian Right attacked Beneš at a moment of extreme crisis.

The scene was now set for the audience of the British and French Ambassadors with President Beneš, which took place, with Hodža's knowledge, shortly after two o'clock in the morning on 21 September. The two ambassadors read out the brief and clear instructions they had received from their governments.

The British Note said that the Czechoslovak Government's reply 'in no way met the critical situation' and that 'the British Government therefore urged the Czechoslovak Government to withdraw this reply and to urgently consider an alternative that took account of realities'. The Note ended with the threat that, should the Czechoslovak Government 'reject this advice, they must of course be free to take any action that they thought appropriate to meet the situation that might develop as a result'.

The French Note was similar both in content and tone, but the threat it carried in conclusion was more concrete and categorical: 'Should the Czechoslovak Government be unable immediately to accept the Franco-British proposals and reject them, and should war result from the situation thus created, Czechoslovakia will be held responsible and France will not join in such a war.'

All the responsibility for an armed conflict was being placed on Czechoslovakia's shoulders. She would be labelled a warmonger and whoever might still want to come to her assistance would himself be branded an aggressor.

The Czechoslovak Government met on 21 September at six o'clock in the morning. Giving way to this overwhelming external pressure it changed its standpoint, stating in brief Notes sent to Paris and London:

> 'Forced by circumstances and by excessively urgent pressure, and as a result of communication with French and British governments of 21 September 1938 in which the two governments express their attitude in regard to assistance to Czechoslovakia if she refused to accept Franco-British proposals and was, as a result attacked by Germany, the Czechoslovak Government accept these conditions of the Franco-British proposals with feelings of grief . . .'

Czechoslovakia had thus been brought to her knees, not by Hitler but by her own allies. But the little country in the heart of Europe still refused to surrender.

The population received the news of the Government's latest reply with feelings of anger and despair. Demonstrators filled the streets of Prague and other cities throughout the country, the demonstrations culminating in a great rally at Prague Castle. The protests went on all night, and on 22 September another huge rally took place in front of the Parliament building. The demonstrators demanded the dismissal of Hodža's Government, the rescinding of the capitulation, and effective measures for the defence of the country against German aggression. From the balcony of the Parliament building the Communist Party leader Klement Gottwald announced the first victory to the assembled crowd.

'Citizens, friends, comrades. The slogan with which you marched into the streets today has become reality. The Government has resigned. At this moment a new Government determined to defend the Republic is being formed, a new Government that relies on the support of the people, the Army, honest democrats of all political parties. The Republic is in danger. However, the people, who have forced the Government to resign and a new one to be set up, will also see to it that the invader does not win. We are in constant touch with London and Paris. The people of London and Paris are on our side, just as the Red Army of the Soviet Union, and the entire democratic world sends us this message: "Hold out, do not surrender." '

The Agrarians had lost their leading position in the Government. A special Committee for the Defence of the Republic was setting up a Popular Front Government that was to defend the country against Hitler. For the first time since the Czechoslovak Republic came into existence the Communist Party was to form part of the Government.

Press agencies throughout the world carried news about the political crisis in Czechoslovakia, saying that the Czechoslovak Government was powerless to deal with the situation. The assertion that the country was on the threshold of a Bolshevik coup gained credence in many quarters. None of this was true, however. The demonstrations had been completely orderly and had only a single aim: to solve the internal political crisis in a way that would ensure the defence of Czechoslovakia against German aggression.

There was no time to be lost. In London an aeroplane was made ready for Chamberlain. And there could be no doubt as to the reason behind his journey.

The new Czechoslovak Government was formed in the evening of 22 September. It was a caretaker Government led by General Syrový and enjoying the support of the Army, which was ready to defend Czechoslovakia's independence. The new Government's first move was to proclaim a general mobilization for 23 September. This action, with Czechoslovak soldiers moving into the strong fortifications in the mountains of the border regions, had an immediate effect on international developments. It struck most where it had been intended to strike, at the talks between Chamberlain and Hitler at Godesberg, helping to break up the Anglo-German negotiations.

When he arrived at Godesberg, Chamberlain told Hitler he was bringing Czechoslovakia's agreement to his annexation of the frontier regions. He then tried to get the Führer to go over to negotiations on the subject of an Anglo-German treaty, which were the main purpose of his visit. But Hitler again refused to negotiate, concentrating once more on the Czechoslovak issue, which had evidently become a question of German prestige. Fresh demands were laid before the now irate and bitterly disappointed Chamberlain. These included Polish and Hungarian, as well as Hitler's own, territorial claims. The German demands were summed up in a special memorandum drafted by Hitler after the talks, and he added a map which showed the territory in question. This territory was divided into two categories – the first, marked in red, was to be handed over by Czechoslovakia at once, the second, marked green, was to be decided by a plebiscite. Hitler's demands here at Godesberg far exceeded those made by him at Berchtesgaden. Particularly in Moravia, the territory marked out for annexation cut so deeply into the Republic that Moravia would have become a mere corridor, between thirty and fifty kilometres wide, linking what remained of Bohemia with Slovakia. Whereas Hitler's *Fall Grün* had envisaged a military pincer movement in Moravia, his Godesberg plan attempted to do the same job without a fight.

The major and decisive difference between Berchtesgaden and Godesberg was that the new plan would involve surrendering all Czechoslovakia's chief fortifications to Germany. This would leave Czechoslovakia completely defenceless, her final liquidation being only a question of time. Hitler demanded that the ceded territory be handed over at once, by 1 October, insisting that the evacuated Sudeten German area be handed over without in any way destroying or rendering unusable the military, economic or transport establishments and facilities. And, finally, no foodstuffs, goods, cattle, raw materials were to be removed.

Just as Hitler was handing Chamberlain his memorandum, at 10.30 p.m. on 23 September, he received the news of Czechoslovakia's mobilization. He was seized by a fit of fury, declaring that this put an end to the whole affair and that Czechoslovakia's step forced him to take certain military measures. Chamberlain had no choice but to state that no further negotiation was possible in the circumstances. The attempt to reach an Anglo-German understanding had failed. It now seemed that the appeasement policy had at last reached an impasse and that a new, favourable situation had been created for Czechoslovakia.

The French Government declared that Hitler's memorandum implied the total destruction of Czechoslovakia and that a new situation had thus arisen in which the French Government would feel obliged to come to her aid. As a result fifteen French divisions were mobilized and sent to man the Maginot Line.

In England there was a wave of opposition to Chamberlain, represented above all by the Labour Party, which organized numerous protest demonstrations. But there was considerable dissension within the Conservative Party itself. Chamberlain's fall became a distinct possibility, with the prospect of Churchill and Eden heading a new Government. England too was preparing for war.

On 25 September the Soviet People's Commissar for Defence informed the French general staff that thirty infantry divisions had been moved to areas adjoining the Western frontier and that the Air Force and tank units were fully alerted.

Czechoslovak-Polish negotiations were started. Her two partners in the Little Entente, Rumania and Yugoslavia, announced that they considered themselves bound to assist Czechoslovakia should she be attacked by Hungary. And throughout the world Czech embassies were getting offers from volunteers wishing to fight on behalf of Czechoslovakia. Encouraged by all these developments, Czechoslovakia now officially rejected Hitler's Godesberg demands.

On 25 September Jan Masaryk handed Chamberlain his Government's reply to the German memorandum. This stated that the memorandum was in fact an 'ultimatum of the sort usually presented to a vanquished nation and not a proposition to a sovereign state'. The German proposals went 'far beyond what was agreed in the so-called Anglo-French plan. They deprived Czechoslovakia of every safeguard for her national existence and forced her to yield up large proportions of her carefully prepared defences and to admit the German armies deep into the country before plans could be made to organize it on the new basis or any preparations for its defence could be made. Her national and economic independence would automatically disappear with the acceptance of Hitler's plan.' On the strength of this argument Jan Masaryk then conveyed to the British Prime Minister the view taken by the Czechoslovak Government.

'My Government wish me to declare in all solemnity that Hitler's demands in their present form are absolutely and unconditionally unacceptable to my Government. Against these new and cruel demands my Government feel bound to make their utmost resistance and we shall do so, God helping. The nation of St Wenceslas, John Hus and Thomas Masaryk will not be a nation of slaves.'

No more words were needed. Czechoslovakia's attitude left no room for doubt.

D.D.—9*

Chamberlain responded by asking that Prague should not, for the time being, make her standpoint public. But Sir Horace Wilson was sent to Berlin with a letter, pressing Hitler to withdraw his Godesberg demands. The Führer was livid with rage. He kept interrupting Ambassador Henderson, and at one point 'left his chair and made to leave the room, muttering that it was no use talking further; the time for action had come. . . .'

Sir Neville Henderson said repeatedly that the British Government would see that the Czechs handed over the territory; they were in a position to put adequate pressure on the Czech Government. Sir Horace Wilson urged that the British and French governments should ensure that the Czechoslovak Government hand over the territory and that the Germans could achieve what they wanted by peaceful methods.

Hitler told Henderson at the end of the audience that unless Czechoslovakia changed her attitude and accepted his Godesberg memorandum by two o'clock on the afternoon of Wednesday 28 September, the German armed forces would strike. A few hours later he made a speech at the Sports Palace which was nothing but a furious attack on Czechoslovakia and in particular on President Beneš, whom Hitler rightly considered his most dangerous and unparalleled enemy in Europe.

Although Czechoslovakia doubted Hitler's determination to fight, considering – rightly, as it turned out later – his timetable to be just a bluff intended to exert pressure on his opponents, she nevertheless made all the necessary preparations.

The Czechoslovak Government, with Beneš presiding, met at 9.30 p.m. on 27 September. The Foreign Minister, Krofta, recapitulated the situation and quoted from a speech by the Soviet People's Commissar Litvinov, who said that war was now unavoidable and that Russia would come to an agreement with France and Britain. Beneš told the Government that Litvinov considered Hitler's demands unacceptable and declared that the Soviet Union would do its duty. The Little Entente would also go along with France and Britain. Should Czechoslovakia be attacked tomorrow, the front had been reconstructed – if there was a war, they had a front reconstructed by superhuman effort and they must look to the future with confidence. The Government session ended at 10.30 p.m.

A little over an hour later, at 11.45 p.m. a Note was sent to the Czechoslovak representatives in Geneva on the orders of the Foreign Minister with instructions that in case of a German invasion it should at once be handed to the General Secretary of the League of Nations. The Note briefly explained the cause of the conflict, concluding with the following words:

'The Czechoslovak Republic has now become victim of aggression and on the basis of Articles 11, 16, and 18, appeals to the Council, asking that it be immediately called into session in order to name the aggressor.

'A crime has been committed against international law, against humanity and justice. Czechoslovakia trusts that the League of Nations will not abandon her.'

This Note was intended to brand Germany as the aggressor and to provide a basis for the application of the Czechoslovak-French and Czechoslovak-Soviet treaties.

Also on Wednesday morning the Soviet Government received Beneš's request for immediate air support, as is shown by the cable message sent from Moscow by Ambassador Fierlinger on 28 September: 'The President's request for immediate air support has been presented. I hope it will be granted.' Everything was ready.

After the failure of the Godesberg talks, the anti-German front concentrated around Czechoslovakia in the week between 23 and 28 September 1938, and Czechoslovakia was well prepared to defend herself. It was basically the same front as had existed in the middle thirties, and now it was partly in arms. It had come into being due to Czechoslovakia's carefully thought-out and highly consistent policy, but it was hard to tell just how genuine it really was. It had been created under the force of circumstances, against the wishes of conservative French and British governments, the result of a desperate fight for survival on Czechoslovakia's part. It concealed within itself many contradictions and many pitfalls. In those tense September days a single false step would have sufficed to turn it against a completely different enemy, and the skein of behind-the-scenes negotiations that went on between London, Paris, and Berlin was a sinister warning.

At a meeting of the French Government on 27 September, Bonnet asserted that France's military and diplomatic situation was so unsatisfactory that it was unthinkable for the country to go to war over some trifling technical disagreements about the annexation of the Sudetenland. On the same day the Czechoslovak Ambassador cabled from Paris:

'Bonnet and those close to him are spreading it round that France will in no circumstances go to war. The fact that he has remained in the Cabinet even after yesterday's London agreement makes it look as if the London decision, the French mobilization, and the British communiqué are just a manoeuvre. . . .'

On 27 September Chamberlain spoke on the radio, saying:

'However much we may sympathize with a small nation that has to contend with a great and powerful neighbour, we cannot, in the circumstances, involve the entire British Empire in war simply on account of such a country. If we did have to fight, it would have to be for a more weighty cause.'

The following day Chamberlain accepted Hitler's invitation to Munich.

The anti-German front had collapsed. A 'peaceful' solution to the crisis had been found. It was simpler and less painful than war. Czechoslovakia was to be the pawn and the ransom.

The international conference that was to decide her fate was the last and final stage of the struggle for the defence of Czechoslovakia in 1938. As soon as France, following Britain's example, had decided to conclude an agreement with Germany against her Czechoslovak ally, the Czechoslovak system of alliances, the only real basis of the country's defence against foreign aggression, fell apart. The Soviet Union now held back and did nothing to intervene in the crisis. The shifting of loyalties at Munich posed a threat to it just as much as to Czechoslovakia. And so Czechoslovakia now found herself in just the situation she had been assiduously trying to prevent. She was completely isolated.

Hitler, Chamberlain, Daladier, and Mussolini met at the conference table on 29 September. Czechoslovakia was not invited, for, to quote Hitler, 'her constant resistance would disrupt the atmosphere where there are no fundamental differences between the individual members'. The conference met to discuss Mussolini's plan, which had been drafted for him by the Nazis and was to provide for the immediate occupation of the Czechoslovak frontier regions on the basis of Hitler's Godesberg memorandum. There was no proper organization, no chairman, and no agenda. The Conference in fact only discussed the proposals laid before it, all the participants having one common aim, which was to accept them. There were altogether three meetings, the first lasted from 2.45 to 3.00 p.m. and dealt primarily with formalities. At the second session, from 4.30 to 9.00 p.m., the actual discussion of the proposal to occupy the Sudetenland took place. The third session ended shortly after midnight with the approval of the final draft and the signing of the agreement.

Once the representatives of the four powers had signed, the agreement became valid. There was no need to ask the Czechoslovak Government for its approval. Thus the four powers by themselves decided the fate of Czechoslovakia. The Czechoslovak Republic, as it had been established in 1918, no longer existed.

On 30 September Kamil Krofta sent his last instructions to the Czechoslovak embassies in Paris and London:

'Remind the Government and the general staff that by the Munich agreement they have forced us to surrender the fortifications undamaged and equipped. Remind them that by their decision they have thus helped further to arm Hitler against themselves, for in the fortifications we are to surrender by 10 October there is two thousand million crowns' worth of cannon, machine-guns, and ammunition.'

But the world rejoiced that peace had been won. Again, as after the Locarno agreement between the four powers, the bells pealed and mass was celebrated in the churches. The League of Nations welcomed the endeavour to safeguard world peace. And Chamberlain joyfully announced that he had saved peace 'for our time'.

# Epilogue

The bells that had celebrated the signing of the Munich Agreement stopped ringing. The wave of enthusiasm subsided. There followed a brief period of calm, of everyday reality. What did Munich mean in the light of that reality? What did it mean for the coming days, weeks, months, and years? Who had won a victory and who had suffered a defeat? Only one of the four statesmen who signed the Munich Agreement was really the victor. Munich represented a great triumph for Hitler's Germany, a victory for which a terrible price was shortly to be paid.

Hitler's policy of daring brinkmanship, relying on the weakness and lack of consistency on the part of the Western powers, had again paid off that September. Once more as at the time of the Rhineland crisis in March 1936, Hitler, moving along a razor's edge, had snatched a victory. His critics in Germany, who had been gaining in strength, fell silent, convinced by the positive results achieved by the Führer.

As in the Rhineland, only this time to a far greater degree, Hitler succeeded in smashing the barrier that had been erected around Germany. By destroying Czechoslovakia he managed to eradicate the nucleus around which, and on whose initiative, the anti-German front of the middle thirties had been resurrected in 1938. And as in the Rhineland, he did so by applying pressure at the weakest point, in the West. This time he disrupted the anti-German front when it was already standing in the trenches.

Hitler succeeded in doing far more than this. His victory at Munich far outstripped his Rhineland triumph. Once Czechoslovakia had been cleared out of the way he proceeded, step by step, to conclude agreements with all the other chief participants of the front. Munich was the beginning of this process.

When two of the four countries, Britain and France, who

on 27 and 28 September were still preparing to go to war against Germany, several hours later signed an agreement sacrificing the third, Czechoslovakia, to aggressive Germany, they were signing an agreement with the enemy. By signing the Munich Agreement they not only openly betrayed their erstwhile ally, they also submitted to Hitler's desires and his will. And by doing so they at the same time signed their own defeat, helping to liquidate a politically and strategically highly important base that had blocked Hitler's expansion, not only into Central, Eastern, and South-Eastern Europe but much farther – his conquest of the world as a whole. How great an Anglo-French defeat the Munich dictate really was became further apparent by the fact that it was not followed by any Anglo-German agreement on the division of the world spheres of influence, which had been the chief aim behind Chamberlain's whole policy.

Munich also meant a parting of the ways between two of the signatories, France and Britain, and the fourth partner in the anti-German front, the Soviet Union. While the solution of the Rhineland crisis had broken up the Franco-Soviet pact, Munich created a wide gulf between the two West European powers and the Soviet Union. At a time when Soviet, as well as Czechoslovak, French, and British forces were preparing to take military action against Germany, an agreement was signed with the enemy, the Soviet Union being neither invited to take part in the negotiations nor even adequately informed about them. The split between Britain and France on the one side and the Soviet Union on the other destroyed the mainstay of the anti-German front.

The Agreement created a deep rift in relations between Western and Eastern Europe, helping to realize an aim which German policy had been following for many years: to divide East and West and to determine their relationship in accordance with her own interests. Munich achieved this aim, and Hitler now took the initiative in relations between Western Europe and the Soviet Union. The world was thus faced with a new threat: the newly-formed political front of the four – Germany, Britain, France, and Italy – was not just an anti-Czechoslovak front but, more important, an anti-Soviet one.

The Munich Agreement was simply a deal between great powers. The signatories of the agreement officially acknowledged Central Europe to be a German sphere of interest, while the anti-Russian bias of the new power-grouping paved the way towards the solution of a number of other world problems, especially in Asia.

Britain was particularly interested in this part of the world, for it was in Asia that the major part of her Empire lay. And it was in this continent that her interests conflicted with those of the Soviet Union, whose power base was also in Asia. That was why Britain had signed the Munich Agreement, giving Hitler a free hand in Czechoslovakia in the hope that with his help she would succeed in breaking Soviet influence in Asia.

The Soviet Union, like Czechoslovakia, was completely isolated internationally as a result of Munich. It now found itself opposed by Germany, Britain, France, Italy, and Japan. These countries, including British colonies in southern Asia, encircled the Soviet Union, and the front created at Munich limited her freedom of political action, ensuring her isolation.

In this power game Czechoslovakia was a mere pawn on the world's chess board. She stood in the way of power interests and the defence of her existence became an embarrassment to her partners. That was why Czechoslovakia had to be crushed at Munich and left to Hitler's mercy.

The situation being what it was, armed resistance to the German tanks which entered the country could only have had a moral significance. Czechoslovak blood would now have been nothing more than an appeal to the conscience of a world whose brutal reality had destroyed the little democracy in the heart of Europe. And in addition, when the Munich Agreement was signed it was not out of the question that the new political front, albeit with various modifications, might still turn into a military one, aimed against Czechoslovakia and the Soviet Union. That was the greatest danger of all. That it did not happen was due to the fact that Czechoslovakia, well aware of the danger, bowed to the Munich dictate. Even as she fell Czechoslovakia was still fighting.

Munich significantly altered the balance of power in the

world and reshuffled the partners in the power game. The existence of an anti-Soviet front forced the Russians to seek a way out of their isolation. They did so by signing an agreement with the victor of Munich, the German-Soviet Treaty of 1939. Hitler's victory at Munich had had very far-reaching consequences.

Nevertheless, if Munich is looked at from the viewpoint of Hitler's plans for world conquest, it is clear that it acted also as a detour and a delay in his aggressive campaign. The long-drawn-out, consistent and extremely cautious defence put up by Czechoslovakia prevented Hitler from ridding himself of this particular obstacle in the lightning fashion he originally had in mind. Unlike Austria, which was occupied in a matter of hours, and Poland, whose turn came a little later and who fell in eighteen days, and Denmark, Holland, Belgium, and even France whose destruction took Hitler only a few weeks, Czechoslovakia made him expend all his energies on a struggle which drove him into a fury.

It was incredible that this country could for so long fight off determined German aggression. The world, or at least its progressive and far-sighted forces, followed the struggle attentively and with bated breath. And if in the end Czechoslovakia fell, it was not because she had shown herself unwilling to fight in her own defence.

Czechoslovak policy made it impossible for Hitler to proceed singlehanded and forced him to find partners who would help him break down Czechoslovakia's resistance. He had to resort to an agreement of the Four, which was never his intention. However, the deep political rift created by Munich in the ranks of his former enemies was sufficient compensation for the detour he was obliged to make.

Munich gave Hitler his greatest political victory, immensely boosting both his power and his self-esteem. And, with the occupation of Czechoslovakia on 15 March 1939, opened the way for his further aggression, giving him a great feeling of confidence; nothing could stop him now. This enabled him to throw all caution to the wind and to make use of Germany's military might in order to implement his plans.

In other ways, too, Munich unleashed the full brutal force of

German Nazism and of all Fascist forces throughout the world. It was shortly after Munich, on 9 November 1938, that an unprecedented Jewish pogrom took place in Germany, the beginning of their systematic mass liquidation.

It was also no coincidence that the destruction of yet another European state which had resisted Fascist aggression – democratic Spain – entered its final phase a few months after Munich. Barcelona fell in January 1939, Madrid on 28 March. And at the beginning of April Falangist Spain joined the anti-Comintern Pact.

After Munich the Europe which had been born in 1918 out of a terrible bloodbath in the name of humanity, justice, and peace became engulfed by the darkness of Fascism. But at the same time, there appeared the first indications of a possible way out of this darkness. Once again Czechoslovakia had a role to play, though this time no longer as a fighting nation but as a defeated, non-existent Czechoslovakia.

The swastika that flew over Prague on 15 March 1939 symbolized the infringement, the discarding, and thus also the annulment of Munich. The political front created shortly before at Munich was disrupted by the German troops marching into the interior of the Republic. March 15 was the best proof of what Munich stood for in Hitler's plans, giving the British and French tangible evidence of the futility of any agreement with him. This was the beginning of the end of the Anglo-French policy of appeasement. The possibility of a new anti-German front was alive again. But a long and bloody road had to be travelled before it became a reality. It was more than two years later, in the summer of 1941, that the anti-German and anti-Fascist front was truly reconstituted, the front which had first come into being in 1935 on Czechoslovakia's initiative, to be reborn thanks to her superhuman efforts in 1938.

It was even more difficult to revive this front in 1941 than it had been three years earlier. It was a long process that began in April 1939 with the annulment of the Anglo-German naval treaty and with the granting by Britain, disillusioned by Hitler's occupation of Czechoslovakia in March 1939, of guarantees against aggression to Poland, Greece, Rumania, and Turkey. The anti-German front was, at the outset, virtually non-existent. Even though in September 1939 Britain and France reacted to Hitler's attack on Poland by declaring war on Germany, Poland was allowed to bleed to death. It was a front that only came into being gradually, mostly as a result of Hitler's continued aggression, his numerous victories and growing power, which was accompanied by ever greater ruthlessness, brutality, and inhumanity. The price was counted in millions of human lives.

With Germany's invasion of the Soviet Union the front was decisively strengthened by the new alliance of Western Europe, America, and the Soviet Union. And even then it took four years to achieve final victory – the crushing of Hitlerite Germany. Czechoslovakia played her part in this struggle, but her energies had been dissipated for a long time by the hard fight she had put up in 1938.

Amidst the general rejoicing that followed the signing of the Munich Agreement there sounded one of the few voices raised in Czechoslovakia's defence, which was however at the same time an obituary of the Czechoslovak Republic created in 1918. This was the voice of Winston Churchill. Speaking in the House of Commons, he said: 'All is over. Silent, mournful, abandoned, broken, Czechoslovakia recedes into darkness . . . It is a tragedy which has occurred . . . At any rate, the story is over and told.'

Munich led to the dismemberment of Czechoslovakia. The German regions were the first to go, but then other claimants appeared, Poland and Hungary. What remained of Czechoslovakia after Munich and the Vienna arbitration was the torso of a state, hamstrung economically as well as politically, and without the means to defend itself. The final blow was dealt on 15 March 1939. The fears of Czech politicians of the nineteenth century, and of Masaryk, Šmeral, Kramář, and others were now realized. The Czechoslovak State had succumbed to German militarism in its new, Nazi guise.

Munich disrupted the unity of the two nations which gave rise to the Republic, that of the Czechs and the Slovaks. This unity was full of mutual conflicts and tensions, caused above all by their different history and the differences in their economic, political and social structure. Their existence side by side in one state had for twenty years guaranteed their freedom and independence. Munich, however, considerably weakened the links between the Czech lands and Slovakia, and the Slovak People's Party, at a rally held in Žilina on 6 October 1938, proclaimed the Manifesto of the Slovak People and Slovakia's autonomy. The new title of Czecho-Slovakia gave expression to this looser association.

In March 1939 relations between the Czech lands and Slovakia were turned into open conflict on the initiative and with the active participation of Nazi Germany. German troops were already marching towards the frontiers of Bohemia and Moravia to occupy what was left of the State after Munich, where the Nazis succeeded – after several refusals and using Hitler's personal influence – in inducing Tiso and Durčanský to proclaim Slovakia's independence. For a time the ways of the the two nations parted.

Munich caused a crisis in Czechoslovakia's internal political development, representing as it did the defeat of all those who had wished to defend the Republic, all the revolutionary and democratic forces in the country. Thus the external intervention of Munich achieved what Czechoslovak reaction and even Henlein had not been able to achieve – a change in Czecho-slovakia's political structure.

The first condition posed by Hitler as a *conditio sine qua non* was the departure from the country of President Beneš, the man who had stood at the cradle of the ·Republic, who had for twenty years been in charge of her foreign policy, and who, in close co-operation with Thomas Masaryk, had influenced, and in the thirties actually determined, the country's internal policies. Edvard Beneš had led the defence of the Republic. He had been one of the few who had the courage to carry on their shoulders the immense weight of responsibility, danger, and risk.

When President Beneš went into exile at the end of October 1938, conservative and Fascist groups headed by the Czech Agrarian and the Slovak People's Party took over the helm of the so-called Second Republic. The former democratic system was replaced by something that was akin to a Fascist corporate state.

One of the consequences of this change was the growing persecution of the revolutionary and democratic forces, who were forced into semi-illegality. The banning of the Communist Party of Czechoslovakia led to its becoming a completely underground organization at the end of 1938. The new regime also meant that many leading representatives of revolutionary and democratic parties sought asylum abroad. All this considerably weakened the country's political life. The way was open for political tendencies which, though they had existed earlier, had throughout the twenty years of the Republic's existence, been kept in the background. After Munich they found expression both in official policies and in a number of political and propaganda campaigns, in coarse, uncouth press campaigns, anonymous letters, and radio sketches. This political decline went hand in hand with the growth of reactionary Fascist forces throughout Europe, which made good use of the Munich crisis and the depression it had engendered. But the new regime was not given enough time to develop. The Second Republic was merely a brief interlude before the final liquidation of Czechoslovakia and the complete disruption of her political life that came with the German occupation of 15 March 1939.

Munich had crushed the Czechoslovak Republic under the brutal steamroller of power, destroying Masaryk's concept of Czechoslovakia as an independent democratic state. It negated faith in a new Europe, in the possibility of the free existence of a small nation. It negated everything that the Czechoslovakia established in 1918 had stood for. Not even the bloody and protracted Second World War could remove the consequences of the catastrophe that destroyed the Europe of the inter-war years.

# Index

D5